Social
SOFTWARE
.in LIBRARIES

Social
SOFTWARE
.in LIBRARIES

Building Collaboration, Communication, and Community Online

Meredith G. Farkas

Information Today, Inc.
Medford, New Jersey

First Printing, 2007

Social Software in Libraries: Building Collaboration, Communication, and Community Online

Library of Congress Cataloging-in-Publication Data

Farkas, Meredith G., 1977-
    Social software in libraries : building collaboration, communication, and community online / Meredith G. Farkas
        p. cm.
    Includes bibliographical references and index.
        ISBN: 978-1-57387-275-1
1. Libraries and the Internet. 2. Telecommunication in libraries. 3. Libraries and community. 4. Libraries--Information technology. 5. Electronic reference services (Libraries) 6. Onlinw social networks. 7. Blogs. 8. RSS feeds. 9. Wikis (Computer science) 10. Podcasting   I. Title
    Z674.75.I58F37 2007
    025.5'24--dc22

                                                                        2007004515

Printed and bound in the United States of America.

President and CEO: Thomas H. Hogan, Sr.
Editor-in-Chief and Publisher: John B. Bryans
Managing Editor: Amy M. Reeve
Project Editor: Rachel Singer Gordon
VP Graphics and Production: M. Heide Dengler
Book Designer: Kara Mia Jalkowski
Cover Designer: Dana Kruse
Copyeditor: Barbara Brynko
Proofreader: Pat Hadley-Miller
Indexer: Beth Palmer

For Adam, with love and gratitude

Contents

Chapter 16 Future Trends in Social Software 269

Appendix: Referenced Web Sites 283

About the Author 297

Index 299

Figures

Acknowledgments

I am grateful to all of the library bloggers who have inspired and challenged me throughout the years. Special thanks to Mom and Dad, Steve Lawson, Dorothea Salo, Paul Pival, Jessamyn West, Sarah Houghton, Greg Schwartz, Jay Bhatt, Laurie Allen, Stephen Francoeur, Chrystie Hill, Aaron Schmidt, Roy Tennant, Megan Fox, Kelly Czarnecki, Chris Harris, Michelle Kraft, Mary Carmen Chimato, Elise Cole, Dave Hook, Brian Mathews, and Ellen Hall. I would also like to thank John Bryans, Amy Reeve, and the talented folks at Information Today, Inc., who helped make this book possible. I am so fortunate to have a brilliant editor, Rachel Singer Gordon, who saw something in me that I certainly never did. I am especially grateful to my husband, Adam, whose support, patience, generosity, proofreading skills, and love made writing this book possible (anyone who lives with a writer should automatically be eligible for sainthood).

About the Web Site
www.sociallibraries.com

This book explores the current landscape of social technologies in libraries and is designed to provide a better understanding of social software and the ways to make good decisions about implementing technology. As with all technology, new tools and new uses for social tools appear constantly. To keep up to date with social software developments in libraries, I have created a Web site companion to the book.

The *Social Software in Libraries* Web site (www.sociallibraries.com) uses some of the social tools described in this book to offer readers a richer experience. The Web site not only includes all of the links mentioned in this book, but also links to other useful resources, new social software tools, and blogs by other librarians. I will be adding new articles, blog posts, and tools to the site as I discover them. I hope that this Web site will become a useful tool for those who read this book and for anyone else interested in technology in libraries.

Disclaimer

Foreword

The Internet's creators thought that moving data from place to place was an essential component of a computer network; file transfer was one of its first applications. It didn't take long, though, for an imaginative and resourceful researcher to create a primitive Internet e-mail system by combining this file transfer component with their local e-mail system. E-mail quickly eclipsed file transfer as the single most important Internet application, and thus was born the first Internet "killer app."

So, from its earliest days, the true power of the Internet lay in the ability of the network to enhance communication. Primitive e-mail was quickly followed by software that enabled rich communities of common interest to thrive. Whether through bulletin boards such as Usenet News or mailing list applications such as LISTSERV, the ability of groups of people to create a community around common ground became one of the single most important aspects of the Internet—as it is to this day.

And although the mostly one-way communication medium of the Web was what brought the Internet into the mainstream, the need for two-way and many-way communication has once again reasserted itself in the form of social software. Social software provides easy-to-use ways to communicate, collaborate, and participate on an unprecedented scale. People are social animals, and the Internet provides a way to be social with whom you want, when you want, where you want, and how you want. It should come as no surprise then that social software applications are at the core of some of the most successful Internet companies today.

As institutions rooted in our communities, libraries are social institutions. Therefore, libraries belong in the social network. We belong where our users can be found—and they are increasingly found online, interacting in completely new ways. A librarian who connects with a local teenager on MySpace.com, helping her find the information she needs to get into the college of her choice, is an invaluable community resource.

Brick-and-mortar libraries are not going away, but they are now not the only way to be there for our clientele. Social networking is a new tool that lets us accomplish many of the same things we've done before, but in new and more effective ways. We need what Meredith Farkas is telling us—we need to be there for our users in the ways that she describes.

And describe them she does. There is no better guide to this brave new world than Meredith. She is not a dewy-eyed technologist who loves any bright thing that comes her way. Instead, she correctly holds any technology up to a hard scrutiny that seeks to know how it can help her fulfill the mission of her institution. If she tells you that a particular technology is useful for libraries, listen. She thinks carefully about costs and implications and lost opportunities. She judges carefully and does not jump on bandwagons simply for the joy of doing so. If she is excited about something, you should likely be excited about it as well.

But more than this, Meredith is a gifted writer. She explains technical topics simply, understandably, and even elegantly. You will enjoy reading this book. This is, of course, much to your benefit, as learning about technical topics can already be a challenge without adding confusion to the equation.

So plunge in, enjoy the ride, and take what Meredith tells you and run with it. Library users—whether actual or virtual—deserve no less.

Roy Tennant
User Services Architect
California Digital Library
University of California

Introduction

The Web has become an integral part of the daily lives of hundreds of millions of people around the world. In the early 1990s, Internet usage was limited primarily to people at academic institutions and those willing to pay a high premium for Web access. With the decreasing cost of Internet access and the growing availability of broadband, people from all demographic groups are now represented online. The World Wide Web has gone mainstream. It has changed the way we look for information; it has changed the way we communicate with others. Every day it opens new worlds for people, brings what was distant closer, and lets us connect with others beyond the barriers of distance or time. The Web enhances many activities that predate the Web; it also enables many activities we could never have done before.

Some people use the Internet as a tool to simplify things they've always done. Where it once was time consuming and difficult to look for a hotel for a vacation, track down articles about an obscure tribe in Africa, find the answer to a home-improvement question, or buy collectible figurines, all these tasks can now be easily accomplished online. Some people spend most of their free time online engaged in a variety of activities, which has led to concerns about the time Internet use takes away from traditional social interactions. However, according to a Pew Internet and American Life study, 65 percent of Americans believe that the Internet has improved their relationships with their friends, and 56 percent feel that it has improved their relationships with family members.[1] The Internet is not simply an isolating influence; it lets people connect to others around the globe. People with obscure interests, rare medical conditions, or beliefs not shared by their family and friends can interact with others online who have similar views or problems. The Internet allows people to both provide support and be supported.

Many people also use the Internet to improve and sustain relationships with people they already know. According to the same study, 84 percent of Internet users belong to online groups; many users were members of these groups before going online. The Internet lets them interact more frequently outside of periodic in-person meetings, making them more productive and more connected. People use the Internet to keep in touch with friends, family, college buddies, former co-workers, and people they lost touch with a long time ago. While the Internet has changed the ways we interact with people, it has also improved our chances of meeting like-minded people and helped us sustain relationships with family and friends.

For some people, the Internet has become just as important to their social lives as the physical world. Many young people often don't have access to a third place, a space where members of a community can go to socialize outside of work and home. This leads them to look to the Internet as a third place, since it is already a seamless part of their lives. Generation Xers have used computers most of their lives. The Millennial Generation (Generation Yers) essentially grew up with the Web—and the Web grew up with them.

These two generations in particular are using the Internet in new and exciting ways, seamlessly integrating social software into their daily lives. They are building their own Web presence with social networking software, blogs, and wikis. They are networking and communicating with friends online, synchronously and asynchronously, through both text and voice. They are expressing themselves creatively by producing audio and video content and making it available online. They are freely sharing content they create and collect, from bookmarks to photos to product reviews. They are gaming in persistent online worlds where they interact with thousands of other gamers and build relationships through the use of avatars (online representations of each player). While members of other generations are also involved in these activities, Gen X and Y have overwhelmingly adopted the Web as a third place, and are pushing the boundaries of what the Web can be.

What were you doing on the World Wide Web 10 years ago? Chances are it was quite different than what you use the Web for now. When Sir Tim Berners-Lee was developing the World Wide Web, he envisioned it as a platform where users could easily add content. The original Web browser was also an editor, so that users could create their own space online.[2] However, the Web was then essentially read-only for most. Unless users had HTML skills and access to server space, it was quite difficult to make a mark. As a result, most individuals originally used the Web as information consumers. While some people still use the Web only as a tool for retrieving information, the Web itself has transformed into a read/write environment during the past eight years. Now both amateurs and professionals can be content creators. An architecture of participation encourages people to add content and take part in conversations online, without needing much more than the ability to type. This transformation is largely due to the development of social software.

This book explores the growing phenomenon of social software and how these technologies can be applied in libraries. Librarians have put tremendous energy into making their libraries the physical hubs of their communities and institutions. However, many librarians have ignored the value of technology in communicating with their patrons and building online communities. This book describes various social technologies, discusses how libraries have effectively used each, and explains how to successfully implement each in your own library. The book is designed to be understood easily by people new to Web technologies, but it also offers veteran social software users plenty of new applications to consider.

The first 13 chapters introduce social software, then explore various tools, starting with blogs and ending with gaming. With the exception of the two chapters devoted to blogs, each chapter describes one technology (or group of related technologies), discusses its evolution, demonstrates its practical applications, and offers tips on how to make it work at your library. If you are interested in a particular technology, you can pick up the book and jump right to that chapter to learn everything you need to know. Chapter 14 offers advice on assessing your patrons' needs and determining which social software technologies would fit the best in your library. Chapter 15 looks at ways to keep up with new developments in library technologies—without spending a lot of money. Finally, Chapter 16 considers what the future of social software may hold.

Social software has tremendous potential for libraries, allowing them to better connect to and provide services for their patrons. By the end of the book, you should feel better equipped when making decisions about what technologies may be right for your library, and better able to implement those technologies successfully.

Endnotes

1. Lee Rainie and John Horrigan, *Internet: The Mainstreaming of Online Life*, Pew Internet and American Life Project, (January 25, 2005): 62,

www.pewinternet.org/pdfs/Internet_Status_2005.pdf (accessed May 28, 2006).

2. Mark Lawson, "Berners-Lee on the Read/Write Web," BBC NEWS August 9, 2005, news.bbc.co.uk/1/hi/technology/4132752.stm (accessed May 26, 2006).

Chapter 1

What Is Social Software?

Social software has played a major role in changing the ways people interact online. It has led to the birth of the read/write Web, where users are both consumers and producers of online content. The term "social software" is difficult to define because it can include so many different tools. Some people argue that social software includes the tools that allow people to connect more easily to each other online, such as wireless Internet access and mobile devices. A more narrow definition may only include software that lets people have a two-way conversation, excluding technologies such as podcasting and screencasting.

Tom Coates, a blogger and Yahoo! employee, created one of the most concise definitions: "Social software can be loosely defined as software which supports, extends, or derives added value from human social behaviour—message boards, music taste-sharing, photo-sharing, instant messaging, mailing lists, social networking."[1] For the purposes of this book, social software is defined as a tool that must meet at least two of the three following conditions:

1. It allows people to communicate, collaborate, and build community online.

2. It can be syndicated, shared, reused, or remixed, or it facilitates syndication.

3. It lets people learn easily from and capitalize on the behavior or knowledge of others.

While some tools (including electronic mailing lists and forum software) have been around for more than two decades, the majority of social software tools have been developed within the past 10 years. These newer tools both help create and benefit from modern ideas about the read/write Web, which promotes collaboration, sharing, and community-building from the bottom up.

Characteristics of Social Software

While social software can include a variety of tools, certain characteristics distinguish it from other technologies.

Easy Content Creation and Content Sharing

Years ago, putting content on the Web was a job for tech-savvy individuals who were familiar with HTML and Web programming languages. With today's social software, anyone can add online content, including photos, text, audio, and video. Blogging software lets anyone create a Web page easily—using the software to write whatever they want and posting it to the Web a moment later. Blogs also allow organizations to develop a Web presence without a Webmaster. Essentially, if you can type, you can produce a blog. Wikis make it easy for groups of people to add content to a single space without needing to know any HTML. Essentially, a group of people can use a wiki to build a Web site together, democratizing the process of content creation.

Photo-sharing software lets people easily upload their digital photos to the Web to share them with family and friends or with the world. Audio recording software made it easy for users to create a digital audio file, but services that can host and syndicate these audio files now make podcasting accessible to everyone. Screencasting software lets people create Flash movies without knowing anything about Flash animation. Video-editing software has become affordable and easier to use. Even people without a server of their own can create a blog or a wiki, develop podcasts and screencasts, and put content online using one of many free storage services. Online directories of blogs, photos, podcasts, and videos let others find this content more easily. In fact, social software has made it easy for everyone to express themselves online, share content with family and friends, and become active developers of the World Wide Web.

Online Collaboration

While e-mail made it easy to communicate virtually, it wasn't easy to work collaboratively online until the wiki was born. Before wikis, collaborative Web development translated to a group of people telling their Web developer what they wanted on their site. With wikis, anyone can add or edit content, letting people create a Web site together and asynchronously. Wikis can be used collaboratively to develop guides and knowledgebases, plan conferences, and edit text. They also offer a terrific space for collecting knowledge from a diverse group of people for everyone's benefit.

but not design? layout?

Conversations: Distributed and in Real Time

Social software allows conversations to occur in many different forms. Blogs that allow comments enable conversation between the author and his or her readers. A more distributed conversation (a conversation held in more than one place), however, can occur when a blogger uses his or her own blog to comment on another person's writing. Permalinks, or permanent links to specific blog posts, let people easily refer their readers to the blog post on which they are commenting. TrackBacks and applications that follow the thread of a conversation across blogs let us know who said what about us, so we can respond to them on our own blog. People can even subscribe to "ego searches" to receive an update every time another blogger refers to them.

Conversations can take place online in real time through the use of instant messaging (IM) or Voice over IP (VoIP). With IM, two or more individuals can type messages to each other in real time, letting them have a synchronous conversation online through the use of text. Voice over IP is an Internet protocol that allows two or more people to talk with each other through their computers. Using VoIP is much the same as talking on the phone, only the signal is transmitted over the Internet rather than a phone line, usually with no cost involved.

Communities Developed from the Bottom Up

People usually think of online communities as groups that are created from above and consciously joined. This type of online community has clear boundaries—you are either a member of a community or you are not. However, many social software tools allow communities to be created from the bottom up, where people are connected in a network by their affiliations to one another, and where boundaries are more permeable and changeable. Bloggers offer an excellent example of a community developed from the bottom up. Hundreds of individuals start their own blogs and write about a certain topic. Somehow, as they link to each other and comment on each other's blogs, a community begins to form. These bloggers begin to feel that they have become part of a community that they did not consciously join, but their connection is based only on their linking behavior and their comments.

These bottom-up online communities are similar to networks, in which people can be connected to each other by third parties, and connections can be either strong or weak. Bloggers may not all know each other, but they are connected by their connections to other bloggers. I may read a blog, and someone else may read the same blog, but we don't read each other's blogs. Yet we are still part of the same community based on our shared connection as readers. Social networking software works in a similar way. One person creates a profile about himself and adds a list of his friends with links to their profiles. He can then see his friends' friends, visualizing how they are connected to others through people he already knows. This lets people connect with friends of friends for dating, friendships, or business in an interconnected web of relationships that somehow forms a community.

Social software helps us build different types of communities. Online community doesn't require a forum, a bulletin board, or an electronic mailing list. Conversations can take place in a wiki, in the comments section of a blog, through photo-sharing software, through linking behavior, or through common tagging of materials. Communities such as this require no maintenance and no central authority. They exist only because people are using the same social tools or taking part in similar activities.

Capitalizing on the Wisdom of Crowds

Not only can we converse, collaborate, and build a community online, but we can learn a lot from the aggregate knowledge and behavior of others. Many social software tools let us learn more as more people participate. Wikis, for example, let tens, hundreds, thousands, or even hundreds of thousands of people add their knowledge to a single Web site, creating a tremendous knowledgebase about a given subject. If your library colleagues recorded everything they know about reference materials and Web sites in an internal wiki, each member of the library staff would essentially have their colleagues' knowledge with them daily at the reference desk. The more people add their knowledge to a wiki, the more useful it becomes.

The wisdom of crowds also shines through in recommendation systems. People always want to know that they are buying the best product or getting the best deal. Before the Web, we used magazines such as *Consumer Reports* or asked friends; now, we all can benefit from the knowledge of millions of other consumers. People write up their impressions of hotels, restaurants, and products and put them online for everyone to see. People can easily assign ratings to the movies they rent and the books they buy. Sites also make recommendations passively based on individuals' purchasing behavior. With this kind of people-driven system, a substandard product will not stay on the market for long.

With tagging, people can make sense of the Web. A tag is basically a keyword, and users are tagging their blog posts, their photos, and the Web sites they bookmark so that people can find them easily. People can search for a single tag and find everything others have tagged under that term. With social bookmarking, people bookmark Web pages that are meaningful to them and tag them with descriptive terms. If someone is interested in wikis, they can call up everything others have tagged with the term "wiki." Ostensibly, the documents that people tag "wiki" are going to be more relevant—and perhaps of higher quality—than those that Google indexes under that term. Tagging helps people make sense of their own resources and, by extension, makes it easier for others to discover the same things.

Transparency

The wisdom of crowds produces transparency. If the quality of a product is poor, a company does something controversial, or a congressman breaks the law, you can be certain that people will find out about it. The reputation of any organization can be ruined by a string of bad reviews online or by a group of bloggers posting negative comments. The crowd can bring a gadget, a book, or a piece of software great fame, or ensure that no one buys it just as easily. While this may be startling to corporations that are used to letting their public relations executives deal with the traditional media, this transparency also presents a unique opportunity. Social software lets organizations connect with customers in a more personal way. In addition to its flashy impersonal Web site, General Motors has a blog (fastlane.gmblogs.com) where company executives write about what's happening behind the scenes. Rather than writing as GM, these people write under their own names, with their own voice, and connect with their customers as human beings. Putting a human face on a large, impersonal company can be difficult, but social software can offer companies—and libraries—the chance to connect with their customers on a personal level.

Personalization

Some people read the newspaper from cover to cover, but many people only read articles on particular topics of interest. However, they still have to go through the entire paper to pick out what they want to read. What if you could tell your newspaper the topics you were interested in and have only articles on those topics delivered to your doorstep every day? RSS essentially lets you roll your own daily news online. RSS is a social software tool that allows users to syndicate content from various sites onto a single Web page or into an RSS aggregator. So if you're interested in technology news, you can subscribe to technology RSS feeds from various sources, including mainstream media like the *New York Times*, blogs, and scholarly journals. Some Web sites even let you subscribe to a search term and receive all the news or blog posts related to that term; you could subscribe to the term "wiki" to have every blog post written about wikis sent to you daily. This leaves you with an online newspaper you would enjoy reading from cover to cover.

RSS is also the technology behind podcasts, audio files that are syndicated on the Web. Many podcasts are designed much the same as radio shows, with music, commentary, and humor. You can subscribe to the podcasts you like best, download them to your MP3 player, and essentially create your own radio station that plays only what you want to hear. RSS enables people to choose what information is pushed to them. They no longer have to hunt for materials on their topics of interest or wade through irrelevant material.

Portability

To use the Internet, we used to be tied to our desks at work or at home. As access became more ubiquitous, people started to take their work with them wherever they went. Unfortunately, most traditional computer applications aren't portable: Desktop applications are installed on one computer and then can be accessed only on that computer. Even if another computer has the same application, you have to bring all of your personal files with you on a portable storage device. Fortunately, most social software applications are Web applications. If you're sitting at an Internet café in Fiji, you can still access your blog to write about your vacation, upload photos to your photo-sharing application, and read all of your favorite blogs and news sources in your RSS aggregator. As long as you remember your username and password for each application, your social software applications can follow you wherever you find an Internet connection.

Beyond using portable Web applications, more people now access the Web through mobile devices such as PDAs and cellphones. These tools can be used to search Google, check movie times, network with friends, send e-mails, take photos or movies and upload them to the Web, and send text messages. More and more Web sites and applications are designed to be accessed by both desktops and handheld devices, making it possible for people to use their handhelds to do many of the same things on their desktop computer. SMS, or mobile text messaging, has become a particularly popular way for young people to communicate with one another, and companies are taking advantage of this by offering services that push information to users via SMS. Web applications, mobile devices, and text messaging provides access to people online 24/7, no matter where they are.

Overcoming Barriers of Distance and Time

Social software does an excellent job of overcoming the barriers of distance and time, giving people a chance to communicate and work together wherever they are. Through IM and VoIP, people can communicate with each other in real time. Libraries with IM reference services can provide the same level of service whether a patron is on the other side of the library or the other side of the world. Using wikis, people can collaborate on a project online without having to be in the same room together or work on it at the same time. These tools make in-person meetings much less necessary.

Why Should Librarians Care About Social Software?

Social software is obviously an important trend, but why should librarians be concerned? First, and most importantly, our patrons are using these tools. No matter what type of library you work in, your patrons will be using some type of social software, whether they IM, blog, or listen to podcasts. It's important to be aware of the tools your patrons use to see if you can provide services using the same tools. If the vast majority of your patrons use IM, it may make sense to offer virtual reference services via IM. If your patrons are avid blog readers, your library might want to start a blog to disseminate information about programs, services, or resources.

While social software tools can improve the ways in which libraries communicate with patrons, they can also improve internal communication and knowledge sharing. Blogs, wikis, and social bookmarking each can play a role. A library wiki knowledgebase can decrease people's dependence on their colleagues' in-person expertise. Blogs are a great way to disseminate news about broken printers or new databases. Social bookmarking can help colleagues share useful Web links. Libraries not only should examine how social software can improve services to their patrons, but they should also consider how these tools can improve internal communication and collaboration.

Finally, librarians often talk about providing outreach to their patrons. This usually means getting out of the library and providing services where patrons congregate. But what if your patrons are hanging out online? Libraries should be aware of their patrons' online social worlds, whether these are Massively Multiplayer Online Games (MMOGs), social networking sites, or other online communities. Whatever your patrons' third place, consider how you can provide services there. Librarians can do market research, build presence, market services, provide reference services, and develop portals to library resources in these online worlds. If patrons spend more time online than they do at the library, it makes sense for libraries to provide outreach online.

Libraries need to look at social software applications as valuable tools for communicating with and serving their current patrons, as well as attracting new library patrons. Social software can provide libraries with a human face beyond their walls. It can provide them with ways to communicate, collaborate, educate, and market services to their patrons and other community members. Social software can also help libraries position themselves as the online hub of their communities. Technology can make libraries more relevant to people who think they can get all their information from the Web, while attracting a brand new population to the library.

Endnote

1. Tom Coates, "An Addendum to a Definition of Social Software," plastic bag.org, January 5, 2005, www.plasticbag.org/archives/2005/01/an_addendum_to_a_definition_of_social_software.shtml (accessed May 26, 2006).

Chapter 2

Blogs

Each year, the *Merriam-Webster Dictionary* publishes its Top Ten words of the year that visitors looked up most often on its Web site. Most of the top words for 2004—an election year—were unsurprising. Words such as incumbent, electoral, and partisan all made the list. Other Top Ten words—insurgent, sovereignty, hurricane, and cicada—were also related to major 2004 world events. The No. 1 word users searched for in the online dictionary that year, however, didn't relate directly to politics or world events. *Merriam-Webster*'s Word of the Year for 2004 was blog.[1]

2004 was a very big year for Weblogs, or "blogs." Bloggers, people who write blogs, were named ABC News' People of the Year.[2] According to the Pew Internet and American Life survey on The State of Blogging, blog readership shot up 58 percent between 2003 and 2004; the number of people creating blogs also more than doubled during those two years.[3] According to Technorati, a company that tracks blogs, about 5 million blogs were in existence at the end of 2004, almost five times the number of blogs at the beginning of the year. According to estimates in 2005, the size of the blogosphere—the community of blogs and bloggers—had been doubling every five months.[4] Political bloggers' activity during the election year and their representation at the Democratic National Convention made them more visible to both the mainstream media and average Internet users. Blogs began to be seen as more than just a vehicle for voicing teenage angst. Even mainstream media outlets and businesses began using blogs to communicate with their customers. People started to see blogs as a legitimate medium for sharing information with others.

What Is a Blog?

Since the late 1990s, many people have tried to define the term blog. We still, however, have no authoritative and concise definition because there are so many different types of blogs and audiences. How can a single definition be inclusive enough to fit both the Becker-Posner Blog (www.becker-posner-blog.com)—written by a federal judge and a Nobel Prize-winning economist—and a blog written by a teenage girl about her personal life? The Becker-Posner Blog, which resembles a scholarly debate rather than a personal journal, would not fit into *Merriam-Webster's* definition of "a Web site that contains an online personal journal with reflections, comments, and often hyperlinks provided by the writer."[5] Many people used to think of blogs as diaries or personal journals, but these definitions ignore institutional and professional blogs. Blogging is simply a technology; it's a medium. The software does not define the content that goes into it.

For the purposes of this book, blogs will be defined more by their structural components than by their content, although blog content will be part of the discussion. Jill Walker wrote a broad definition, inclusive enough to fit most blogs, but exclusive enough not to include other types of Web sites, for the *Routledge Encyclopedia of Narrative Theory*:

> A weblog or blog is a frequently updated website consisting of dated entries arranged in reverse chronological order so the most recent post appears first.[6]

Blogs can also be characterized as a low-threshold technology. Blogging software is quite easy to set up, and blogs are easy to update without knowing anything about Web design. The internal interface on most blogging software consists of a text box for adding content, a small text box for a title, and various formatting buttons for adding links, bulleted lists, and other styles. (See Figure 2.1 for an example of an internal blogging interface.) Essentially, if a person can type a sentence, she can probably use a blog.

A number of structural components characterize today's blogs (Figure 2.2), including:

- *Archives* – Listings of past blog entries are usually organized by date, although some software also lets readers browse by category.

- *Dated entries* – All entries are dated and usually also have a time stamp.

- *Permalinks* – Links that let others link directly to each post.

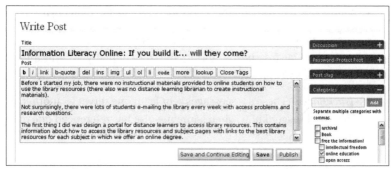

Figure 2.1   Most blog interfaces, such as this one from WordPress, consist of a simple interface with buttons to format the text.

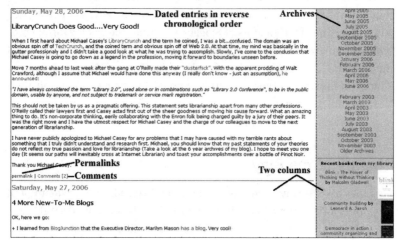

Figure 2.2   This screen shot from the popular Library Stuff blog shows many typical components of a blog. (*Reproduced with permission.*)

- *Reverse-chronological postings* – Postings are arranged in reverse chronological order.

- *Two- or three-column format* – Most blogs have a large column for blog posts and one or two columns on the sides of the screen for additional information about the blog or its author.

Other structural components appear in most but not all blog software:

- *Categories* – Archiving blog posts under certain categories makes it easier to retrieve them at a later date.

- *Comments* – Users can post comments to specific blog posts.

- *Search functionality* – Many bloggers today let readers search their archives for specific terms; this functionality is built into most blog software.

- *TrackBacks* – These are messages sent from one server to another, letting a blogger know when someone else has referenced one of their blog posts.

Blogs are clearly more than the sum of their parts. Professional and personal blogs also differ so greatly that they can hardly be considered part of the same genre; blogs as a medium are defined by their structure, but individual blogs are defined by their content and audience. Meg Hourihan, one of the creators of Blogger, says that "the weblog format provides a framework for our universal blog experiences, enabling the social interactions we associate with blogging."[7] While a working definition of "blog" is important, blogs are truly defined by their content and their community interactions.

History of the Blog

Blogs had already been around for several years by 1997, when Robot Wisdom's Jorn Barger coined the term "Weblog." He described a Weblog as "a webpage where a weblogger (sometimes called a blogger, or a pre-surfer) 'logs' all the other webpages she finds interesting."[8] The first Web site with blog-like characteristics was the National Center for Supercomputing Applications' (NCSA) What's New page. (NCSA created Mosaic, the first graphical Web browser.) From 1993 to 1996, NCSA's Web site provided links to new pages on the Web in reverse chronological order. By 1996, so many new Web sites had appeared that it was impossible to keep track of them all in one place. A number of notable Weblogs sprang up in the late 1990s, designed to point bloggers' friends to new Web sites of interest. At the beginning of 1999, only about 23 Weblogs existed. That year, the world of Weblogs would be forever changed with the advent of blog software.[9]

Before 1999, anyone who wanted to create a blog had to build it from scratch. It wasn't particularly complicated to develop a simple HTML page and call it a blog, but it was a large roadblock for people who knew nothing about Web design. Bloggers at that time tended to be involved in the Web design, networking, or software development fields. In mid-1999, both Pitas.com (www.pitas.com) and Blogger (www.blogger.com) released free blogging software. This eliminated the biggest barrier to entry, attracting an entirely new population to the blogosphere (world of blogs). This new population also changed the very definition of blogs. Rather than linking to interesting news stories, some of these new bloggers used their blogs as personal journals or public platforms to opine on topics of interest. Many of them weren't even interested in technology, but simply used technology as a tool to disseminate information to friends and family. A definite gulf sprang up between those who wrote journal-type blogs and those who wrote link-type blogs.

In the year 2000 (by which time there were thousands of blogs), another technological innovation changed the way people blog: the permalink, which is a permanent link that points to a specific blog post. These let bloggers link to a single blog post easily. Before this, they would have had to link to a blog's main page, making it difficult to find the one particular post they were referring to. By making linking to blog posts as easy as linking to mainstream news stories, permalinks helped encourage distributed conversations. Rather than a conversation living and dying on a single blog, others would pick up the conversation where the original author left off, linking to the original author's post with a permalink. That same year, many blogs let readers comment on posts, enabling blog readers to take part in the dialogue.[10] By 2002, the blogging platform Movable Type (www.sixapart.com/movabletype) came out with TrackBacks, which alert bloggers when someone else references their blog posts.[11] TrackBacks enable more interactive conversations. Permalinks, comments, and TrackBacks were largely responsible for fostering the blogging communities we know today.

By 2004, the landscape had changed again, but this time not through technological innovation. The U.S. presidential election polarized the nation, inspiring a new group of politically active individuals to start blogging. The number of blogs grew at a tremendous pace, and their power could be seen throughout politics. Candidate Howard Dean mobilized significant grassroots support, largely through his Blog for America (www.blogforamerica.com). Bloggers were given press passes to attend the Democratic National Convention in Boston. The first major political impact of blogging came when bloggers influenced public opinion to force Senator Trent Lott's resignation in 2002. A similar episode occurred in 2004 when a blogger discovered that the documents Dan Rather used in an anti-Bush *60 Minutes* story were false. Instead of being seen as diaries for teens, blogs began to be viewed as vehicles for citizen journalism. Bloggers began to be compared to the muckrakers of the early 1900s who exposed corruption in business and politics.

Today, there are millions of blogs, and the blogging population is far more diverse than it was only a few years ago. Many U.S. soldiers in Iraq have blogs discussing their experiences at war. Anchorman Brian Williams and other important players at NBC News give viewers a behind-the-scenes look at how news is made in their blog The Daily Nightly (dailynightly.msnbc.com). Upper-level executives at General Motors write about new developments at GM in their FastLane Blog (fast lane.gmblogs.com). Stanford Law School professor Lawrence Lessig blogs about intellectual property issues (www.lessig.org/blog), and many other academics also blog about their areas of interest. Elementary school classes blog, as do their teachers. Teenagers are still active in the blogosphere, as are people working in the technology sector. But the playing field has grown to accommodate many different types of blogs and many different types of bloggers. Communities have developed around certain areas of interest, and blogs are now being used for things people never imagined in the 1990s. Blogging's sheer ease of use makes it a natural fit for a public forum, a closed discussion, or information sharing.

Types of Blogs

In 1999, the two major types of blogs were personal journals and blogs linking to other stories. It is much more difficult to categorize the millions of blogs now in existence. Just as with books, blogs can be defined by genre, style, format, and author. Also like books, some blogs can defy categorization. In a 2004 genre analysis of blogs, Herring, et al. defined three types of blogs:[12]

- *Filters* are blogs that essentially filter the Web by providing links to and commentary on interesting Web sites.

- *Personal journals* are diary-like blogs with postings about the author's everyday life.

- *Knowledge logs* are blogs used to create original knowledge online.

While Herring, et al. separated blogs in their survey into these three predefined categories, many blogs would fit into two or all three. Blogs can also be characterized by their subject matter or by author. While most blogs are written by a single individual, some are written by several people or by an organization. Blogs can be personal or professional, official or unofficial, signed or anonymous.

Types of Blog Posts

Two bloggers can use the same software and write about the same topic, yet their blogs may seem quite different. Posting format is the manner in which people write blog posts, which considers factors such as length and linking behavior. Amy Gahran, author of the blog Contentious, describes seven types of posting formats:[13]

- *Link only* – These posts only contain a link and a title.

- *Link blurb* – A link is followed by commentary.

- *Brief remark* – This is a short post that can contain commentary, links, and/or personal reflections.

- *List* – Several links are grouped together in one post on a particular topic.

- *Short article* – This is a short essay-type post.

- *Long article* – This is a longer essay-type post.

- *Series postings* – This group of essay-type posts follows a single topic or argument.

Many blogs use a variety of posting formats. When bloggers find an article of interest, they may simply link to it and provide some commentary. However, when they feel particularly passionate about a topic, their postings may instead take the form of a long article or a series.

Blogs and Community

It can be difficult to imagine a community sprouting up around blogs written by individuals. After all, each person writes in isolation and often doesn't personally know any of the other bloggers. The public nature of blogs, however, indicates a desire to communicate. Because blogs are social, people with common interests will often comment on others' blogs. They may continue a thread of conversation on their own blogs, which the original blogger will discover through TrackBacks. These distributed conversations can occur across multiple blogs as people continue the topical thread in both blog posts and comments. In their study of blog communities, Efimova, et al. liken blog communities to life in the public spaces between buildings in a city:

> As in cities, *blogger communal spaces* are not evenly distributed: some neighbourhoods are full of social activities and conversations, while others look like a random collocation of houses where inhabitants have nothing in common. Blogger communal spaces may have visible boundaries (e.g., NetRing for Knitting Blogger community, Wei, 2004), but more often indicators of a community are subtle and difficult for a non-member to distinguish.[14]

In analyzing linking behavior in a particular blog community, Efimova, et al. discovered that blog communities might have certain "A-list" blogs, but that community activity goes on in all of the blogs, no matter how small the audience. They discovered mini-clusters of mutual linking within communities that indicated subgroups focused on a particular interest, and they found that the boundaries between blog communities are quite fluid. During one conference, bloggers in attendance from various communities linked heavily to one another. When the conference ended, some of those links remained, while others went back to linking and being linked only to the communities to which they belonged prior to the conference. Groups will link to each other more and less intensely at times, but some type of community always exists, due to general interest and linking behavior. Community formation is entirely organic, and these distributed conversations are the hallmark of an online community.

Creating a Blog: Practical Considerations

The first step to creating a blog may be deciding that a blog is the right tool for you or your library. You should be able to answer a number of questions before creating any blog. These include:

- What is the focus of the blog?

- What are your software needs?

- How will you deal with security issues?

- What amount of interactivity do you want?

- How will you get people to read it?

If you create a blog without really knowing what your intended audience wants, you probably will have a blog that no one reads. Blog posts can be fun to write, but blogs should always fill a need rather than simply satisfy their author's technolust. Successful bloggers know their audience and how to engage them. You simply need some careful planning and an understanding of your audience's needs to develop a successful blog.

Focus

First you need to determine the scope, audience, and focus of your blog. Who are you writing this for? Your audience should determine your focus. Are you creating a blog for staff members? Think about what information they might need. You could create a reference blog that collects useful resources, a blog for professional development, or a blog to share library news and announcements. The institutional culture at your library and the interests of your colleagues should determine your focus. Are you writing for your patrons? If so, which patrons? A children's blog should be significantly different from a teen blog, which should be different from a blog for adults. It is difficult to write a blog for patrons of all ages, because you will not be able to speak to the entire audience in every post. A blog trying to be all things to all people usually ends up being useful to no one.

Once you have determined your specific audience, think about what they would enjoy reading about in a blog. Perhaps parents would enjoy a readers' advisory blog that helps them choose children's books. Or teens at your library may want to learn about the latest gadgets and games. You may be interested in technology, but if you work with a population that couldn't care less about computers and gadgets, then you probably shouldn't blog about them. People will not read a blog that doesn't interest them, even if you think the topic would be good for them. Think about what patrons do at your library. Consider what books they check out, what programs are well attended, and how they use the Internet. Once you have determined the focus of your blog, make sure you can state that focus concisely. It's a good idea to have a statement of purpose on your site so that people know what to expect on your blog. If you know your patrons well enough and tailor your blog to their needs, you can make your blog an integral part of your library's online presence.

Software

A variety of blogging software platforms are available, and it can be difficult to determine which one will be right for your purposes. If you are handy with HTML, you can conceivably build a blog yourself, but this is not the route most bloggers take anymore. To create a blog, you certainly don't need to know anything about HTML (or that many software platforms use a database such as MySQL to store information and PHP to publish data dynamically onto your Web site); most blogging software keeps all the technical stuff behind the scenes. All you need to do is type your blog posts into a text box and click the "post" button; the rest is automated.

First, determine where your blog will be hosted. Your decisions will quickly narrow down your software choices. Blogs must be hosted on a server, whether it's your own server, a hosting company's server, or the server of the company whose software you are using. Pros and cons come with each approach. If you are running a blog on your own server, you will be responsible for maintaining the blog and server, which can involve frequently updating software and dealing with any unforeseen technical snafus. On the other hand, you have total control over your blog. If you are creating a library blog and have a systems librarian or network administrator already administering a server, this can be a good option. If you are running your blog yourself without experience administering (or access to) a server, you should probably consider hosting your blog elsewhere.

Many hosting companies will host your blog on their servers for a monthly fee, just as they would any other Web site. You can expect to pay anywhere between $5 and $50 per month, though prices will be greater for high-traffic blogs. This arrangement is beneficial because someone else deals with the headaches of server administration, and you can still choose a software platform that gives you more control over the end product. You also have ownership of your data, so if you are unhappy with your hosting company, you can take your business (and your data) elsewhere.

Many popular blog platforms offer free hosted versions of their software, meaning that your blog is hosted on the software company's servers. The greatest benefit of this arrangement is that setup usually involves little more than filling out a registration form and choosing a title for your blog. This means that anyone can easily create a blog, though; the volume can slow down the servers. Some free hosting companies may add advertisements, which will look unprofessional on a blog representing your library. Depending on the software, it can be difficult to move your data if you decide later to switch to a different company. You should research all of these issues before deciding where to host your blog. Some for-pay hosted blog options ostensibly offer better quality and service, but you should still determine how portable your data will be if you decide to move to another service.

Before choosing blog software, make sure you can answer the following questions:

- Does the software have thorough documentation? Can you easily find the help file and is there someone you can contact about problems? Some software platforms have forums where users can help each other with their problems. This can be tremendously helpful to bloggers who may not understand the inner workings of the software.

- To what extent can you customize the look of the site? If you want to make your blog match the style of the rest of your Web site, you need a software platform that lets you alter its style sheets.

- Is it easy to create and delete a post? If you make a mistake in a post or write something you later regret, can you easily go in and edit the post or delete it?

- Are posts archived? Is it easy for people to find the archives? Are they searchable?

- Can you assign categories to posts? This will help people to find older posts of interest. With categories, if a reader wants to see all of your posts about children's books, they only need to click on that category to list all your posts on that subject by date.

- Can you easily back up and restore your data? How portable is your data?

- Does the software allow comments? Can you turn them off if you don't want them? Can you require people to register before they comment or prevent anonymous commenting?

- What sort of spam protection does this software offer?

- Does the blog software create a permalink for each post? (If not, people won't be able to bookmark or link directly to any specific post.)

The three most popular blogging platforms are WordPress (word press.org), Blogger, and Movable Type, but other options are available. It may be helpful to read reviews of the software platforms you're considering. Searching online for "software name review" usually retrieves many reviews. Some Web sites also compare software platforms side-by-side; two excellent resources here are the blog software comparison chart from the Annenberg Center for Communication (www.ojr.org/ojr/images/blog_software_comparison.cfm) and Web Log Software/Platform Reviews from About.com (weblogs.about.com/od/softwareplatformreviews). Look carefully at the features each review describes to see if these are features you need; a bad review shouldn't unduly influence your opinion. One reviewer may not like limitations on editing the look of a blog, but you may not care about this. If possible, test-drive several software options for a better idea about the features that are important to you. Once you commit to a specific software platform, it can be difficult to switch.

Posting and Comments

When you first start your blog, it is very important that you post frequently and regularly. People may not return to a blog that is sometimes updated once every couple of weeks and sometimes every couple of days; they appreciate consistency. When you are not writing about something that really interests you, blogging can quickly become tedious. Before you start your blog, consider whether you can imagine yourself writing on this topic for years. Your focus can change to some extent as you write, but it's best to consider the interests of your intended audience.

Establishing credibility with your audience is important, and this depends on who your target audience is. For an adult audience, this may mean appearing knowledgeable through your writing. For a teen audience, it may mean using language and grammar they use in their own blogs. You also may wish to establish a personal code of blogging ethics. For example, these could include not writing negative things about others, not taking money from companies to recommend their products, and always checking your facts before you write. Simply think about what you absolutely should and should not do in your blog, and hold yourself accountable to those standards.

The focus and audience of your blog will help you determine if you want to keep comments open. If you want your blog to generate conversations online, you will want to keep comments open. If you think your readers might have questions for you, that's another good reason to allow comments. If you only want to inform your patrons or friends about news and events, it may not be as important to have people comment on your posts. You can deal with comments in a number of ways: You can let everyone post comments freely on the blog, you can moderate comments yourself, or you can require people to register before they can add comments. Look for a software platform with good spam filtering capabilities, or you may find yourself manually deleting hundreds of spam comments and TrackBacks each day. Spam usually originates from computerized spambots that can easily send hundreds of spam messages to thousands of blogs each day. Spam filtering software has to be continually improved to keep up with the underhanded tactics of spammers. Some software platforms have plug-ins that can help your blog distinguish a machine posting from a human posting. This may include asking a commenter to enter some graphical text displayed on the screen that can only be read by humans. If spam is overwhelming your blog, you may need to close your comments, but many options make spam a more manageable problem.

Jessamyn West on Planning
for a Successful Library Blog

Purpose – This is often summed up with Walt Crawford's words, "first have something to say." Figure out why you want a blog and try to plan what you would like it to do and what would be a desirable outcome. While it's fine to jump in feet first and learn as you go, trying to get a group blog going is often easier when people know exactly what it is they're contributing to. Being clear about your purpose also helps readers know why they might want to read it. Is the purpose to highlight library events? Will it be a new titles list? Does it track the ongoing library renovation? Is it a gathering place for teen patrons?

Function – How do you want your blog to work? This can help you make software decisions, bring other people on board to help, and help you make some introductory decisions that help you get started. Do you want comments? How about anonymous comments? Moderated comments? Image posting? External links? Is the site part of a larger Web site, or *is* it the Web site? Starting with a simple style guide helps everyone understand some ground rules and can make unfamiliar territory a little clearer for novice bloggers. While it's good to let some guidelines grow organically, look at other library blogs to get an idea of how blogs can work, so that you can more usefully guide how yours will work.

Connection – It's all about the links. Make sure your blog is linking to your Web site, to your community, to other information on the Internet, to itself. Encourage contributors to your blog to interact with other blogs—library blogs or otherwise—to get a feel for the blogosphere and the people who inhabit it. Learn about social spaces online and figure out how to interact with them. Your patrons are already there; think about whether you should be, too.

Voice – Blogs are a great, personalized complement to an existing Web site. They can help make staff seem approachable and knowledgeable at the same time. Encourage staff to develop their own voices on the blog and to experiment.

Develop it as an official outreach tool, an online public face of the library.

Assess – As with any new endeavor, check to see how the project is going. Does your staff have time to contribute? Are they enjoying their roles on the site? Are there things you could be doing to make the blog more connected, more enjoyable, more noticed, more prominent? Your blog is one of the few technology-related things in the library that requires little money to maintain, but it does require enthusiasm, determination, and a bit of stick-to-itiveness. Make sure you're keeping an eye on the project and collecting both internal and external feedback as it continues.

Jessamyn West is a community technology mentor at the Randolph Technical Career Center in Vermont. She is the founder of the blog librarian.net, one of the first librarian-created blogs.

Marketing

Whether you write for your patrons or for other librarians, you need to determine a strategy for getting people to read your blog. Blogs don't often attract a significant number of readers without marketing; you'll need at least to send out an e-mail announcement and link to your blog from your library's Web site. Marketing is an essential part of starting a blog, whether you merely tell your family and friends you have a blog or mount a full-blown marketing campaign. The intensity of your efforts depends on your audience's prior familiarity with blogs and the reach you would like your blog to have.

Many of your patrons may not be familiar with blogs yet. So, the first hurdle is simply getting them to understand what a blog is, and why it is worth their time. This explanation needs to be concrete and based on real applications that your patrons would appreciate. For example, if you are writing a readers' advisory blog for parents of small children, you can highlight its value as a one-stop shop for children's book recommendations. You can also offer workshops on blogs to help educate your patrons, using your library's blog as an example. A library can promote a blog through its newsletter, on its Web site, through an intranet, or by sending an e-mail announcement to teachers and colleagues. If your library is willing to invest some money in promoting the blog, you can create posters, fliers, or bookmarks to display and distribute. A bookmark with the name and URL of your blog can be an excellent marketing tool since people are likely to take bookmarks home and use them.

But you don't necessarily need to market your blog as a blog. Using RSS—a format for syndicating content on the Web—you can take content from your blog and automatically place it on your Web site using a free service like Feed2JS (jade.mcli.dist.maricopa.edu/feed) or RSS-to-JavaScript (www.rss-to-javascript.com). (RSS will be covered in more detail in Chapter 4.) This way, you can benefit from the ease of use of the blog software's internal interface, but your patrons will just see another Web page on your site, with information posted in reverse-chronological order. This approach is useful for blogs with the primary goal of disseminating information. If you want to encourage patrons to post comments, you should link to your blog itself rather than putting its content on your site. Through the use of style sheets, you can make your blog's look and style consistent with the design of your Web site. The more consistent and integrated your blog is with your Web site, the more comfortable your patrons will be with using this new resource.

If you are writing for other library professionals, you can increase your blog's visibility in several ways. First, you can comment on other people's blog posts. Comment forms usually ask for the URL, or Web address, of a person's blog or site. If your comment piques the interest of the author or other readers, they may click through to your blog. You can also get involved in a distributed conversation. If a notable blogger writes something that interests you, link to their post and comment on it in your own blog. People like to read things about themselves and may even have an "ego feed" set up to notify them of blog posts that mention them—so they will likely visit your blog if you write about them. Installing a "blogroll"— a list of links to people whose blogs you read—will also get you on people's radar. But simply linking to someone in a blogroll is less effective than writing about them. The best way to increase traffic to your blog is to create frequent, interesting, and well-written posts. Develop your unique voice rather than parroting the peanut gallery. If you can distinguish yourself from the pack—if you offer readers something no one else does—you will attract your desired audience.

Endnotes

1. "Merriam-Webster's Words of the Year 2004," Merriam-Webster Online, November 2004, www.m-w.com/info/pr/2004-words-of-year.htm (accessed November 25, 2005).

2. Elizabeth Vargas, "Internet Phenomenon Provides Unique Insight Into People's Thoughts," *ABC News*, December 30, 2004, abcnews.go.com/WNT/PersonOfWeek/story?id=372266&page=1 (accessed November 26, 2005).

3. Lee Rainie, *The State of Blogging*, Pew Internet and American Life Project, January 2005, www.pewinternet.org/pdfs/PIP_blogging_data.pdf (accessed December 1, 2005).

4. David Sifry, "State of the Blogosphere, March 2005, Part 1: Growth of Blogs," Sifry's Alerts, March 14, 2005, www.sifry.com/alerts/archives/000298.html (accessed November 22, 2005).

5. "Merriam-Webster's Words of the Year 2004."

6. Jill Walker, "Final Version of Weblog Definition," jill/txt, June 28, 2003, huminf.uib.no/~jill/archives/blog_theorising/final_version_of_weblog_definition.html (accessed November 22, 2005).

7. Meg Hourihan, "What We're Doing When We Blog," O'Reilly Web DevCenter, June 13, 2002, www.oreillynet.com/lpt/a/2474 (accessed November 22, 2005).

8. Jorn Barger, "Weblog Resource FAQ," Robot Wisdom, September 1999, www.robotwisdom.com/weblogs.

9. Rebecca Blood, "Weblogs: A History and Perspective," *We've Got Blog: How Weblogs Are Changing our Culture*, Ed., Editors of Perseus Publishing, Cambridge, MA: Perseus Publishing, 2002.

10. Rebecca Blood, "Hammer, Nail: How Blogging Software Reshaped the Online Community," Rebecca's Pocket, December 2004, www.rebeccablood.net/essays/blog_software.html (accessed November 21, 2005).

11. Mena Trott and Ben Trott, "A Beginner's Guide to TrackBack," Six Apart News and Events, March 24, 2003, www.sixapart.com/about/news/2003/03/a_beginners_gui.html (accessed November 20, 2005).

12. Susan Herring, Lois Ann Scheidt, Sabrina Bonus, and Elijah Wright, "Bridging the Gap: A Genre Analysis of Weblogs," *Proceedings of the 37th Annual Hawaii International Conference on System Sciences, 2004*, csdl2.computer.org/comp/proceedings/hicss/2004/2056/04/205640101b.pdf (accessed November 19, 2005).

13. Amy Gahran, "Blogging Style: The Basic Posting Formats (Series Index)," Contentious, September 22, 2004, blog.contentious.com/ archives/2004/09/22/blogging-style-the-basic-posting-formats-series-index.

14. Lilia Efimova, Stephanie Hendrick, and Anjo Anjewierden, "Finding 'The Life Between Buildings': An Approach for Defining a Weblog Community," November 21, 2005, staff.science.uva.nl/~anjo/aoir_2005.pdf.

Chapter 3

Blogs in Libraries: Practical Applications

Libraries are always looking for new ways to disseminate information and attract new patrons. Static Web sites, however, lack the dynamism to entice patrons to return to see what's new. Patrons may visit a library's Web site to use the online catalog and databases, but these tools fail to put a human face on the library. Blogs add value to a library's Web site. They can give the library a human face, allowing librarians to put more of themselves and their library into their site. A blog can provide a forum for librarians to educate their patrons and can be an ideal space for disseminating news and other information. Many of your patrons may already read blogs regularly, so it makes sense to use that same technology.

Just as blogs help you share information with patrons, they are also excellent tools for sharing information with other librarians. Blogs can be used both within libraries and within the profession as a whole. Many librarians blog to share information with colleagues around the world, build community, and promote themselves. Never has professional dialogue been so open, so immediate, and so international; blogs have become a popular and accepted professional development tool among many librarians. No other tool is as effective in keeping us current and in enabling timely profession-wide discussions about the issues affecting our field.

How Libraries Can Use Blogs with Their Patrons

All kinds of libraries now use blogs. Special libraries provide relevant subject news, school media centers provide readers' advisory services, academic libraries promote new databases, and public libraries create forums to discuss community issues. The uses of blogs in libraries are almost limitless, and their simplicity makes them easy to implement. The burden of updating a blog is fairly minimal, but its impact can be significant.

News Blogs

How do you share library news with your patrons? Do you have an online monthly newsletter in PDF format? Do you add news on your Web site but fail to update it frequently because only one person on your staff knows HTML? Realize that people are more likely to visit pages that are updated frequently and regularly; news page visitors who find outdated information may never come back. How do you let patrons know about changes in storytime hours, or about author signings and book discussions? Many libraries don't include this information on their Web sites, but disseminate it only via fliers in the library. Imagine how many people miss valuable information because they don't visit the library regularly. Someone in your community may rarely come in but may happen to love an author who will be speaking next week. It's unlikely he or she will ever find out about the event. Libraries miss out on many opportunities to share information with their patrons and market the library to potential patrons. Blogging, however, makes it easy to post and update online news and promote events.

Mabry Middle School in Marietta, Georgia, has an impressive Web presence that capitalizes on many social software technologies. One component is a Media Center blog (mabryonline.org/blogs/media) authored by the school librarian, Gail Hendrix. She uses the blog to post important school announcements, upcoming classes at the center, library news, and a book of the week. She also provides information literacy instruction, advising her students on how to correctly cite resources and evaluate Web sites. Children often forget to inform their parents about book fairs or class trips, and this blog lets parents keep track of events at their child's school without relying on the child to tell them.

The Marin County Free Library in California uses its blog (marincounty freelibrary.blogspot.com) to provide news about upcoming events. Posts cover library exhibits, lectures, classes, storytime, and book club selections. Included are links to library-related topics of interest, such as information about the latest *Harry Potter* book and links to works by the winner of the Nobel Prize in literature. The librarian bloggers at the Marin County Free Library also include photos of events and exhibits, which help humanize the library's Web presence. This news blog offers important information about changes in classes or events for regular library visitors and provides infrequent visitors with useful information about events they may wish to attend. If people can simply visit a library's blog to find out about events, these events may be better attended.

The West Virginia University Library replaced its newsletter, *Ex Libris* (www.libraries.wvu.edu/exlibris), with the West Virginia University Library News blog (www.libraries.wvu.edu/news). This blog offers information about new databases, exhibits, events, changes in library hours, and library services. Many posts are more detailed than traditional blog posts, frequently resembling newspaper articles. Articles written for newsletters generally tend to be more polished, but *Ex Libris* was only published two or three times a year, making it an inappropriate vehicle for time-sensitive news. Many West Virginia University Library News posts are similar to newsletter articles; they simply appear in a timelier manner. Members of the university community are free to add comments on the blog, making it a two-way communication vehicle. Newsletter content needs to be written before the newsletter is formatted and printed, and space constraints make it difficult to add new information as it comes up. Blogs let libraries add new information on the fly. If information changes, blog posts can be edited easily.

Subject Blogs

Subject blogs, which offer news and information on a single subject, are particularly useful for academic liaison librarians, medical librarians, law librarians, corporate librarians, and special librarians who focus on a specific subject. However, they can be used in any library with the need and the staff to run blogs on several different subjects. A school librarian could run blogs on each major academic subject, highlighting relevant research books and Web sites; a public librarian could create similar subject blogs for frequently requested topics or annual projects at local schools. However, most current library subject blogs have been created by academic libraries, law libraries, and special libraries.

Georgia State University (www.library.gsu.edu/news) is a model for the use of subject blogs in academic libraries. The library offers 22 blogs on various subjects that range from economics to African-American studies to general library news. Each blog contains a variety of content, including new subject-specific databases, calls for participation and requests for proposals, subject-related world news and studies, book reviews, conference announcements, and relevant library news. Authors and librarians

Doug Goans and Teri M. Vogel discussed the decision to use blogs as a way to deliver library news and resources to students and faculty in the sciences in their *Internet Reference Services Quarterly* (*IRSQ*) article "Delivering the News with Blogs: The Georgia State University Library Experience":

> Even if newsletters are abandoned and e-mail is used only for the most important or time sensitive alerts, librarians still need to keep patrons informed about library news and resources pertinent to scholarly activities. The challenge for libraries is to find or develop a system that combines the permanence and patron-specificity of newsletters with the ease and immediacy of e-mail, while avoiding the drawbacks of either format. Blogging has emerged as a possible solution.[1]

Binghamton University in New York also has an excellent Science Library Blog (library.lib.binghamton.edu/mt/science), which focuses primarily on highlighting databases, journals, and news of interest to science faculty and students.

Many law and special libraries use subject blogs to disseminate useful information to their patrons. First Reading from the Hawaii Legislative Reference Bureau Library (www.hawaii.gov/lrb/libblog) is designed to provide news, announcements, articles of interest, and lists of recent titles to the legislative community of Hawaii. The blog's authors essentially act as information filters for busy legislators. Other excellent law blogs (or "blawgs") include WisBlawg from the University of Wisconsin Law Library (www.law.wisc.edu/blogs/wisblawg) and the Stark County Law Library Blawg (temp.starklawlibrary.org/blog) for the legal community in Stark County, Ohio.

Chad Boeninger, the business and economics bibliographer at the Ohio University Libraries, developed a Business Blog (www.library.ohiou.edu/subjects/businessblog) to communicate with business students:

> I originally set up my Business Blog to serve as sort of an online FAQ. Since many of the students that I deal with are all working on very similar projects, sometimes it is useful (and much easier on me) to post some hints online. Now I don't tell the students the page numbers of books that have the particular statistic that they need, I just point them to appropriate

resources for the project. This saves them time and in turn, it saves me from answering the same question over and over again.[2]

The Business Blog (Figure 3.1) is much more focused than most other subject blogs because it is designed to help students with specific research projects. This gives students a more compelling reason to read the blog, which is essentially a just-in-time subject guide created on the fly as Boeninger learns about assignments. He also puts his photo and contact information at the top of the page, which quite literally puts a human face on the blog and encourages students to ask him business-related questions. The Business Blog also includes a link to an explanation of what a blog is and the specific goal of his blog. Many subject librarians know in advance about important papers that students in their subject have been assigned. A blog with helpful information about relevant resources could save both librarians and students time and energy.

Figure 3.1   The Ohio University Libraries Business Blog offers just-in-time resources and research tips to business students. (*Reproduced with permission.*)

Blogs to Supplement Workshops

Many librarians provide patron instruction of some kind, from biblio-graphic instruction for freshmen, to classes on database and Internet use, to classes instructing faculty or colleagues about new technologies. Whatever the purpose of a class, if the audience can access the Internet, a blog can be an excellent way to supplement a workshop and reinforce skills. For every one-hour class, librarians often have at least another hour's worth of information they would like to offer; much of this infor-mation can go into a blog. For a basic Internet skills class, a blog could offer useful tips, suggested Web sites, and instructions for specific tasks. For an information literacy class, a blog can include the resources dis-cussed in class as well as additional resources and research tips the librar-ian didn't have time to discuss. A blog is far more permanent than a paper handout (which most students will probably lose!).

A workshop blog could even be used during a class. Rather than using Microsoft PowerPoint or other presentation software, librarians can put their content and Web links into a blog. This lets students use the librar-ian's notes and links after the class is finished. Librarians could also use the blog to record questions asked and answered during the course of the class. By allowing people to post comments, they can continue educating patrons long after classes are finished.

Reference Blogs

A reference blog is similar to a subject blog, but it provides links to interesting articles and Web resources on multiple subjects. Similar to the eclectic questions librarians are asked at a typical reference desk, a refer-ence blog includes an eclectic assortment of resources. Reference blogs let librarians play the role of a filter, pointing patrons to interesting and qual-ity content on the Web. Reference blogs are perfect for public, academic, and school libraries, where patrons have a variety of interests. Patrons may not be interested in every resource listed on a reference blog, but they will often find a hidden gem they would not have otherwise uncovered.

In a single week on the h2Oboro lib blog (www.waterborolibrary.org/blog.htm), a blog for patrons of the Waterboro Public Library in Maine, readers could find information on Generation Y, booklists of current events, lyrics of original nursery rhymes, sites about the economist Peter Drucker, *Empire Magazine*'s 50 Greatest Independent Films, town news about garbage pickup, and local election results. The blog, created in 2002, has been around longer than most library blogs. Its author, library volunteer Molly Williams, explained the goals of the blog and how she finds materials in a 2003 interview:

> [It's] a place to inform patrons, readers, librarians, educators, researchers, writers, and others about news relevant to reading, books, literature, libraries, bookstores, and to some extent, Maine, as well as to note our own website offerings, all in one place. Sometimes I also throw in news and information about my personal interests, such as gardening, botany, rural and coastal living, England, animals, sustainable living practices, and of course, crime novels and mysteries. I create the weblog daily using news that's emailed to me and using some of the several hundred Web pages I have bookmarked as "blogfodder."[3]

Special libraries also have blogs that act as information filters for the range of subjects in which their patrons are interested. The United Nations' Dag Hammarskjöld Library in New York City has its own blog, UN Pulse (unhq-appspub-01.un.org/lib/dhlrefweblog.nsf). Its authors provide links to reports, articles, and Web sites of interest to U.N. employees and diplomats. Most links point to groups affiliated with the U.N., because in such a large organization, it's easy to miss an important report. Topics covered include human rights issues, literacy, world health, disaster relief, the environment, and terrorism.

Book Club Blogs

Library book clubs are very popular, but some people who enjoy discussing books cannot physically attend discussions. A book club blog is an excellent alternative or supplement to an in-person book club and can be as unstructured or structured as the participants prefer. The club could be assigned a particular book each month, with a different member acting as a facilitator. The facilitator (or facilitating librarian) would start off the discussion in a blog post, and other members could continue the discussion in the comments section. A less structured online book discussion blog allows members to post book reviews and others to discuss those books in the comments. Blogs can also serve as online supplements to book clubs that meet in person. People can start online discussions before their meetings and continue them online after a meeting is over.

The Roselle Public Library in Illinois established a Blogger Book Club (www.roselle.lib.il.us/YouthServices/BookClub/Bloggerbookclub.htm) for children in 2003. When the club first started, a specific book was chosen each month that the children would discuss, with librarians facilitating. Any child who was a member of the Roselle Public Library could register for the book club. After almost two years, the librarians decided to change the format and make the club less structured. Rather than choosing a specific book to discuss each month, registered members can now write reviews of any books they have read. Membership requirements have been relaxed to let any children's book lover and library cardholder in the country register. The Blogger Book Club is an excellent example of both structured and unstructured online book clubs.

Readers' Advisory Blogs

Readers' advisory is an integral part of many librarians' jobs. A patron will come up and say, "I'm looking for a murder mystery book," or "I liked *Plainsong*, what else do you have like that?" Librarians in public and academic libraries, in particular, are often in the position of suggesting particular books to patrons. Some libraries have taken readers' advisory online with blogs. Readers' advisory blogs again turn librarians into filters for patrons who don't have the time to read the *New York Times Book Review* or *Booklist*. Readers' advisory blogs highlight books that patrons might otherwise miss, by posting book reviews, best-seller lists, and/or lists of books on specific themes.

The Harris County Public Library eBranch Blog (www.hcpl.net/ebranch/news) is intended to be just another branch of the Harris County Library System in Houston, albeit online (Figure 3.2). The blog includes elements of typical readers' advisory, including book reviews, listings of best sellers, and reading suggestions on specific themes. At the time of Rosa Parks' death, the blog suggested seven books about Rosa Parks for children, young adults, and adults. For Halloween, it listed suggested horror books and movies. This is a rare example of a blog that provides readers' advisory for both young people and adults.

Bookends (library.coloradocollege.edu/bookends) is a readers' advisory blog from librarians at the Tutt Library of Colorado College. The blog

Figure 3.2   The Harris County (TX) Public Library eBranch Blog provides reading lists on a variety of themes for readers of all ages. (*Reproduced with permission.*)

provides brief reviews of both fiction and nonfiction books, helping people find books they may otherwise overlook. Each review is categorized by genre and review author so users can browse the archives based on the type of book they're looking for. Many readers' advisory blogs at public libraries also offer book suggestions for children and young adults; this can be useful at school libraries, helping librarians positively influence children's reading choices.

Marketing Blogs

Blogs can be used to give libraries a human face online and to market their services to community members who don't normally visit the library. Marketing blogs encourage patrons to use resources and attend library events, while trying to attract new patrons. News blogs and marketing blogs overlap quite a bit. The Old Bridge (NJ) Library Weblog (obpl.blogspot.com) engages its readers through photos. This blog markets upcoming events, but it also describes past events. Because it describes and includes photos of past events, patrons can see what these events are like before committing to attending one. Each blog post includes a photo or graphic to create visual interest for an event or an exhibit. When librarians moved the science fiction books to another part of the library, they even included a picture of the shelves with a description of where the books could now be found. Photos catch the eye and make it more likely that users will read a post.

The St. Joseph County Public Library in Indiana uses a different method to humanize its online presence in SJCPL Lifeline (www.library forlife.org/blogs/lifeline/). The language used in a blog—formal or familiar—largely determines its tone. Formally written blogs may be more professional, but they may not really engage the reader. The librarians who write for the SJCPL Lifeline use familiar language when addressing readers, as if they are writing for friends. This makes readers, or community members, feel as though they are part of the family. Here is a post by one librarian about the movie *Charlie and the Chocolate Factory*:

> Ok, I hate to admit it but I broke the firm resolution I made to myself of never seeing a remade Hollywood classic that I loved growing up. Then Tim Burton has to come along with his amazing style and phenomenal cast and makes *Charlie and the Chocolate Factory* ... From the very opening sequence of rich, wonderful Wonka Bars being made in the factory on, I was an addict! Like other Burton films this movie was dark and colorful, both literally and figuratively. Burton has a way of making the creepy fun! This it true not only with his incredibly visual sets and costumes, but also with his stellar cast.[4]

This type of writing engages the reader with its familiarity. Rather than a dry factual review of the movie, the author's post feels more like someone talking to an old friend. By extension, it makes the library seem as though it's an old friend to the reader.

Blogs to Build Community

Currently, very few library blogs can be considered online communities in and of themselves. With the exception of book club blogs, most library blogs inform instead of inviting discussion. The danger when opening a blog up to public comment is that patrons or other individuals will post inappropriate content. However, one benefit of a true community blog is an engaged population that feels it has a voice in the future of the library. After all, a library is a community institution; it makes sense to include patrons in what amounts to the library's online branch.

Some library blogs do allow patrons to comment on posts, but these comments are rare—if not nonexistent—for several reasons. Not every library blog includes posts that really invite comment. People rarely feel compelled to comment on items in a reference or news blog. Blogs also sometimes fail to occupy a prominent spot on a library's Web site; their placement makes them appear unimportant to the Web site as a whole, and not worth reading. Lastly, patrons simply may not be engaged enough to take interest in discussions. A library blog must have a combination of engaging posts and an engaged population to become a successful online community.

Users who visit the front page of the Ann Arbor (MI) District Library (AADL) Web site (www.aadl.org) find themselves on a blog—a very attractive page that is visually consistent with the Web site's design, but still a blog. In fact, there are many blogs on the library's Web site, with little to distinguish them from the rest of the site. The blogs are integrated, and integral, parts of the library's online presence. As Library Director Josie Parker stated in an interview with *Library Journal*, "we wanted our Web site to be interactive with the public and chose blogs as the major form of communication ... The major point is to make the library transparent."[5] AADL achieves this transparency by encouraging online interaction. Users can register to post comments to the blogs, which they have done in large numbers. Ann Arbor is a particularly civic-minded community, which is well suited to this kind of forum. Even the library director has a blog (www.aadl.org/taxonomy/term/86) where she discusses issues that affect the library and the community on a macro level (Figure 3.3). Almost all of her posts have received thoughtful comments from Ann Arbor citizens.

The other community that has formed around AADL's Web site has nothing to do with civic issues. The library's teen services department, AXIS, most notably includes online information on their gaming tournaments. (For more on these tournaments, see Chapter 13.) The AXIS blog (www.aadl.org/axis) exists to communicate with teenage patrons, but blog posts about gaming tournaments have become a social hub for the gamers. There were 355 comments attached to one blog post about an

Figure 3.3   The Director's Blog at the Ann Arbor (MI) District Library
receives a great deal of comments from members of the
community. (*Reproduced with permission.*)

upcoming tournament, all in the form of a spirited conversation about
gaming. AADL librarians—who clearly enjoy gaming as much as their
patrons—speak the teens' language in their blog posts, making it a safe
environment for teens to be themselves.

Developing an interactive online library community around a blog can
greatly improve communication between a library and its community.
Librarian bloggers can solicit patron feedback about collections, services,
and programming, giving the library valuable information about the needs
of their patrons and helping to humanize its online presence. When giving
their feedback, patrons would likely feel more invested in their library.
Libraries must be cognizant of possible abuses when allowing comments,
but as AADL has shown, the potential benefits of building community
online are tremendous and the potential drawbacks can be managed.

How Librarians Can Use Blogs

Librarians need to communicate effectively with colleagues and others in the profession just as much as with their patrons. Internally, it's

important to find effective and nondisruptive ways of disseminating information. Externally, librarians can learn a great deal from other members of the profession. All over the world, librarians are introducing innovations in their libraries. Many libraries have created tremendous programs and services—many of which are not known to anyone outside of their immediate community. At the same time, others are trying to accomplish the same things. Why reinvent the wheel? Librarians need tools that let them communicate and share their success stories. Blogs can help librarians share information, learn from one another, and build community online.

Internal Staff Blogs

Keeping track of internal library communications and announcements can be difficult. Internal communications usually consist of casual conversations, the occasional staff meeting, paper memos, and mass e-mails. These e-mails can generate countless replies that are sent to everyone on the original list, whether or not they are relevant to everyone. It can be difficult to keep up with daily e-mail in even a mid-sized library, and it is quite easy to delete an important message accidentally. Blogs can help librarians avoid e-mail overload. An internal blog, such as a news blog, can include news and announcements of interest to library staff. Librarians can use an internal blog to announce meetings, discuss problematic issues, and even pose questions to other staff members. With a blog, there is no danger a reader will accidentally delete something important, and announcements will be archived for later use. Posts can also be categorized so people can easily determine which ones are relevant to them. Blogs ensure that people aren't inadvertently left out of the loop by not being included in an e-mail. All the replies to a post will be tied to the post itself so people can easily follow the thread of conversation. But it's important to make sure the staff makes a habit of checking the internal blog daily. Make it part of the staff home page or a prominent link on your Intranet.

At the Bethel Park Public Library in Pennsylvania, busy children's librarians use a blog to make announcements, requests, and share basic information. As they work different shifts, the Children's Department Paperless Notebook (bpchildrens.blogspot.com) is an excellent way for staff to ask if someone could cover a shift or let people know about an upcoming meeting. The Reference at Newman Library blog (reference newman.blogspot.com) at Baruch College (NY) includes announcements about printer status, database access, and computer use policies (Figure 3.4). Librarians at Baruch also post articles that may interest their colleagues. This creates a central repository of relevant information for reference staff and eliminates the need to hold onto countless e-mail messages. Staff members could use a blog to collect useful reference resources or articles for professional development, assigning categories to posts to easily find relevant resources when needed.

Staff can also use blogs when working together on projects. The number of e-mails sent to project members tends to grow exponentially; a blog keeps all of the information and announcements in a central location. Issues could be discussed in the comments section, and all of the team members could be given the right to post to the blog. Blogs are an ideal

Figure 3.4   Internal blogs, such as the Reference at Newman Library blog at Baruch College (NY), can help improve staff communications. (*Reproduced with permission.*)

tool for any type of internal communication. They centralize communications—both the original post and the following comments—and archive them for future use. They can make the effective flow and storage of information far more manageable.

Reading Blogs to Keep Up

These days, keeping up with the flow of information in the library field is virtually impossible. New technologies come out, new studies are published, and librarians introduce new offerings at their libraries every day. Just keeping up with the professional news is a full-time job in itself, but librarians are usually too busy even to read the journals to which their libraries subscribe. Blogs offer an easy way to keep up. Librarian bloggers act as filters for their readers, writing only about the items they find most compelling. Rather than taking the time to read a entire journal article that may turn out to have little or no relevance to you, you can read a blogger's synopsis of that article to see if you might find it useful. They do the research, so you don't have to. On the other hand, blogs reflect each author's subjective viewpoint. If you rely solely on blogs for your news, you may miss out on important information. Each blog will only give you one side of any story, unless it's a collaborative blog. Blogs can be very useful and informative, but readers must view them with a critical eye.

Bloggers use different posting styles. Some primarily link to interesting articles in the field; others write more about what is going on in their libraries; and some write longer reflective posts about the state of the profession. Many bloggers use a combination of posting styles depending on the topic, their interests, and their time constraints. Different librarian bloggers also focus on different issues. If you are interested in learning more about using IM in libraries, read Aaron Schmidt's Walking Paper (walkingpaper.org). If you are interested in creating a podcast, David Free's David's Random Stuff (davidsrandomstuff.blogspot.com) is the place to go. If you want to learn what's new in bibliographic classification and metadata, visit David Bigwood's Catalogablog (catalogablog.blogspot.com). There is a blog for almost every library-related interest, and topical blogs can be very useful when you're looking for information in a specific area. A good place to discover blogs of interest is LibWorm (www.libworm. com), which lets you search over a thousand library blogs and library-related sites for specific terms. This helps users find blogs about their topics of interest. If you are interested in virtual reference services, just search for "virtual reference" and see which blogs discuss the subject. More general blog search engines will help you discover blogs from outside the library world. Tools such as Technorati (technorati.com), BlogPulse (www.blogpulse.com), and Feedster (www.feedster.com) let people search blogs for a specific term. This is a great way to discover new blogs and track conversations in the blogosphere.

Once you find a few blogs that interest you, those blogs will subsequently introduce you to the entire world of library blogs. A link in a blog post at Walking Paper will lead you to an interesting post at Jenny Levine's The Shifted Librarian (www.theshiftedlibrarian.com), which will lead you to another blog, and so on. You will see distributed conversations about library topics in various posts on various blogs. The blog posts will also link to interesting articles, Web sites, and Web applications you may never have found otherwise. Following the links in blogs is a great way to contribute to your own professional development.

Many library bloggers write about their own experiences, and readers can learn a lot from these posts. Librarians write about looking for library jobs, dealing with their administration, implementing new technologies, trying new types of programming with their patrons, and many other experiences. Often they write about things no one has tried before. By writing about these innovations in their blogs, they can assist and inspire others to copy their efforts. This is only one example of the information that is shared when librarians blog.

Blogging to Build Community and Contribute to the Profession

Many librarians have started blogs over the past few years. While each blogger writes an individual blog or contributes to a collaborative blog, the community of librarian bloggers, sharing ideas and success stories, is closely connected. The distributed conversations among blogs have been compared to the citation networks of scholarly writing, although the dialogue occurs at a quicker pace in the blogosphere.[6] In the blogosphere, ideas are collaboratively processed over a few days or weeks, as opposed to the years it can take scholars to publish and respond to the ideas of their colleagues.

The power of library blogs is especially apparent during a library-related conference. Previously, those unable to attend a conference would often hear little about what took place there. Perhaps they would read a conference report from a colleague or an article in a journal, but these really didn't capture the flavor or conference zeitgeist. As more librarians began to blog, more conference reports appeared. Bloggers write about the sessions they attended, what was said, and their personal impressions. They also write about what goes on between sessions, those social moments when so many of the most interesting discussions take place at conferences. In 2005, group blogs began to form to cover conferences. These include the PLA Blog (www.plablog.org), the LITA Blog (litablog.org), the NJLA Blog (blog.njla.org), and the Information Today, Inc. Blog (www.infotodayblog.com). While some of these offer sporadic posts year-round, the start of a conference is always marked by a flurry of coverage by regular authors of the blog and/or volunteers. Conference blogging still appears on individual blogs as well, and bloggers at many conferences choose to tag relevant posts with a mutually agreed on Technorati tag. (A tag is a piece of metadata that you can add to a post to make it easier to find; see more on tagging in Chapter 8.) For example, at the Computers in Libraries conference in 2006, all blog posts about the conference were tagged "CIL2006." This way, people could visit Technorati and easily access all of the posts tagged CIL2006 on various group and individual blogs.

Blogging provides an excellent opportunity for online networking with librarians working in different positions and interested in many different aspects of librarianship. Some of the field's most influential practitioners and scholars now blog. People can develop important friendships with the librarians they share ideas with online. There may be professional benefits to making contact with the online movers and shakers of the library world.

Blogging can also help you hone your writing skills. Many new bloggers consider their online activities good practice for more professional or traditional writing endeavors. Writing daily or weekly about issues in the profession not only can make you a better writer, but can help you to reflect upon your own views about the profession. Sometimes people don't think about their opinion on a particular issue until they are forced to defend or reflect on their view. Writing about many different subjects is also a great way to keep current with what is happening in the profession.

Just as a blog is a great marketing tool for a library, it also can be a great marketing tool for a librarian, when used sensibly. In a tight job market, librarians need to do whatever they can to distinguish themselves from the pack. A blog is an excellent way to show a potential employer your intelligence and passion for librarianship. However, blogging could potentially hurt as much as it can help. If the tone of your blog is negative or offensive—or if a potential employer disdains blogs—this could hurt your chances of employment. Librarians must be mindful of the ways they represent themselves online, whether through blogging, participating on discussion boards, or posting to e-mail lists.

Blogging can be personally and professionally rewarding. It allows bloggers to make new friends and share ideas with colleagues. It can increase their visibility in the profession and bring them new opportunities. It can help them improve their writing skills and learn more about the profession. Although blogging has many potential benefits, bloggers must be aware of what they write and remember that whatever they write may be seen by potential employers.

Blogs have come a long way since they were initially used as mere lists of links in reverse chronological order. Blogs, now used in many areas and for many different purposes, have become a powerful force for self-expression and an excellent tool for sharing information. In libraries, blogs can make it easy for librarians to disseminate news and information to their users and help them develop online communities with their patrons. Personally, blogs can be used as tools for professional development and keeping up with the profession. While blogs are not intended to replace scholarly journals and books, they are an excellent way to stay informed about what's happening in the field. When deciding whether to start a blog, it is important to evaluate what you hope to accomplish and whether a blog is the best tool for your needs. Blogs are not the solution to every information-sharing problem, but they are certainly flexible enough to solve many of them.

Endnotes

1. Teri M. Vogel and Doug Goans, "Delivering the News with Blogs: The Georgia State University Library Experience," *Internet Reference Services Quarterly* 10.1 (2005): 9.

2. Chad Boeninger, "Business Blogging Tips," *Library Voice* 1, February 2005, libraryvoice.com/archives/2005/02/01/business-blogging-tips (accessed November 25, 2005).

3. Marylaine Block, "Molly Williams: Library Volunteer Extraordinaire," Ex Libris 167 (2003), marylaine.com/exlibris/xlib167.html (accessed November 26, 2005).

4. Franklin Sheneman, "Better than the Original?" SJCPL Lifeline, November 8, 2005, www.libraryforlife.org/blogs/lifeline/?p=393 (accessed November 27, 2005).

5. Brian Kenney, "Ann Arbor's Web Site Maximizes Blogging Software," *Library Journal*, September 1, 2005, www.libraryjournal.com/article/CA6251465.html (accessed November 25, 2005).

6. Tom Coates, "Discussion and Citation in the Blogosphere," Plasticbag.org, May 25, 2003, www.plasticbag.org/archives/2003/05 (accessed December 1, 2005).

Chapter 4

RSS

The Web contains a tremendous amount of information on almost every subject imaginable. More and more, people depend on the Web for news, professional development, and education, but its continuous growth makes it nearly impossible to keep up with news stories, scholarly studies, and blog posts. Many people have sources they turn to for news and information, which are often bookmarked in their browser for easy accessibility. However, users still need to visit each Web site frequently to see if new content has been added. This can be time-consuming and frustrating, especially when some Web sites and blogs are updated infrequently.

Many librarians read blogs to keep track of important trends in the field. The number of librarian-written blogs grows every day, offering more content and choice to readers. In a 2005 survey of librarian bloggers, more than 30 percent stated that they read more than 100 blogs on a regular basis.[1] While it isn't difficult to visit five or 10 blogs regularly to search for updated content, it would be nearly impossible to visit more than 100 blogs a day by physically going to each site. Fortunately, RSS has helped automate the process of keeping up with news and information online. Now users can subscribe to blogs, news sites, and other Web content and receive the updated content in a single place. Instead of having to visit the same Web sites every day, any new content is delivered to the user as soon as it is added. RSS is the key to staying informed and preventing information overload.

What Is RSS?

RSS is a format for syndicating content on the Web. Based on XML, RSS breaks Web sites into discrete chunks of information, such as a single news story or a single blog post. This frees the content from the page, since RSS "feeds" only include the content from a given site, not any information about how that content is to be displayed. This means that content can be made available on other pages via RSS, and its look can be tailored to any of these sites. Instead of checking a Web site daily for updates, people can subscribe to the site's RSS feed (the method by which RSS is delivered). When new information is posted to the Web site, RSS lets this information be accessed through an aggregator, via e-mail, or on an entirely separate Web page. The separation of content from format means that RSS feeds can be combined and syndicated in novel ways.

RSS 0.90 was originally designed by Netscape in 1999 for the purpose of gathering content from disparate sources to develop portals. Once Netscape left the portal market, the project was picked up by UserLand for use with blogs, and by the RSS-DEV group, which built RSS 1.0. This created two separate lines of development. In 2002, UserLand's Dave Winer unveiled RSS 2.0. Both RSS 1.0 and 2.0 are now used to syndicate Web sites, blogs, and other content.[2] The acronym RSS has come to stand for a variety of things: "Rich Site Summary," "RDF Site Summary," or "Real Simple Syndication." Real Simple Syndication is the most popular, as it is a truly functional description of RSS.

The majority of people use RSS as consumers. RSS consumers don't need to understand how RSS works; they only need to know what they can do with it. RSS makes information portable, so that it can be read in different places and used in multiple ways. Most people use RSS to read content from multiple Web sites, all on the same page. This way, users can keep track of frequently changing Web content and information without actually having to visit every site. Many news outlets, blogs, and other Web sites offer RSS feeds for their content. For example, CNN (www.cnn. com/services/rss), the *New York Times* online edition (www.nytimes. com/services/xml/rss/index.html), and the *Washington Post* online edition (www.washingtonpost.com/wp-dyn/rss/index.html) each have RSS feeds for sections such as U.S. News, World News, and Technology. You can get RSS feeds of the weather in your area or of package shipments you are tracking. Most Web sites offering RSS feeds display a small orange rectangle reading "XML" or "RSS." This icon can usually be found on the top, bottom, or sidebar column of a Web page. A new square orange icon is becoming the standard RSS indicator and is used by the Internet Explorer and Firefox browsers. If a site has an RSS feed, the icon will be visible in the browser toolbar in IE7 and Firefox 2.0 or later.

When you access an RSS feed in a regular browser, it looks like incomprehensible code, rather than a readable page (Figure 4.1). This is because RSS, like XML, is devoid of presentation information. You will need an aggregator to display RSS feeds so they look like any other Web page. An aggregator (also referred to as a "news reader" or "feed reader") is software or a Web site that consolidates all your feeds so you can read them in one place. It allows users to get news from hundreds of Web sites on a single page. Users can subscribe to an individual Web site's RSS feed in their aggregators, and when another article or post is added, they can read the content in their aggregator. So rather than visiting a blog or Web site to see if there is any new content, users can simply subscribe once to its RSS feed and receive any new information automatically. Many people subscribe to dozens—or even hundreds—of RSS feeds in their aggregator.

With the variety of aggregators available, each has its own pros and cons. Aggregators can be found in your browser, on your desktop, in your e-mail client, on your mobile device, or on a Web portal. Some people use desktop aggregators, which are downloaded to a user's computer. These

```xml
<!-- generator="wordpress/2.0.3" -->
- <rss version="2.0">
  - <channel>
      <title>Information Wants To Be Free</title>
      <link>http://meredith.wolfwater.com/wordpress/index.php</link>
    - <description>
        A librarian, writer and tech geek reflecting on the profession and the tools we use to serve our patrons
      </description>
      <pubDate>Mon, 05 Jun 2006 02:34:09 +0000</pubDate>
      <generator>http://wordpress.org/?v=2.0.3</generator>
      <language>en</language>
    - <item>
        <title>Test</title>
      - <link>
          http://meredith.wolfwater.com/wordpress/index.php/2006/06/04/test-2/
        </link>
      - <comments>
          http://meredith.wolfwater.com/wordpress/index.php/2006/06/04/test-2/#comments
        </comments>
        <pubDate>Mon, 05 Jun 2006 02:34:09 +0000</pubDate>
        <dc:creator>Meredith Farkas</dc:creator>
        <dc:subject>hi</dc:subject>
      - <guid isPermaLink="false">
          http://meredith.wolfwater.com/wordpress/index.php/2006/06/04/test-2/
        </guid>
      - <description>
          I just upgraded Wordpress and I want to make sure everything is still working right.
        </description>
      - <content:encoded>
          <p>I just upgraded Wordpress and I want to make sure everything is still working right. <img
          src='http://meredith.wolfwater.com/wordpress/wp-includes/images/smilies/icon_smile.gif' alt=':)' class='wp-smiley' /> </p>
        </content:encoded>
      - <wfw:commentRSS>
          http://meredith.wolfwater.com/wordpress/index.php/2006/06/04/test-2/feed/
        </wfw:commentRSS>
      </item>
```

Figure 4.1   The RSS feed from Information Wants to Be Free as viewed in a Web browser. Most people view RSS feeds in an aggregator or on a personal start page. (*Reproduced with permission.*)

are available as part of an e-mail application, such as Mozilla Thunderbird or Microsoft Outlook, or as stand-alone software, such as NewzCrawler (www.newzcrawler.com) or BlogBridge (www.blogbridge.com). Desktop aggregators are safer and more private, because they reside on your own computer and information about your subscriptions is not on the Web. Your subscriptions also will continue even if the company that developed the aggregator goes out of business.

The main problem with desktop aggregators is their lack of portability. You can download the application to one computer and add your RSS feeds, and that will be the only place you'll be able to read them. If you use someone else's computer at school, work, or a conference, you will not be able to access your subscriptions. If your hard drive crashes, you may lose all the feeds you were tracking, and you will also have to download any software upgrades and patches yourself. However, if you lose Internet connectivity, you may still be able to access your feeds; many desktop aggregators let you read feeds offline. Portability of your RSS feeds from one application to another is also a concern; investigate this before choosing an aggregator.

Some people use Web-based aggregators, which can be accessed from any browser without downloading. Popular Web-based aggregators include Bloglines (bloglines.com; see Figure 4.2) and Rojo (www.rojo.com). The advantage here is that Web-based aggregators are portable; they can be used from any computer with an Internet connection and a browser. If your hard drive has a meltdown, you won't lose all your feeds. Web-based aggregators are easy to set up, have simple interfaces, and don't require a software download. But Web-based aggregators have no provision for offline reading. If you decide to save all your online reading for a vacation but don't have Internet connectivity while you're away, you won't be able to read any of the posts you saved. Just as you won't be able to access your subscriptions offline, you also won't be able to access them if the company with the application goes out of business. With any aggregator, make sure you can export your RSS feeds in a format—usually OPML (Outline Processor Markup Language)—that can easily be imported into another aggregator. It makes sense to make a backup of your subscriptions in any aggregator, just in case there's a dot-com bust or a hard-drive meltdown.

According to a study by Ipsos Insight and Yahoo!, only 12 percent of the population has heard of the term RSS, but 27 percent has actually used

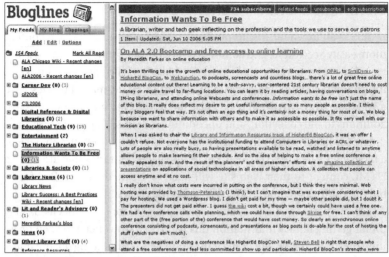

Figure 4.2   The same RSS feed from Figure 4.1 as viewed in the popular aggregator Bloglines. (©2006 Bloglines)

RSS without realizing it.[3] When a Web site such as My Yahoo! (my.yahoo.com) offers content from a variety of Web sites, it is often using RSS-syndicated content. RSS is designed to be integrated into people's daily lifestyle, which is why so few actually know when they are using an RSS aggregator. With RSS, you can view content in a personalized start page like My Yahoo!, listed with other RSS feeds in an aggregator, embedded in a Web page or courseware, or on the page from which the content originated. RSS provides the flexibility to choose the tool you wish to use to view the content you want to see in your daily life.

RSS is not the only XML-based format for syndicating content. Atom feeds, which are functionally similar to RSS feeds, are also used frequently to syndicate content from blogs and wikis. OPML, another format involved in syndication, is used to create a hierarchical list of multiple feeds. Users often use OPML to export all the RSS and Atom feeds from one aggregator and import them into another. If people want to share a reading list of blogs they enjoy, they can also create an OPML file that others can import—with all of the feeds—into their own aggregator.

Librarians as RSS Publishers

RSS is an excellent way to push content to our patrons, make content more easily accessible, and combine content from various sites onto a single page. Most content that can be broken up into discrete chunks of information can be syndicated via RSS. For example, many libraries have a Web page describing what's new at the library, including news, events, additions to the collection, and upcoming programs. This is a natural candidate for RSS; whether the page happens to be a traditional Web page or a blog, an RSS feed can push its content to users. Libraries that are adding HTML content to their Web site will need to create their own RSS feeds, but blog software comes with built-in RSS feed capability.

Library patrons who already use an aggregator for other RSS feeds may prefer getting library information this way. They won't need to keep revisiting the library's Web site to see if there are new events going on; the information will be pushed to them. Parents, for example, could subscribe to an RSS feed for children's events to keep up with the latest programs and cancellations. The Winnetka-Northfield Public Library in Illinois (www.wpld.alibrary.com/rsspage.asp) publishes several news feeds targeted to specific groups. The library has feeds for general library news, the adult book club, the youth book club, upcoming adult programs, upcoming youth programs, and its One Book Two Villages program. The information in these feeds can be found on the library's Web site; however, users can also subscribe to the specific feeds that interest them to get news without visiting the site.

Libraries can also use RSS to publish news content to other pages. Libraries that use a blog to disseminate news can let their blog software create an RSS feed automatically, then take the resulting feed and use JavaScript to publish it to their Web site. This lets libraries integrate their blog content into their main site, making it easier for patrons to find it. Librarians don't necessarily need to know JavaScript to display an RSS feed on their library's Web site; they can simply use a tool such as Feed2JS (feed2js.org) or RSS-to-JavaScript (www.rss-to-javascript.com). These tools automatically create JavaScript that can be pasted into a Web document, letting users add the contents of an RSS feed to any page.

Libraries that provide services to distance learners through online courseware, such as WebCT or Blackboard, can use this approach to communicate with their patrons. Many online courseware packages don't allow users to create blogs within the courses, so this is an ideal way to publish outside blog content inside courseware. At Norwich University, I was looking for an effective way to communicate directly with distance learners online. This was difficult since I didn't want to send out mass e-mails, and our version of WebCT didn't offer support in creating blogs. Instead, I created a news blog outside of WebCT. Rather than directing students to the blog, I used Feed2JS to syndicate the blog content onto the pages in WebCT that distance learners used most often (Figure 4.3). Since I syndicate the RSS in several places instead of creating blogs in WebCT, the content is dynamically updated in multiple places without any human intervention. As soon as I post something on the blog, it appears in every distance learning classroom. The students don't need to know about blogs, RSS, or JavaScript; they just see a Web page with library news listed along the side.

Libraries have also started to use RSS to provide lists of new books and other materials to the public. This is particularly useful in public libraries where some patrons just want to see a list of new books and browse the list

Figure 4.3   The library news on the right side of this page in WebCT from Norwich University (VT) is actually syndicated from a blog outside of the courseware.

without coming to the library. Patrons can also place their holds based on books they've seen on the list, rather than only those that happen to be physically located in the library at the time the patrons visit. In academic libraries, sorting the lists of new books by subject could make them a more valuable resource for faculty members. For example, a physics professor could see what's new in his or her field by browsing the list of new physics books. The University of Alberta (www.library.ualberta.ca/newbooks/index.cfm; see Figure 4.4) offers feeds of new titles at its libraries, organized by library and by subject (call number). Each new book includes basic citation information, the location of the book, and an image of the book cover when it is available. Faculty and graduate students can subscribe to the RSS feeds for their areas of interest to have information on the newest books on their subject at the library pushed to them regularly. The Seattle Public Library offers RSS feeds for dynamically created reading lists (www.spl.org/default.asp?pageID=collection_readinglists; see Figure 4.5). These reading lists include the newest materials in all genres and the most popular materials (in terms of holds placed) in all genres. This way,

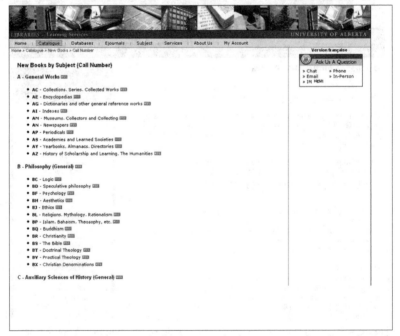

Figure 4.4   The University of Alberta (Canada) lets patrons subscribe to lists of new books by library or subject. (*Reproduced with permission.*)

teens can find out which books other teenagers in Seattle are currently reading, and people of all ages can be the first to get on the reserve list for a brand new book.

Users have been able to subscribe to searches in certain databases and Web sites for some time. After performing a search, users could register their e-mail addresses with the Web site to receive a periodic e-mail message with any new results of that search. When users search for "librarian" on the *Chronicle of Higher Education*'s Chronicle Careers Web site (chronicle. com/jobs), the results are shown with an option to create a search agent. Once you have submitted your e-mail address to the *Chronicle of Higher Education,* you will receive daily or weekly e-mails with your most recent search results. This is an excellent way to keep up with various job sites without having to visit them over and over again. However, creating such a search agent involves disclosing your e-mail address, which can result in

Figure 4.5   The Seattle (WA) Public Library uses RSS to create dynamically updated reading lists of new books for various populations and interests. (*Reproduced with permission.*)

your mailbox being clogged with e-mails from various sites. RSS is a natural alternative to such e-mail subscriptions.

Some libraries offer RSS feeds for catalog searches. When searching the catalog at the Seattle Public Library (www.spl.org), users will see an orange XML button at the bottom of each results page. They can then subscribe to a feed for that particular search by clicking the button and pasting the resulting URL into their aggregator. From then on, any new materials at the library matching their search criteria—whether a title, keyword, subject, or any other kind of search—will show up in the patron's aggregator. The Hennepin County (MN) Public Library (www.hclib.org/pub/search/RSS. cfm; see Figure 4.6) also offers search feeds for its catalog, and offers feeds for searches made in its listing of events and classes. Some people will remember to check the library Web site frequently for any new materials or upcoming events of interest, but many will not. Feeds ensure that information targeted to patrons' interests gets to them automatically without the patrons having to come to the library or check the Web site.

Libraries can also offer RSS feeds that help patrons keep up with their library account. The Hennepin County Public Library and the Seattle Public Library both offer RSS feeds of the books patrons have checked out of the library and feeds that notify patrons when their holds arrive. To get these feeds, patrons just need to enter their library card number and PIN number. Patrons no longer have to wait for a notification from the library that their books are overdue or their holds have come in. They also won't have to go through the process of logging onto the library's Web site to view their record.

Privacy is one potential concern in regards to RSS feeds of patron information. Third parties who are able to access the RSS feed for a patron's account can view a list of what he or she has checked out. These feeds could be accessed by parents who wish to see what their children are reading, or by government agents looking for suspicious borrowing behavior. RSS feeds can sometimes be discovered by others, especially when patrons use Web-based aggregators. The Seattle Public Library addresses these privacy concerns on its Web site:

> **Important Privacy Notice**: The Seattle Public Library cares about the privacy of your personal information. Patrons who use public RSS aggregator Web sites, such as Bloglines, Rojo or Feedster, are cautioned that some of these services allow other users of the service to read your RSS feeds. This means that

Figure 4.6   In the Hennepin County (MN) Public Library catalog, users can
subscribe to alerts that notify them when the library purchases
new materials matching their search criteria. (*Reproduced with
permission.*)

other people can view information regarding items you have
checked out or have placed on hold. Usually you can control
this by using an option in your profile or in the setup of the
feed to mark it "private" or "public."[4]

Some individuals and third-party companies have created hacks to log
remotely into a patron's record and retrieve information, using a card number and PIN provided by the patron. These third parties are not affiliated
with libraries or library vendors, but they provide an attractive service to
people whose libraries don't provide RSS feeds. LibraryElf (www.libraryelf.
com) is popular among frequent library users who want to keep track of
their records easily. Whenever a third party has access to your login information, however, they also have access to your data; while they probably
won't give it out to others, this is still a concern. Users should always be
warned to read the privacy policies of any company with access to their
personal information.

Many libraries have developed subject guides that list useful Web
resources for their patrons. If these are updated frequently, it may make
sense to provide RSS feeds for each of these individual subject pages. This

way, patrons could keep track of new and useful Web resources in their subjects of interest. These subject guides can also include new subject databases and books. The Kansas City Public Library (www.kcpl.lib. mo.us/guides) has created a comprehensive list of subject guides, each with its own RSS feed. Patrons can subscribe to the feed(s) they are interested in, and each time a new Web resource is added, it will appear in the patron's aggregator. Some academic libraries have created RSS feeds that include Web resources and news from other sources. Georgia State University Library (www.library.gsu.edu/news) offers a number of frequently updated subject blogs that contain relevant news. Each has an RSS feed so that students and faculty can get the news filtered from a variety of sources in a single RSS feed in their aggregator.

Librarians as RSS Middlemen

Libraries can syndicate and remix existing feeds from a variety of sources to provide useful information for their patrons. Database vendors and journal publishers are increasingly recognizing the value of RSS in delivering information to users. Patrons in academic, corporate, medical, special, and law libraries keep up-to-date with specific journals in their subjects of interest and would appreciate having information about current journal issues delivered to them in a timely fashion. Journal publishers are starting to provide RSS feeds to alert readers when a new issue is published; some provide RSS feeds of tables of contents and article abstracts for new issues. Individuals can subscribe to the RSS feeds for journals they are interested in to receive current information in their aggregator.

Database vendors have also recently started using RSS. In 2005, ProQuest released Curriculum Match Factor (www.proquest.com/ syndication/rss), which provides curriculum-specific RSS feeds. In each feed, ProQuest provides the titles of and links to journal articles from the best journals for that subject via a computerized search for specific subject terms. ProQuest does the searching, finds relevant articles, and provides feeds for students and faculty to subscribe to in their aggregators. In

Jay Bhatt on RSS

What would you say are the most important uses of RSS in libraries?

RSS feeds can play a vital role in helping researchers keep up with new information as it is published. Researchers worldwide now need information quickly from a multitude of resources to conduct and publish high-quality research. With more resources beginning to provide RSS feeds of research keywords used in a query and more electronic journals now beginning to provide feeds of their new journal issues, researchers can keep up-to-date with new information quickly by subscribing to these feeds from their research interest areas. Information professionals and librarians can benefit by keeping up with the availability of new information tools for their users so that knowledge updates can happen immediately. In addition, feeds of new books and other materials acquired in the library can further motivate users and make finding materials more convenient.

What can librarians do to get their patrons reading RSS feeds?

Librarians can create innovative classes incorporating discussion on how RSS feeds can help students to quickly retrieve scholarly information. Creating flyers and simple handouts that describe the benefits of RSS and offer instructions on using RSS feeds can inspire patrons to use RSS. Librarians need to proactively promote the use of RSS feeds while discussing this topic during faculty and staff meetings and by e-mailing instructional tips to all faculty members and students. Announcement of the availability of new RSS feeds with instructions in library newsletters can make users aware of the availability of new resources and corresponding RSS feeds. Librarians can meet with various student organizations on campus to promote the use of RSS feeds.

What do you use RSS for in your everyday life?

I use RSS in my daily life to keep abreast of new information related to libraries, new books, and engineering resources and tools. I monitor international news every day through RSS feeds and also keep up-to-date on sports and new Bollywood movies. My personal list of feeds (www.bloglines.com/public/bhattjj) illustrates how I keep up with new information from a variety of sources in a very short time.

Jay Bhatt is the Information Services Librarian for Engineering at Drexel University. He is the author of the Englibrary Blog (www.library.drexel.edu/blogs/englibrary) and has written a number of articles on the use of RSS for science librarians.

2006, EBSCO began offering registered users the ability to subscribe to RSS feeds of specific searches in EBSCO databases.[5] This way, when a new article on the subject a patron subscribes to is added to the database, the patron will be notified in his or her aggregator.

Librarians can obviously capitalize on these RSS feeds from journal and database providers by integrating their content or by informing patrons of their availability. Librarians can add lists of relevant journals offering RSS feeds to their existing subject guides. The University of Wisconsin's (UW) Ebling Library (www.hsl.wisc.edu/bjd/journals/rss/index.cfm) has created a page of RSS feeds for a large number of journals in the biomedical and health sciences. Each RSS feed contains a list of the journal's most recent articles with a brief description of each article. UW librarians simply took existing journal RSS feeds and compiled them on the same page. OhioLINK (journals.ohiolink.edu) offers RSS feeds of the table of contents of any journal in its Electronic Journal Center to patrons of OhioLINK member libraries. Libraries could also create aggregated pages of subject-specific information or provide an OPML file with all the journals in a single subject so patrons could subscribe to all their RSS feeds at once. Some tools combine multiple RSS feeds into a single feed, such as RSS Mix (www.rssmix.com) and KickRSS (www.kickrss.com). Using one of these tools, a library could create a single-subject feed with multiple journal feeds. This way, patrons would only have to subscribe to a single feed to see the tables of contents from multiple journals—and the content would be dynamically updated (Figure 4.7). Librarians could syndicate the tables of contents from popular journals on a subject resource page and mix database feeds, news, and other subject resources into a single feed to display on their pages as well.

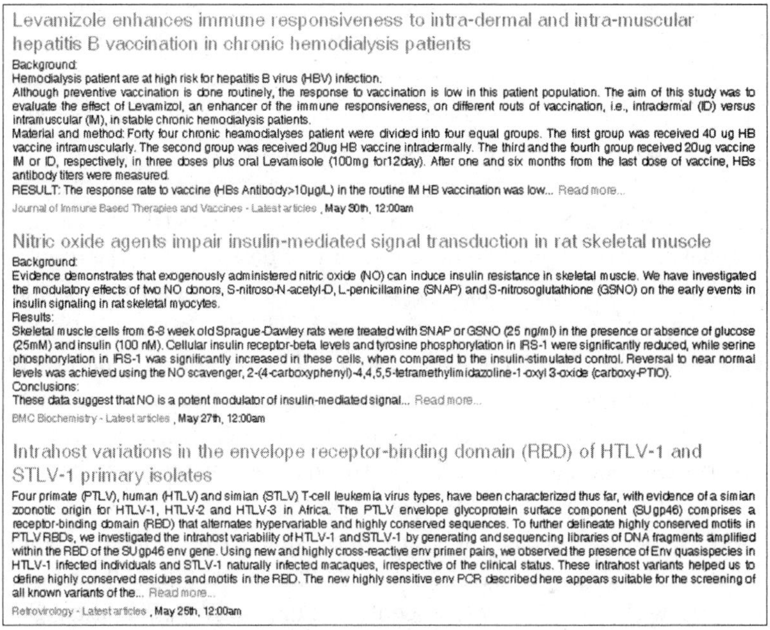

Levamizole enhances immune responsiveness to intra-dermal and intra-muscular hepatitis B vaccination in chronic hemodialysis patients

Background:
Hemodialysis patient are at high risk for hepatitis B virus (HBV) infection.
Although preventive vaccination is done routinely, the response to vaccination is low in this patient population. The aim of this study was to evaluate the effect of Levamizol, an enhancer of the immune responsiveness, on different routs of vaccination, i.e., intradermal (ID) versus intramuscular (IM), in stable chronic hemodialysis patients.
Material and method: Forty four chronic heamodialyses patient were divided into four equal groups. The first group was received 40 ug HB vaccine intramuscularly. The second group was received 20ug HB vaccine intradermally. The third and the fourth group received 20ug vaccine IM or ID, respectively, in three doses plus oral Levamisole (100mg for12day). After one and six months from the last dose of vaccine, HBs antibody titers were measured.
RESULT: The response rate to vaccine (HBs Antibody>10µg/L) in the routine IM HB vaccination was low... Read more...

Journal of Immune Based Therapies and Vaccines - Latest articles , May 30th, 12:00am

Nitric oxide agents impair insulin-mediated signal transduction in rat skeletal muscle

Background:
Evidence demonstrates that exogenously administered nitric oxide (NO) can induce insulin resistance in skeletal muscle. We have investigated the modulatory effects of two NO donors, S-nitroso-N-acetyl-D, L-penicillamine (SNAP) and S-nitrosoglutathione (GSNO) on the early events in insulin signaling in rat skeletal myocytes.
Results:
Skeletal muscle cells from 6-8 week old Sprague-Dawley rats were treated with SNAP or GSNO (25 ng/ml) in the presence or absence of glucose (25mM) and insulin (100 nM). Cellular insulin receptor-beta levels and tyrosine phosphorylation in IRS-1 were significantly reduced, while serine phosphorylation in IRS-1 was significantly increased in these cells, when compared to the insulin-stimulated control. Reversal to near normal levels was achieved using the NO scavenger, 2-(4-carboxyphenyl)-4,4,5,5-tetramethylimidazoline-1-oxyl 3-oxide (carboxy-PTIO).
Conclusions:
These data suggest that NO is a potent modulator of insulin-mediated signal... Read more...

BMC Biochemistry - Latest articles , May 27th, 12:00am

Intrahost variations in the envelope receptor-binding domain (RBD) of HTLV-1 and STLV-1 primary isolates

Four primate (PTLV), human (HTLV) and simian (STLV) T-cell leukemia virus types, have been characterized thus far, with evidence of a simian zoonotic origin for HTLV-1, HTLV-2 and HTLV-3 in Africa. The PTLV envelope glycoprotein surface component (SUgp46) comprises a receptor-binding domain (RBD) that alternates hypervariable and highly conserved sequences. To further delineate highly conserved motifs in PTLV RBDs, we investigated the intrahost variability of HTLV-1 and STLV-1 by generating and sequencing libraries of DNA fragments amplified within the RBD of the SUgp46 env gene. Using new and highly cross-reactive env primer pairs, we observed the presence of Env quasispecies in HTLV-1 infected individuals and STLV-1 naturally infected macaques, irrespective of the clinical status. These intrahost variants helped us to define highly conserved residues and motifs in the RBD. The new highly sensitive env PCR described here appears suitable for the screening of all known variants of the... Read more...

Retrovirology - Latest articles , May 25th, 12:00am

Figure 4.7 This combined RSS feed contains article abstracts from the most recent tables of contents of four science journals.

Librarians as RSS Consumers

Chapter 3 discussed blogs as an excellent way for librarians to keep up with the latest library trends and issues. (See the "Reading Blogs to Keep Up" section on page 43 for more ideas.) Of course, the more blogs a librarian reads, the more difficult it becomes to visit them all regularly. RSS is a great way to keep current with your favorite blogs, journals, and news sites, consolidating all your online reading in a single place. Whenever a new post or article is written on one of your subscription sites, it will be added to your aggregator. RSS is the ultimate tool for preventing information overload.

RSS isn't just for blogs, databases, and journal content; it is the backbone of most social software. RSS feeds allow people to make their content from various sites more portable and easier to collect in one place. Many people now have personally collected content tied up with different Web applications, ranging from favorite Web links cataloged on social bookmarking sites, to photos stored on photo-sharing sites, to discussions in online communities, to posts and comments on blogs where people share their ideas. People's online selves tend to be fragmented, trapped in a number of diverse applications. Many of these offer RSS feeds so people can syndicate their content onto other sites and pull content from these various applications together in one place. A variety of newer services lets users create a virtual desktop using RSS feeds, including Netvibes (www.netvibes.com) and Pageflakes (www.pageflakes.com). In a virtual desktop, RSS feeds can be combined visually on a single page where a user can view photos, blog posts, bookmarks, calendar of events, and many other pieces of the user's virtual self. These virtual desktops can also be used to create pages with favorite blogs and news sources or topical pages. Users can also combine RSS feeds to group blogs together. If one group is blogging about a certain library conference, for example, the feeds to all of their blogs can be combined using a service like Blogdigger (www.blogdigger.com), RSS Mix, or KickRSS; that way, people can visit a single Web site for conference commentary. Some services even offer a single RSS feed of the combined content. Using RSS in this way lets people pull diverse Web content together into a single page to categorize and group the content they read online.

RSS can be both a push and pull technology: It is a push technology when new content of interest is constantly pushed to users via a Web site or an aggregator; it is a pull technology when users combine diverse RSS feeds onto a single Web site. The amount of Web content that can be syndicated via RSS is growing, letting librarians push subject-specific content to their patrons and receive relevant content to keep themselves up-to-date. RSS makes it easier for people to keep up with the constant flow of information online.

Endnotes

1. Meredith Farkas, "Survey of the Biblioblogosphere: Attitudes and Behaviors," Information Wants To Be Free, September 12, 2005, meredith.

wolfwater.com/wordpress/index.php/2005/09/12 (accessed November 27, 2005).

2. "RSS," Wikipedia: The Free Encyclopedia, en.wikipedia.org/wiki/RSS (accessed November 28, 2005).

3. Joshua Grossnickle, Todd Board, Brian Pickens, and Mike Bellmont, RSS—Crossing into the Mainstream, October 2005, publisher.yahoo.com/rss/RSS_whitePaper1004.pdf (accessed November 28, 2005).

4. "What Is RSS?" Seattle Public Library, catalog.spl.org/hipres/help/local/rss.html (accessed November 30, 2005).

5. "EBSCO Supports RSS Feeds," EBSCO Support News, March 2006, support.epnet.com/support_news/detail.php?id=204&t=h (accessed May 1, 2006).

Chapter 5

Wikis

"Web design" was previously only attempted by people with specific technological knowledge; they controlled the design of our Web sites and, in many cases, controlled the content. Over the past decade, however, various tools have leveled the playing field a bit, giving almost anyone the ability to develop a Web page. In spite of these newer WYSIWYG (What You See Is What You Get) editors, a single person is still often in charge of adding content to Web sites for most organizations. So many Web sites only reflect the vision of a single person or a small handful of people. People throughout an organization may have great ideas on improving its Web presence, but they are excluded from the decision-making process because they lack technical skills. If changes need to be made to the Web site, only the person in charge is able to make them. If that person is busy, it can take quite some time before those changes go live. *busy person*

Wikis level the playing field even further than WYSIWYG editors, democratizing the process of Web content creation. Wikis give everyone the ability to take part in creating and editing Web content. With simplified, easy-to-learn text-formatting rules, wikis truly put experienced Web designers and Web novices on an equal footing. In libraries, where the technological skills of employees can range from expert to nonexistent, a wiki allows everyone to give input on the Web site's content. Resulting content would then reflect the imagination and good ideas of the entire organization, not just a select few who have the requisite technical skills.

For libraries, wikis offer endless possibilities. The community of users who add content and edit a wiki has a large part in defining its scope and structure. At their most basic, wikis are spaces for quick and easy Web publishing and editing. At their best, they can become true community resources that position a library as an online hub of its local community.

What Is a Wiki?

Shortly after the birth of the World Wide Web in the early 1990s, a computer programmer named Ward Cunningham was looking for a simple solution to the problem of collaborative Web publishing. Cunningham wanted to publish software patterns to the Web, but rather than creating his own Web site, he wanted the site to be developed collaboratively by the community of software developers. This idea spawned the Portland Pattern Repository (c2.com/cgi/wiki), the first WikiWiki Web site or wiki. First published to the Web in 1995, the Portland Pattern Repository is still a vibrant and growing wiki community today.

Wikis let a group of people with no knowledge of HTML or other markup languages develop a Web site collaboratively. A wiki is infinitely expandable and its pages are created and connected to one another through hyperlinks. As a result, the structure of a wiki is not predefined, but is developed by the linking behavior of its users. Wikis are simple and lightweight solutions. According to Cunningham and Bo Leuf, they can be identified by the following characteristics[1]:

- A wiki invites all users to edit any page or to create new pages within the wiki Web site, using only a plain-vanilla Web browser without any extra add-ons.

- A wiki promotes meaningful topic associations between different pages by making page link creation almost intuitively easy and by showing whether an intended target page exists or not.

- A wiki is not a carefully crafted site for casual visitors. Instead, it seeks to involve the visitor in an ongoing process of creation and collaboration that constantly changes the Web site landscape.

Essentially, a wiki is a perpetual work in progress where anyone can add content, edit content, and create relationships between content through hyperlinks. Wiki, meaning "quick" in Hawaiian, was developed for easy and fast collaborative development and editing of a Web site. Collaborators may know each other or they may be strangers with common interests working toward a common goal. Wikis, which usually start as a blank slate, are developed by the community of users who choose to participate. Wikis are also completely democratic so that anyone in the community can add to or edit anyone else's writing. In theory, the final content should represent a sort of community consensus.

Wikis and blogs are similar in that they both encourage communication, but they also differ in many important ways. A blog usually belongs to one person or a small group of people, and each person signs what they write. In a wiki, no one person owns the content—and yet, everyone owns the content. Blog entries are organized in reverse chronological order, meaning that the most recent entries get the most attention at the top of the screen. Wikis have no predetermined structure; they are organized by the links that users create between articles. With blogs, only author(s) are allowed to write posts; others can only comment on those posts. With wikis, no one owns the content, so anyone can add to or change whatever they want. With blogs, the author seldom edits the post once it is written. Because a wiki is a perpetual work in progress, content can be edited at any time. Blogs are good for individuals who want to disseminate information or start a dialogue. Wikis are good for groups of people working collaboratively toward a specific goal.

As originally developed by Cunningham, wikis were meant to have very simple syntax and few text formatting options. However, some of the more recent wiki incarnations include many ways to format text. While basic wiki syntax is still quite easy to learn, differences in syntax often vary from one wiki to the next. While one wiki might have users enter two single quotations (") to denote italics, for example, another wiki might use a completely different notation. Fortunately, most projects require minimal knowledge of formatting rules; the most important formatting, such as links, bullets, and headings, is usually easy to create. Some wikis offer WYSIWYG functionality, meaning that people simply have to click a button to format text. Most wikis will likely have this functionality in the future, making content creation in a wiki as easy as in any word-processing program.

Cunningham originally envisioned wikis to be completely open to anyone who wanted to add and edit content. He later recognized the need for limitations in some cases, although he believed that "adding extra layers of security adds complexity, and access restrictions are always an inconvenience to users."[2] Some wikis are open to everyone, including the most well-known example, Wikipedia (en.wikipedia.org). Wikipedia is an encyclopedia created by the online community, where any individual is allowed to create, add to, or edit any entry. The more popular Wikipedia entries have been edited hundreds of times by dozens of people. This openness can become problematic when spammers or malicious individuals vandalize entries, but these entries are often quickly fixed by concerned members of the wiki community. The community enforces behavioral norms so that the wiki doesn't become a free-for-all, an example of self-organizing group behavior in action. Other wikis are open only to specific groups, such as librarians, software developers, or students taking a particular class. These wikis are used for a specific project or purpose, so access is usually limited to those involved.

People often have trouble getting used to the idea of a Web site that anyone is allowed to add to or edit. The notion of private property is so deeply embedded in our society that it's difficult to imagine going onto someone else's Web site and changing its content, even when you are invited to do so. People are accustomed to Web sites where some authority is the final arbiter on what can or cannot be published. With a wiki, everyone has that authority. If you don't like what someone entered into the wiki, you can change it. If someone doesn't like what you wrote, that person can make his or her own changes. Wikis develop organically to reflect the interests and needs of the groups that work on them.

Why Choose Wiki? Why Not?

A wiki can be an excellent tool for many kinds of collaborative work, but it is not the right tool for every project. Cunningham wrote that "not every situation benefits from becoming an open discussion or collaborative forum."[3] The following are some common reasons why people adopt wikis for their professional and personal online collaborative work, as well as some reasons why others might choose not to use wikis. Some people prefer using wikis for precisely the same reasons others object to their use.

Ease of use is the most attractive feature of wikis; the learning curve involved is very small. Ease of installation and set-up differs depending on the wiki implementation, but one factor common to all implementations is the ease of adding and editing text. Wikis have a simple interface (Figure 5.1), where users simply have to click an Edit button to edit the page, type in their changes, and click the Submit or Save Page button to submit their work. Some wikis have other controls, such as History, which shows the edits to the page chronologically, and Discussion, where users can discuss the page. All wikis have a page called Recent Changes where users can see what changes have recently been made to the wiki. This helps the community keep up with what's new on the wiki and quickly detect spam or vandalism.

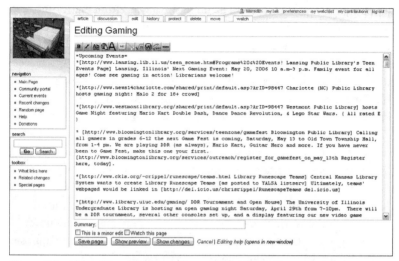

Figure 5.1   The editing interface of a page in Library Success: A Best
Practices Wiki.

As their name implies, wikis allow for quick editing. In the past, people had to wait for their Webmaster to make changes to their Web site, but now, everyone can quickly and easily add content to a wiki. Fixing a typo on a Web site can involve firing up a WYSIWYG editor, making the change, and then uploading the page onto a server. With a wiki, no uploading is necessary; all of the work takes place right in the Web browser. Wikis also have flexibility other Web publishing applications lack. Where a blog has a very specific format, a wiki can become anything the community wants; structures and hierarchies are created as people develop the content. As Brian Lamb writes, "The structure of wikis is shaped from within—not imposed from above."[4]

Many companies and institutions use enterprise solutions including Microsoft Outlook and Lotus Notes for collaborative work. However, this software is expensive and complicated. People need to spend a great deal of time learning how to use these particular products. Since most aren't Web-based, they aren't as portable as Web applications. Most wikis, however, are open source software and are free. For such a scalable tool, wikis are also amazingly simple. Since these products are Web-based, they can be used on any browser and any computer.

The most important feature distinguishing wikis from many other collaborative tools is that wikis are truly democratic. With no imposed structure, users can decide for themselves what a wiki will become, based upon
their needs and goals. Wikis develop organically and often grow to be very
different than their creators originally intended. Most Web pages reflect
the limited vision of just a few people, but wikis can capitalize on the
knowledge and imagination of a large group of people.

Groups decide against using wikis for a number of reasons. The lack of
imposed structure can lead to problems keeping track of a wiki's content.
Some wikis have no index, table of contents, or hierarchy, so it can be difficult to know what pages are available. The search function and the
Recent Changes page are useful, but without some sort of organization—
just as with the World Wide Web as a whole—some pages may never be
found, except by their author(s). However, the lack of a structure imposed
from above does not mean that users can't create their own. Most wikis
have hierarchies, assigned categories, or an alphabetical index, so people
can see just what pages are available.

Probably the most common reason that people decide against wikis is
due to their openness. It can be difficult to trust a group of people, especially when that group happens to include anyone on the Web. If people
can add or edit content, they can also destroy content. People often feel
attached to their writing and don't want to see it changed by someone who
doesn't know their topic as well. Wikis are also perfect targets for vandals
and spammers, and few truly open wikis have avoided becoming the vic-
tims of spam. Spam can often be controlled by plug-ins designed to prevent or kill it, but spammers are constantly working to break through
wikis' defenses. In healthy online communities with many members,
spam and vandalism usually disappear quickly. When people feel committed to their community, they will not allow vandalized content to stay
up long. Most wikis also include mechanisms for rolling a page back to
earlier versions so that nothing can be irreparably broken (this is called
version control). However, in some communities, only a few members are
committed enough to remove spam and vandalism. As the amount of
spam grows, it takes longer and longer for these people to keep up with it.
Without a strong community commitment to keep the space free of spam,
access to the wiki may have to be restricted.

Restricted access can take various forms. The most basic restrictions
require users to register before they can add content to the wiki. This may

deter spammers, but people who want to vandalize the wiki still might be motivated enough to register. Many wikis only allow people with passwords to edit the wiki, while everyone can read the wiki. Others require a password to even look at the wiki. Passwords are useful for group projects or policy manual development, where the content is only of interest to those working on it. Wiki developers who have certain pages they don't want others to change can also lock those specific pages in the wiki. Since each wiki implementation has its own options for restricting access to the wiki and its functionality, it's important to ensure the wiki software you choose is able to restrict access in the manner you want.

A wiki is a collaborative document, so no one gets individual credit for its contents. How can people take credit for their writing when others are able to change their work? If people need to take credit for the things they write, a wiki is probably not the best tool. This lack of individual ownership of work in a wiki can also bring up intellectual property issues. Who owns the content in a wiki? Do others have the right to copy the contents of the wiki and publish them elsewhere? When a group creates a wiki, it may want to place its content under some sort of license. Many use the GNU General Public License (www.gnu.org/copyleft/gpl.html) or one of the Creative Commons licenses (creativecommons.org/licenses).

How Libraries Can Use Wikis with Their Patrons

Since wikis are so flexible, libraries can use them with patrons in many ways. Many libraries position themselves as the physical hub of their communities through programming, collection development, and marketing. However, some have overlooked the value of making their Web sites the online hub of their communities. A community wiki can help make a library's Web site a place people visit for more than simply searching the online catalog; a library can become a one-stop-shop for community information. By capitalizing on the input of community members, wikis can become an amazing resource for the community and its visitors. Want to find the best mechanic for fixing old Toyotas? Check the automotive reviews on the wiki. Want to know when your child's next Little League game is? Check the team information page the coach set up on the wiki. Want to find the spiciest Thai food in town? Read the member reviews in the restaurant section.

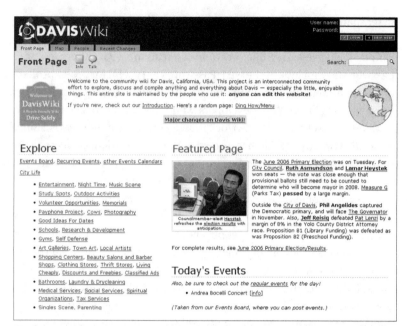

Figure 5.2   The Davis (CA) Wiki lets members of the community add content to this comprehensive local guide. (©2006 Davis Wiki)

The Davis Wiki (daviswiki.org; see Figure 5.2) collects information from residents about culture, food, stores, events, and more in Davis, California. Anyone can add information and photos to this comprehensive, growing resource. A community wiki can become whatever the community needs it to be, reflecting the unique and local knowledge of its members. Your library could team up with other local organizations to develop, maintain, and add content to a wiki, but the bulk of the content will come from community members. Opening a community guide to the public creates a grassroots repository of community information, making the library's Web site a true community resource.

Just like community wikis, subject guide wikis can capitalize not just on librarians' subject expertise but also on that of its patrons. Librarians have been creating subject guides on the Internet even since before the creation of the World Wide Web. Since most librarians have to wear too many "hats" in any given day, updating these guides may not be a priority. Subject guides can languish with dead links to defunct Web sites and without links to new useful sites. This may be because librarians don't have time to update them, or because any updates must be given to someone else who actually puts them on the Web.

A wiki is a great technology for research and subject guides. Because wikis can be edited by anyone, patrons can add to the collections of useful resources and help prune the dead links. A librarian can moderate the wiki and decide what Web sites should stay in the guide or can decide to let everyone contribute freely. This lets librarians develop a subject guide that truly represents the interests of its users and also removes some of the burden of finding Web sites. In college, university, and school libraries, faculty input can make the subject guides more useful, since they are the true subject experts. Even without asking for user input, a wiki lets librarians with little Web savvy update a subject guide quickly and easily. Chad Boeninger, Business Librarian at Ohio University, created the Biz Wiki (www.library.ohiou.edu/subjects/bizwiki) to update his subject guides easily and let students and faculty add to his lists of useful links. Organized hierarchically by topic, the Biz Wiki offers location information and descriptions for each resource. So far, Boeninger has been the only person adding to the wiki, but it is still a useful format because it is completely searchable and can be updated quickly. For this wiki, findability and easy editing make it a valuable tool.

SJCPL's Subject Guides (www.libraryforlife.org/subjectguides/index.php/Main_Page), created by the St. Joseph County Public Library in Indiana, is another useful subject guide wiki that includes guides to subjects of interest to public library patrons (i.e., crafts, local history, and business). These librarian-created subject guides are full of local information and useful Web links. Library patrons cannot make changes, but they can provide comments from the discussion tab on each page, where they can suggest new resources and communicate with the librarians. Both the Biz Wiki and SJCPL's Subject Guides were developed using MediaWiki (www.mediawiki.org), the same software used by Wikipedia.

Many library catalogs contain only the most basic information about materials. Each item's record includes only the elements of a MARC record: title, subject(s), author, year published, etc. When patrons use an online catalog, they may not know if they've found the sort of book they were looking for until they actually pull it off the shelf. If patrons are looking at the catalog on their home computers, they may not be motivated to visit the library for a book that may or may not be relevant. But when users go to Amazon.com, they find a book synopsis, cover art, and reviews from people who have already read the book. This extra content gives a reader a better sense of whether a given book will meet his or her needs. Adding wiki functionality to a catalog lets users post synopses and reviews. We can capitalize on the reading experiences of our patrons, helping them make informed reading decisions from the library catalog. OCLC has given registered users the ability to add reviews, tables of contents, and notes to records in WorldCat. Letting patrons add synopses, reviews, and other information to a common pot where the content could later be imported into individual libraries' catalogs lets all libraries benefit from that content.

In some libraries, none of the staff members have the skills to create or update a Web site. Some libraries have no Web site at all, and others have a very basic Web presence or one that was created years ago and never updated. Since wikis do not require any knowledge of HTML, libraries could use wikis to create their primary Web presence. Essentially, the wiki would be a content management system that librarians could use easily to add and update online content. While it's possible that librarians may need help initially to set up the wiki, they should be able to manage pretty well on their own with minimal training. The Web site of the Gregg-Graniteville Library at the University of South Carolina Aiken (library.usca.edu; Figure 5.3) looks as though it is a normal library Web site with links to the library catalog, databases, research guides, and other library resources. However, the entire Web site is powered by wiki software, which lets the library staff update the Web site as needed with ease. (Since access is restricted, there is no visible link to edit the wiki.)

Since wikis have the flexibility to become almost anything participants need them to be, they have the potential to fill many educational needs. For information literacy classes (or any class for that matter), they could replace courseware. Faculty members could create pages for announcements, assignments, and lectures. Instead of writing papers, turning them in, and never thinking about them again, students could post their papers to the wiki and start a dialogue about them with their fellow students. In grade schools, students could use wikis to create collaborative stories where each child is responsible for adding something to the story. Wikis are also a great tool for group projects. Writing a group paper often involves e-mailing different versions of one document back and forth. It can be difficult to reconcile those versions and create a document that satisfies everyone in the group. When groups use a wiki, the document is online for

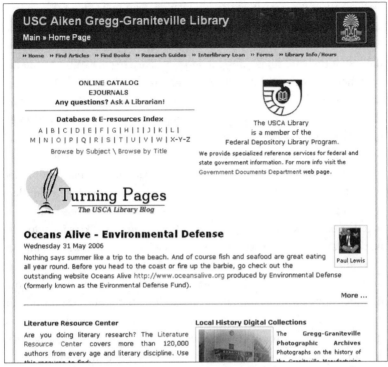

Figure 5.3   The Web site for the Gregg-Graniteville Library at USC Aiken
(SC) was actually created using a wiki. (*Reproduced with
permission.*)

everyone to edit. With version control, students can roll back to previous
versions if they're unhappy with a recent edit and discuss changes in the
same space. The key is that the document and corresponding discussions
are in one place, resolving the issue of reconciling various versions at the
end of the project. In some cases, wikis may be preferable to structured
courseware because of their flexibility and scalability. Rather than having
to fit class content into the structure of their courseware, faculty members
could structure a wiki based on their content.

How Librarians Can Use Wikis

Wikis have many applications for use in libraries and in professional
development work. A wiki is an excellent format for a staff intranet. The

University of Minnesota Libraries Staff Home Page (wiki.lib.umn.edu) contains library information, strategic planning documents, and internal library project information. Developed using PmWiki (www.pmwiki.org), the staff intranet has been designed to look like a regular Web site, but any staff member with a valid username and password can edit it. While anyone can view the content, the password protection could also be extended to read access if the staff wants to have a private wiki. With a private internal wiki, staff can make announcements, discuss internal issues, and work on projects. Within larger nonlibrary organizations, wikis can be an excellent way to communicate with patrons throughout the organization and solicit feedback. In the same vein, wikis lend themselves to the development of policy documents and manuals. A group of librarians could work together on a wiki to develop a reference e-manual. A wiki is ideal for this work because the expertise and insights of all of the librarians can be capitalized on and the document can be edited all in one place. Wikis are also useful in creating and editing policy documents. Rather than every group member physically meeting at the same time, the group responsible for developing a policy can work on the document, edit each other's work, and discuss the policy within the wiki. The work the members do in the wiki will save them considerable time when the group is able to meet in person.

Reference librarians often have to answer questions on a variety of topics, some of which they are familiar with, others that they know nothing about. In most libraries, each librarian has different subject strengths. When someone comes to the reference desk with a question about architecture, the librarian who knows a lot about architecture will often be called on for help with relevant resources. What if someone poses a question at night when the architecture librarian is at home? It makes sense to find a way to make this information accessible without depending on others' in-person expertise. A wiki is an excellent repository for collective knowledge. A reference wiki could be organized by subject and by assignment. The librarian who knows about architecture could put his or her knowledge about architecture resources into the wiki. The librarian with expertise in Web resources could add links to the ones that he or she uses frequently. When a number of students come to the desk with the same assignment, the librarian on duty could enter information about the assignment and resources used so the next librarian at the reference desk would have this information ready and avoid duplicating efforts. Putting this information into the wiki is much the same as having all your colleagues at the desk with you each time you answer a reference question.

The wiki as knowledge repository could be used in many situations. Each year, dozens of library conferences take place in cities around the world. The librarians attending these conferences have often never been to the cities they are visiting. They may have a difficult time finding the best places to eat, stay, and visit—especially on a limited budget. At a large conference like the ALA annual conference, new attendees may be overwhelmed by its size and not know how to make the most of their time. Librarians who are experienced conference-goers and librarians who live in the city where the conference is taking place have useful knowledge that could benefit others. A wiki can solve the problem of connecting these two groups.

I developed the ALA Chicago 2005 Wiki (meredith.wolfwater.com/wiki/) to supplement the ALA's annual conference information and capitalize on the knowledge of experienced conference-goers. The wiki included restaurant reviews, a guide to wireless Internet access in Chicago, tips on getting around the city, advice for conference-goers, a list of unofficial and official conference events, librarians' conference schedules, and much more. I originally created the wiki with a limited vision of what it could be, but other members of the library community added elements I had never considered. Some added a conference tip or the name of a favorite restaurant, while others added entire sections. All of these contributions, no matter their size, added up to a truly useful resource for attendees. In 2006, I worked with the ALA to create the ALA 2006 New Orleans Wiki (meredith.wolfwater.com/ala2006/; see Figure 5.4), a guide to that year's conference.

Since the creation of the ALA Chicago 2005 Wiki, a number of wiki knowledge repositories have been developed to collect best practices in different areas. Library Success: A Best Practices Wiki (www.libsuccess.org) was designed as a one-stop-shop for great ideas for librarians. Librarians who have done something successful at their library or have materials and Web sites to recommend can add these to the wiki. The goal of the wiki is to help librarians replicate the successes of others so that no one has to reinvent the wheel. The Library Instruction Wiki (instruction wiki.org) was developed by the Oregon Library Association for a similar purpose—to collect useful advice, ideas, and materials about providing library instruction. Since many instruction librarians struggle with the same issues, it makes sense to share ideas and success stories. Similar

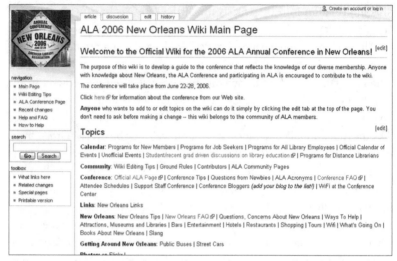

Figure 5.4   The ALA 2006 New Orleans Wiki was a guide to the annual conference and to New Orleans that could be added on to by anyone.

wikis could address any area of librarianship, such as cataloging, marketing, and readers' advisory.

Implementing a Wiki: Practical Considerations

Once you have decided that a wiki is the right tool for your job, the next step is choosing the software that best meets your needs. Different wiki implementations are available. First, determine whether you will host the wiki on your own server, or if you want to use wiki software hosted by the company that developed the software. If you do not have access to a server, then a hosted wiki, or a wiki farm, is a good option. Hosted wikis range from being free, with very basic functionality, to being very expensive, with lots of features and flexibility. If you don't need much functionality other than the ability for everyone to create, add to, and edit pages, then a free wiki should meet your needs. For larger, complicated projects that require sophisticated permissioning schemes, it may make sense to look into the for-pay models.

If you choose to host the wiki on your own server, you will have far more choices available. Each wiki implementation has different strengths and weaknesses. The right choice depends on the features most important to you. Here are some variables you should consider before making your choice:

- *Programming language* – While Ward Cunningham created his wiki using Perl, most wikis today are developed using PHP, which may be an easier language to learn and use. However, some wikis are still developed using Perl, as well as Ruby, Python, and Java. You don't need to know any programming languages to install and manage a wiki. But if you are a programmer, you're probably better off with a wiki based on a language you know.

- *Security and permissioning* – If you want to limit people's ability to change things on the wiki, make sure the software you choose offers some mechanism for setting permissions. Some allow sophisticated permissioning schemes, while others do not. For spam protection, many wikis either come with the ability to block IP addresses or to create a blacklist of words banned from the content. Other wikis have optional plug-ins that provide more sophisticated spam protection. While you may not think about spam when you first start a public wiki, you may later regret not installing wiki software with mechanisms for dealing with spam.

- *Ease of installation* – While some wikis are easy to install, others are notoriously difficult. Is there good documentation on how to install the wiki software? Take a look at that documentation and see if it looks like something you can do. If you have trouble, is there a forum or someone to contact who can help?

- *Ease of use* – Wikis are known for their ease of use. If you need to spend a lot of time reading instructions before you are able to enter content into the wiki, then it's probably not the right one.

- *Cost* – This really depends on your budget and comfort level with technology. Wikis that cost money are usually easier to use because they're often marketed to businesses and contain more documentation. When you pay for a wiki, you'll probably have someone to contact if there are any problems. However, MediaWiki, which is open source, has so many people using the software that the documentation and forums for asking other users questions are extensive.

- *Wiki syntax* – The biggest problem with different wiki implementations is the lack of standard syntax rules for formatting a document. Some wikis have simple syntax rules, while others, in an effort to provide a lot of options, have syntax rules that are unintuitive and hard to remember. Take a look at a wiki that uses the software you're considering to see how its pages are formatted. If your user population is intimidated by new technologies, look for a wiki with WYSIWYG functionality.

- *Version control* – If you want to roll back to previous versions of each wiki page, then version control is an essential feature. Version control means that you can see all of the previous versions of the page and can change the page back to an old version (Figure 5.5). If you expect to get spam and vandalism or even if you expect to have heated debates about the documents in the wiki, it's a good safety net to have because any changes made to the wiki can always be reversed.

- *Discussion section* – Most wikis have a space where people can discuss a particular page. This can take the form of a discussion tab that goes to a separate page or an area under each page that allows for threaded discussion. If you think people will want to discuss changes to the pages in the wiki, make sure its software has a discussion area.

- *RSS* – If you want to track changes made to the wiki in your RSS aggregator, be sure that the wiki provides RSS feeds. Some wikis provide RSS feeds for every page created, while others provide feeds only for recent changes.

- *Ability to customize look* – Most wikis are not very aesthetically pleasing in their native form. If you want your wiki to have a particular look, make sure you can customize it using Cascading Style Sheets (CSS).

The WikiMatrix (www.wikimatrix.org) is an excellent tool for determining which software is right for you. The WikiMatrix lets you compare more than 50 different wiki platforms side-by-side. Comparisons include more

Figure 5.5   With version control, if someone deletes all the content from the main page, community members can easily restore the content from previous versions.

than 100 variables, so users can get a detailed summary of each tool. WikiMatrix's Wiki Choice Wizard asks users questions about what they want out of a wiki and then presents a list of wikis that meet their requirements. The WikiMatrix can make a difficult decision far easier.

After you have chosen and installed the software, there are other considerations in implementing any wiki. Since the idea of private property is so ingrained in our society, it can be difficult to convince people that you really want them to add to and edit your Web pages. Remember that a wiki must have a specific purpose. You simply can't offer a wiki to a population as a blank slate and expect them to know what they should add to it. Even when the wiki has a specific purpose, it's good to create some sort of structure so that people will feel comfortable posting. Users can always post whatever they want and change the structure of the wiki later on, but it can be difficult to get people to start posting without any structure. You may want to consider seeding the wiki with some initial content before making it public. Most people are polite, and if they're the first person posting to a wiki, they want to make sure they're posting the "right" sort of content. Even if there really is no "right" or "wrong" content, people may need some concrete examples before they feel confident enough to add material.

Be explicit with instructions and disclaimers. You need to make the guidelines for adding content to the wiki very clear, or you may receive a flood of e-mails where patrons or staff members ask you to add things for them instead of doing it themselves. On public wikis, you should develop a disclaimer making it clear that the library is not responsible for all the content. Copyright is an issue that should be addressed in terms of the license governing content on the wiki and content added to the wiki that may be restricted under copyright.

Wikis are very different from traditional models of Web content development. Giving everyone the freedom to add or change anything on a Web page goes against the idea of a single point of authority on a Web site. At their best, wikis can encourage content creation in a way that traditional Web sites cannot. However, wikis are not the best solution for every situation. In certain environments, wikis can be a disruptive technology that can get out of hand if spammers and vandals start destroying content. Without a committed community, wikis can end up resembling an Old West town without a sheriff. However, loyal users policing the wiki make this problem manageable. If you need a way to collaborate with a group of people online, and you trust this community enough to give them the right to edit each other's content, a wiki is ideal. Wikis are the best tools for capitalizing on the collective knowledge of a group when creating a knowledge repository or when adding value to an already existing database. They also offer an excellent way to get patrons involved in content creation and build the library as an online community hub.

Endnotes

1. Bo Leuf and Ward Cunningham, *The Wiki Way: Quick Collaboration on the Web*, Upper Saddle River, NJ: Pearson, 2001: 16.
2. Leuf and Cunningham, 278.
3. Leuf and Cunningham, 30.
4. Brian Lamb, "Wide Open Spaces: Wikis Ready or Not," *EDUCAUSE Review* 39.5 (2004): 40.

Chapter 6

Online Communities

Libraries have always been more than mere book repositories. Their role as a place that is open to all community members—regardless of race, gender, or socioeconomic status—puts libraries in an ideal position to become community hubs. Libraries have worked to sustain and improve their communities in a variety of ways. Reference librarians connect patrons with vital information. Children's reading programs give kids a place to be after school and expose them to the joys of reading. Adult literacy programs decrease social exclusion and increase opportunity. Information literacy instruction can help turn nervous freshmen into confident researchers. Library programs for job-seekers and grant-seekers offer community members ways to improve their economic situation. Computer education classes open up whole new worlds to people, allowing them to connect to distant loved ones and find support online. Libraries also often serve as meeting places for other community organizations; some libraries are designed with large areas where community members from all walks of life can congregate and get to know one another. While library collections are crucial to fulfilling libraries' missions, libraries can offer so much more to their communities.

Just as a library is more than a repository for books, a library's online presence can also be more than a space to describe the library's collections and programs. Libraries can use social software to build community with their Web presence. A library's online presence can become a community forum, a space to share ideas, and a place where community members can connect with one another. Learning from existing online communities, libraries can find ways to connect with their patrons and develop online communities of their own, providing a vital online resource. This chapter looks at the various types of online communities. Patrons connect with others online in many different ways, and it's important for libraries to learn how they can capitalize on the growth of online communities.

What Is an Online Community?

People think about communities in different ways. Most commonly, communities are defined geographically: A community is the group of people who lives around you, pays taxes to the same local government, and has similar local concerns. Other communities are defined by an individual's personal characteristics, such as religion, ethnicity, sexual orientation, and interests. These groups can be both local and global. While a Jewish community can be located in a specific geographic area, its members are also members of the global Jewish community. People often belong to many communities, some by choice and others by circumstance. Community ties differ in strength, depending on which are most meaningful to us. We may have strong ties to one community, while feeling less connected to others.

Online communities, however, are always joined by choice. A man may be African-American by birth, but he does not have to become a member of an online community for African-Americans. As a result, online community membership usually reflects the parts of a person's identity that he or she identifies with most intensely, or the things people are most interested in or concerned about. An online community is simply a group of people who gather online for a specific purpose. They may come together to discuss issues, support one another, share photographs and other media, or collaborate on projects. The Internet can help people meet others who share common interests or are in similar situations. It can also help people to strengthen and maintain ties with those they already know.

In this chapter, I will define four primary types of online communities: communities of interest, sustaining communities, communities of action, and local communities. The first type, a community of interest, is based on a specific interest or concern. This is the largest type of community and includes ethnic and religious communities, support groups, fan communities, media sharing communities, lifestyle communities, and professional communities. Members of these communities may live all over the world, and may or may not already know each other.

In the second type of community, which is known as a sustaining community, the participants already know each other; people join these communities specifically to stay connected. These sustaining communities maintain already existing connections. Alumni of a high school or college, family members, and former co-workers can create sustaining communities to keep in touch with each other.

Communities are not always formed simply to communicate online; some are formed to coordinate online and offline action. These communities of action recognize the difficulties of single individuals accomplishing large tasks and try to mobilize like-minded people through an online community. They can include people collaborating to develop a software application or creating change in government policies. Members of this community may all live in the same place—especially if the issue is local—or all over the world. They are tied together by a common interest to create change in a certain area.

Finally, communities can be based on geography. People who live close to one another often share similar local concerns. These local communities can discuss public schools, local government, the local music scene, and other interests or issues. They may also come together online to share practical information about the community or to sell things to one another. Members of this type of community may not know each other before they venture online, but they are more likely later to meet face-to-face because of their proximity. Obviously, many communities fit into more than one category. But in all these cases, people are coming together based on a shared sense of identity or a shared sense of purpose.

The online medium has given people a chance to find a sense of belonging they may never find in their local area. Some people have interests or belong to groups that are not well-represented locally. A young gay teenager in a conservative religious community may not find many other gay teens in his area. Similarly, the mother of a child born with a serious illness may only know people with healthy babies. Before online communities were established, these people often felt isolated and alone; they didn't know anyone who shared an important part of their identity. Since online communities consist of people from all over the world, plenty of gay teens can find others worldwide, and can band together online to support one another. Similarly, a young mother is likely to find strength in a community of other mothers from various locations facing the same challenge. People are no longer limited to making connections and finding support in their geographic communities; they now have the entire world.

In addition to support, the collective knowledge of these communities can offer practical insights into problems. A software developer could work on a problem for days or weeks on his own, or he could ask a community of developers for advice. Someone else has probably already dealt with the same problem and will be able—and willing—to help. A librarian can post to an e-mail list asking about collection development policies, and other community members will probably be happy to share theirs. This way, community members can help each other work more efficiently instead of reinventing the wheel.

Online communities can take many forms, and members can have varying levels of intimacy. On an e-mail list or a forum, people may hardly know each other, but they can still collaborate for a specific purpose. For example, Jane may post to an electronic mailing list and ask for advice about a problem at her library. Other contributors may not know Jane, but are still willing to offer their insights. This advice is offered under the assumption that Jane would also be willing to offer her advice if they needed help. Individual relationships may form in these communities, but they're not usually overt or necessary to the community's success. Other communities let members get to know each other better through blogs, profiles, and photos.

Online communities are becoming a regular part of people's daily online activities. According to a Pew Internet and American Life report, "Internet: The Mainstreaming of Online Life," 84 percent of U.S. Internet users (nearly 100 million people) belong to a group with an online presence.[1] These people use online groups for everything from getting news and information and discussing issues to getting involved in group activities and creating or maintaining relationships. Years ago, the majority of those who used online communities were white, wealthy, well-educated, and tech-savvy. Today, online community members are coming from all age groups, ethnicities, educational backgrounds, and socioeconomic strata. Whether you are a librarian in New York City or Cody, Wyoming, many of your patrons are likely to be part of these online communities.

Types of Online Communities

Online communities are based on interest, location, prior membership, or desired action. People come together for many different reasons and with different tools. Some communities are built from the top-down; others are developed from the bottom-up by individuals who see a need for a certain type of community. Some use existing community creation tools, others repurpose other software, and still others create their online community from scratch. Blogs, wikis, forums, e-mail lists, Web sites, and other tools have been used to create online communities. Some communities allow users the flexibility to add features such as subgroups, personal pages, and calendars. Some encourage users to get to know each other by creating profiles and using instant messaging (IM). The e-group culture and the kind of software used affect the overall flexibility of the community.

Communities of Interest

Communities of interest let people band together based on common interests, goals, or life situations. Online communities of interest can range from support groups for people with mental illness, fan clubs for actors, or discussion groups for politically minded people. They represent the majority of online communities and use many formats to encourage social contact online.

Many communities use forum software for online discussions. Forums are usually tied to a specific Web site, and many companies use them to get people to visit their site. Internet forums are discussion boards where one user can post a message on a given topic, then others can comment on that topic by replying with their own posts. Usually, these comments are threaded, so that they are organized by the post the user responds to rather than the date on which they were posted; some software also lets users sort the posts by thread or by date. Many free and low-cost software options allow anyone with some technical savvy to set up a forum. The ForumMatrix (www.forummatrix.org) helps users choose forum software based on their needs, allowing users to compare forum software side-by-side based on a large number of variables.

Forums usually have different topics that users can post under, and some software makes it easy for anyone to create a completely new topic. The Inside Line Forums at Edmunds.com (www.edmunds.com/inside line/do/ForumsLanding) are well-known forums that have stood the test of time. Edmunds is a site devoted entirely to vehicles; people can research cars they are interested in buying, find the value of their own car, and get tips on keeping their vehicles in good working order. The forums let car enthusiasts, those considering buying a car, and those having problems with their current car communicate online. There are many different forums, organized by vehicle and by topic. Each forum has several topics that people can post to, or they can create a completely new topic; some topics contain more than 10,000 posts! People who have car problems can ask questions on the forums that will usually be answered by an expert, an enthusiast, or someone who had the same problem in the past. People use the forums to argue, post reviews, support one another, and discuss topics of interest. The Inside Line Forums, which started around 1996 (though the name was recently changed), receive thousands of posts each day. Many car companies have representatives who visit the Edmunds forums to offer advice and information to their customers.

Beyond forums, blogs can also be a community affair in two ways. First, some blogs become so popular or controversial that long discussions occur in the comments section. The Ann Arbor District Library's blog for their gaming tournaments (www.aadl.org/aadlgt) has turned into a community for young patrons who use the comments section of each post as their own discussion board.

But second and more commonly, blogs can become a community when any member can post. Slashdot (slashdot.org; see Figure 6.1), developed in 1997, is the first and most notable example of the blog/community hybrid. People can post excerpts or brief synopses of news stories related to technology; other members are allowed to comment on their posts. Anyone can submit stories to the Slashdot moderation queue, where they are either accepted or rejected for publication by the editors. The accepted posts are published on Slashdot, and both members and nonmembers can then comment.

The Slashdot moderation scheme weeds out unhelpful and malicious comments that may crop up in open forums. Moderators are given five points that they can use to promote or demote postings. Moderators are chosen randomly from the pool of people with good "karma" and can only moderate comments for three days. Karma is a number assigned to each user based on how other moderators have rated their previous comments. This gives members in good standing the chance to become moderators. Slashdot members can choose a threshold for comments, where any comments rated lower than that threshold will not appear, and they can also look at items below their threshold that meet certain conditions. This model for moderation allows the most trusted and well-liked members of the community to get the most attention, and allows other members to personalize their Slashdot based on their personal threshold for bad comments. A variety of other communities use

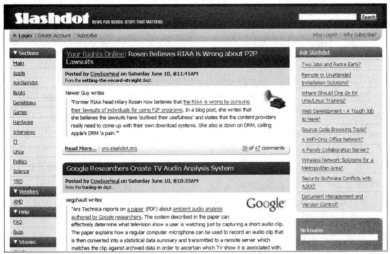

Figure 6.1   Slashdot is one of the most popular online communities.
(Reproduced with permission. ©2006 OSTG)

Slashdot's software, slashcode, including LISNews (lisnews.org), which covers library-related news.

More people now see the value of using more than one type of tool in an online community. Communities could use a forum for discussions, a wiki as a collective knowledgebase, a regular Web site for articles, profiles to help members get to know each other, IM for personal communication, and blogs as personal spaces. The March of Dimes Share community (www.shareyourstory.org) combines different collaborative tools to create a very personal support site. The Share community is a place where parents of premature babies can share their stories and support each other. The site uses discussion boards, blogs, and chat rooms to let these parents connect with each other in whatever way they feel comfortable. A Community Center lets members introduce themselves and discuss changes made to the site. The Parent to Parent area contains discussions on parenting topics ranging from birth defects to nutrition. The Get Involved area allows parents to get involved in advocacy, education, and local issues. Beyond the discussion boards, parents can also share their continuing stories in their own blogs, or they can create a "Short Story," where parents write once about their experience. Blogs provide a personal space for mothers and fathers to write about their experiences and for others to add comments, while discussion boards give parents a place to discuss specific issues. While both tools could serve the same purpose, parents seem to use both seamlessly in the community. There is also a chat area that allows for formal discussions with experts and informal chats with other members. All of these tools combine to form a community that gives members a great deal of self-expression.

Electronic mailing lists (e-mail discussion lists) have existed since before the World Wide Web, and they are still a very popular tool for building online communities. All of the discussions on an electronic mailing list are delivered to each member's e-mail inbox. When a member wants to add a new post or a reply, he or she just needs to send an e-mail to the mailing list's address to post it to the entire community. Users can have each post and comment sent to them as a separate e-mail, or they can choose to receive digests of multiple posts. Electronic mailing lists now often have searchable Web-based archives organized by thread and date. One of the benefits of an electronic mailing list is that users don't need to visit a Web site to see what the community is talking about; the information is pushed to them. One of the disadvantages of electronic mailing lists is that each user receives every post, whether or not these are relevant to him or her. It can also be difficult to follow the thread of a single conversation since posts arrive chronologically. PUBLIB (lists.webjunction. org/publib), which was started in 1992 to give public librarians a place to share ideas online, is a very active electronic mailing list, averaging between 350 and 400 messages per month.[2] In this space, librarians discuss policy issues, collections, trends, problems, and news, as well as provide each other with useful feedback and spark lively debates. The electronic mailing list is still a popular format among librarians, with lists for almost every conceivable niche topic in librarianship.

Photo-Sharing Communities

Digital photography has changed the way we take, store, and share our photos. When you can see your photos before getting them developed, why not take multiple shots, hoping that at least one of the shots will look good? In fact, if you can view your photos on the computer, how many of them need to be printed at all? This kind of reasoning results in people filling their computer hard drives with digital photos of which they have no hard copies. These photos will never become part of an album or be seen by friends and family. The tremendous growth of digital photography has led to the development of photo-sharing Web sites. Many of these initial sites were slow and required people to register before viewing someone else's photo album. People could also only look at photo albums they were invited to view, requiring digital album owners to send e-mails to all of their friends and family members. Over the past few years, photo-sharing software has become more streamlined, acting more like an online community than a personal photo album. Newer photo-sharing software lets people keep their photos private, but they are by default freely viewable by all. Photo-sharing communities allow people to seamlessly share photos with family and friends and connect with other photo-sharing enthusiasts.

The most popular photo-sharing Web site, Flickr (flickr.com), makes it very easy to upload and share photos. The site, which was bought by Yahoo! in early 2005, had about 1.5 million users by the end of that year. Its popularity stems from its incredible ease of use. With Flickr, a user can sign up for an account, upload photos from a computer or mobile device, and make those photos available to others. Users can make individual photos public, limit access only to friends and family, or make their photos completely private. Thanks to the AJAX interface, which makes only the necessary parts of a Web page reload, it takes no time to rotate photos, add titles and captions, or change the order of the photos. Photos can also be organized into topical sets where they can be viewed as a grouping of photos or as a slideshow (Figure 6.2).

Flickr users can add additional context to their photos by "tagging" them. Tags are user-created metadata about a given photo. If a user assigns the tag "dog" to all photos of a pet, clicking on that tag will bring up all photos of the dog, no matter when they were taken. Others can also add context to photos they view by adding tags or commenting on them. With Flickr, users can send photos to their blog with a Blog This button. Users just need to provide Flickr with basic information about their blog to create a post with photos and text from Flickr. Users can also post their photos to groups inside Flickr itself, such as groups of car enthusiasts, gardeners, cat owners, and individuals who live near each other. If a group doesn't exist for your interest, it's easy to create a new one. People can keep up with the photos their friends are taking with an RSS feed for each user's account, called a Photostream.

For many Flickr users, the site becomes more like an online community than a simple photo-sharing site. While most people first come to Flickr to share photos with their friends and family, many begin looking at other people's photos. People living in a specific area may join a Flickr

Figure 6.2   On Flickr, the popular photo-sharing Web site, users can organize photos into topical sets. (*Reproduced with permission. ©2006 Yahoo! Inc.   FLICKR and the FLICKR logo are trademarks of Yahoo! Inc.*)

group for that area, making it easy to find pictures of their hometown by visiting that group. Golden retriever enthusiasts can easily find photos of these dogs either by searching the tags people assign to their photos or finding a golden retriever group. Members who like someone else's photos can add them as a contact or as a friend to find that person's photos at a later date. This also builds a community of people who may not know each other in the physical world but who enjoy sharing photos because of some common attribute or interest.

Whether or not a user wants to share photos, Flickr offers an excellent place to store pictures for those without server space. Each photo has an individual URL, and there are separate URLs for different sizes of the same photo, making it easy to post photos from Flickr onto another Web site.

Flickr offers two membership options: The free option lets users upload 20MB of photos each month, with limits on the ability to create sets and on how many photos can be stored; the Pro Account, which costs $24.95 per year, includes a 2GB monthly upload limit without limits on storage and set creation. Both accounts give users many options for printing photos.

While Flickr is the most popular photo-sharing community, many others offer most of the same features with a few minor differences. Zoto (www.zoto.com) resembles Flickr in many ways, although its free package offers a 2GB monthly upload limit that sets it apart. SmugMug (www.smugmug.com), which has photo storage packages starting at $39.95 per year, offers a number of options for professional-quality photo printing. Photo enthusiasts can find many other options, some geared toward mobile users, some toward professional photographers.

"Photoblogging" and "moblogging" (blogging from mobile devices) have become very popular, as more and more mobile phones and PDAs come with cameras built in. Many photo-sharing services such as Flickr let users upload photos and then send them to a blog, but some let users blog photos and other media in one easy step. Textamerica (www.text america.com) lets people register for moblogs that they can then populate by e-mailing photos and text to the service. The blogs live on the Textamerica site, which is useful for users who don't already have a blog. Nokia Lifeblog (europe.nokia.com/lifeblog) is a service for Nokia users where every photo—and any accompanying text—is automatically added to their Lifeblog. Photos and text can also be posted directly to any TypePad (www.typepad.com) blog.

People with traditional blogs may want to blog their photos there rather than starting a separate blog for media. On Kablog (www.kablog. org), users can send photos and blog entries directly from a handheld to any of the major traditional blogging platforms. Users can also e-mail moblog entries directly to their blogs without using a third-party provider.

Sustaining Communities

Over the past few decades, people have become more mobile and most no longer spend their entire lives in the same place. People often move far away from their childhood homes for college or for a career. Each time they move, they leave behind a circle of friends with certain shared memories.

While it makes sense to stay in contact with family and close friends through e-mail, this quickly becomes unmanageable with large numbers of acquaintances. Online communities provide an excellent method for keeping in touch with groups of people, whether family members or friends from high school, college, or a former job.

Many colleges and universities develop their own systems for alumni to stay connected. This is in a college's best interest since the school can also use the space for fundraising efforts. Alumni communities usually include an alumni directory, message boards, and a career-assistance networking area. A good example of an online community for alumni is the Fulbright Web (www.fulbrightweb.org). This community for past and current Fulbright Scholars includes bulletin boards, chat rooms, news, lifetime e-mail, event listings, and an alumni directory, providing a space for Fulbright Scholars to network, share their experiences, and connect with old friends.

Alumni of high schools, colleges, and companies without official alumni communities have many options for creating their own. Many alumni Web sites have been developed on Yahoo! Groups (groups.yahoo.com) and MSN Groups (groups.msn.com). Both Yahoo! and MSN offer free, easy ways to start an online community. Each lets users create discussion groups, chat rooms, photo albums, member directories, calendars, and a file-sharing area. However, Yahoo! Groups also has the characteristics of an electronic mailing list in that people receive an e-mail every time a message is posted. Alumni could also create electronic mailing lists and forums using free software packages, though those options require more set-up and maintenance.

Local Communities

People often connect online with people in their local area. Some local online communities are simply online versions of physical communities: churches, schools, and activity groups with an online presence where members continue conversations. This is practical when people have busy schedules and don't always have time to meet in person. Other online communities let people meet others in their local area who share similar interests. craigslist (www.craigslist.org) is a series of local online communities for various areas across the world. The site first started in the mid-1990s as space for people in San Francisco to connect, find housing, buy and sell things, and have online discussions. It has recently expanded to include all major metropolitan areas in the U.S. as well as rural areas and cities outside the U.S.[3] Each craigslist has the same basic features, including classified ads for buying and selling items, personals, job listings, housing listings, discussion forums, and community listings of events, activities, and more. Posting an ad in most regions is free, except for job ads in some metropolitan areas. That fact, along with the existence of forums, distinguishes craigslist as a community, as opposed to a simple commerce site.

People can also connect locally through social event calendars. These let members know what events are happening in their area and who will be attending. If you want to go to a concert and don't know anyone else who is going, a social event calendar is a great way to find out who is planning to go or to put out a call for others to join you. Upcoming.org (upcoming.org) is a social-events calendar where users can post upcoming events in their area, from parties to book signings to concerts. Members can comment on events, sign up for events, and see who else is coming. Users can also assign descriptive tags to events so people can find them easily. In addition to being able to search by event, users can search by member to see what their friends are doing. Upcoming.org was bought by Yahoo! in 2005. A similar social-calendaring Web application is Eventful (eventful.com), which offers more ways to search and display events. Eventful is notable not only because it includes people's profiles, but because people can also create custom calendars listing the events they are attending or where they are traveling. The site also has groups that list events by topic, such as literary events, celebrity appearances, and political events.

Communities of Action

Communities of action exist to mobilize people to accomplish a specific task; they can exist as a local electronic mailing list, a blog, a Yahoo! or MSN group, or a large professionally developed Web site. The specific format depends on the size, needs, and intent of the organization. One particularly successful grassroots online community of action is MoveOn (moveon.org; see Figure 6.3). MoveOn was originally developed as an e-mail petition against President Bill Clinton's impeachment in the late 1990s. Later, MoveOn began mobilizing people who signed this original

Figure 6.3   MoveOn is a community that encourages people to become
politically active online. (*Reproduced with permission. ©2006
MoveOn*)

petition to fight for progressive causes in Congress. The group developed
a Web site that rallied support and encouraged people to join, then mobilized their members to contact Congressmen, donate money, and go
door-to-door in an effort to get John Kerry elected in 2004. Since the 2004
election, MoveOn has continued its grassroots lobbying and asks its members to contribute in some small way to the cause. Members can easily
e-mail their Congressmen on specific issues by filling out a form on the
Web site. Members are also encouraged to contribute money to and
e-mail friends about causes that matter to them, such as corruption in
Congress and the war in Iraq. People who are more committed to these
causes can also volunteer their time working for MoveOn.

One reason why MoveOn is successful is that it offers opportunities for
people to get involved with varying levels of commitment. Amnesty
International (www.amnestyusa.org) takes a similar approach, asking its

members to provide support at several levels. People can send e-mails to their Congressmen, donate money, or volunteer with a local Amnesty International group. Amnesty also hosts topical forums where people can discuss issues and ways to take action, both locally and globally.

People go online for many different reasons, but the abundance of online communities makes it clear that many go online to connect with others—in their local communities or across the globe. They meet online to share ideas, find a date or a friend, give and receive support, and take action. Community members use a variety of tools to accomplish this, each with its own set of pros and cons. The success of any online community depends on many factors, including the target audience, the tools used, how the site is administered, and its goals. The previous success stories should offer many useful lessons to libraries and other institutions now contemplating building online communities of their own.

The Role of Libraries in this Landscape of Connection

Library systems and consortia first became involved in online community-building with the development of Freenets in the early 1990s. These local networks let users dial in to use e-mail, Telnet, IRC chat, and Usenet newsgroups. In many cases, Freenets were created and maintained by local library systems and consortia. These Freenets offered local information, including event calendars, lists of local organizations, educational information, and employment resources. Local organizations such as a Girl Scout troop or the Rotary Club could have their own page within the Freenet to provide information to members and potential members. Most Freenets eventually shut down because of competition from ISPs (Internet Service Providers) and the graphical Web. However, some are still in existence now letting people dial in for access to the World Wide Web.

Since many of the Freenets of the early 1990s became redundant, most libraries have taken a less active role in building local online communities. Generally, a library's Web presence consists of an online catalog, databases and e-books, Internet links by subject, a listing of events, and basic information about the library. Some libraries' sites have a bit more content, but even some of the most technologically advanced libraries still do not offer a place on their Web site that could be considered an online community, as there is no space for public dialogue. Libraries that have developed blogs and provide a space for commentary come the closest to encouraging dialogue, but most library blogs are more suited to outward communication. When dialogue does occur, as seen on the Ann Arbor District Library site, it is inherently uneven, because librarians can post while patrons can only comment. Libraries are missing out on an important opportunity to position themselves as the online hub of their community and to create a space that can improve community welfare and cohesiveness.

Libraries can accomplish many things with online communities. Communities can be used to better understand the needs of patrons by observing their online behavior. Librarians can build up the library's presence in spaces already used by patrons. Finally, libraries can provide a public space for patrons online that meets their needs. Librarians can also use online communities to share ideas with colleagues, helping them develop better services for their own patrons. In capitalizing on the growth of online communities, libraries can develop a public space for patrons while also enhancing the reputation of the library as a place where patrons can find much more than books.

Building Presence Where Your Patrons Are

When companies want to build visibility and market their products, they try to build presence in places where their potential customers are likely to visit. Similarly, libraries can build a presence in any online community that their patrons use. Online photo sharing has great potential for allowing libraries to connect with patrons beyond their own Web sites. Since it has such a large user base, Flickr (flickr.com) in particular offers libraries an excellent opportunity to develop a presence in an online community that their patrons use. Imagine looking for photos of your community and finding that your local library has a Flickr account. This may help change the perceptions of community members who think that libraries are out of touch with technology. Photos of events, staff members, and everyday life at the library build a sense of community cohesiveness, helping the library become more transparent and more welcoming to patrons. The Bloomington Public Library in Illinois (flickr.com/photos/bloomington library) displays photos of staff members, library events, and its library expansion project. The LaGrange Park Library (flickr.com/photos/60582448@N00), also in Illinois, has photos of its remodeling project and community programming. If posted in a timely manner, these pictures can act as a news source, letting people know what is happening at the library. Photos put a human face on these two libraries, visually depicting them as vibrant community resources. Using Flickr also creates an online archive of photos that can then be used on a library's Web site.

When using photo-sharing software, consider the privacy and legal issues that may arise when your library puts content on another company's server. When your photos are on someone else's server, your library has less control over what happens to them. Before placing your photos online, read a site's terms of service and its privacy policy. Know what rights the company has to your information and what will happen if the company goes out of business or is sold. How does the service protect your library's privacy, and how easy is it to pull your content from the site? When putting photos of patrons on a photo-sharing service, consider the legal issues involved. You may need permission from parents to take and post photos of children online, or you may need to delete photos or other content about patrons at their request. Make sure you are using a service that lets you delete content if necessary.

Developing Online Communities

In any local community or institution, libraries are in an ideal position to develop an online community, as they are one of the few institutions that everyone uses. The library is the most socially inclusive institution in any community. In academia and hospitals, students, faculty, and clinicians all use the library for their research needs. In public libraries, all ages are represented, from young children to the elderly. Special and corporate libraries serve everyone at their institution. Some libraries have already positioned themselves as an online resource. The San Francisco Public Library's Web site hosts the San Francisco Community Services Directory (http://sflib1.sfpl.org:83), which provides detailed information about every San Francisco community service agency and is searchable by subject, program, and organization. Many library-sponsored Freenets offered community information with special pages for different community organizations. However, few libraries have created a space where community members can connect and communicate online. Libraries that create a true online community provide a valuable public space, open to the community.

When developing an online community, a library should consider its goals. Do you want a space where you can have a dialogue with your patrons about the library? Do you want a space where people in the community can discuss community issues? How about having subject spaces where people can discuss local events, sports, music, and other interests? What if you had a space where people could recommend their favorite restaurants, the best mechanic in town, or the clothing store with the best sales? Do you want people to advertise on your site? Do you want to create support groups? It is important to define the goals and scope of your community, both when designing the space and explaining this goal to your patrons. If you want to limit the space to one where people can only discuss the library and local community issues, you probably won't want to allow people to create their own forums. If you want the site to meet the needs of patrons no matter what subjects they choose to discuss, you may want people to develop topical forums. But that freedom requires extra attention to ensure that people don't create inappropriate forums.

Once you know what you'd like your community to be, you need to consider which type of software would do the job best:

- If you only want discussion spaces, forums are probably a good option, because they live on your Web site and you can create numerous forums on different topics.

- If you only want to discuss a single issue, a forum would work but so could an electronic mailing list. Mailing lists, however, require a committed group of people who want to discuss your desired subject. Signing up to receive e-mail messages from a mailing list requires a commitment that browsing a forum on the Web does not. But this might be a good option if your community has a group of people who are passionate about discussing local government issues or other local concerns.

- If you want people to offer advice on restaurants, retailers, and other local topics, a wiki is a good option. Since a wiki can become anything the community wants it to be, baseball fans could create a space devoted to baseball and vegetarians could create a vegetarian recipe archive. However, wikis such as this require closer moderation, and are only effective in communities committed to adding content. Wikis also can be more confusing than forums for people to use.

- Blogs can be useful if your goal is a controlled discussion of library issues. Librarians can post topics to the blog and patrons can discuss the topics in the comments section. A blog like this, however, does not give patrons a feeling of equal ownership of the medium, and many may not participate for this reason.

Another option is using free software such as Yahoo! Groups and MSN Groups. These groups let people share photos, allowing people to add photos of the local community. This can create a feeling of cohesiveness in the group, but would also require careful moderation. The Ann Arbor District Library has successfully used photos in its pictureAnnArbor project (www.aadl.org/services/products/pictureAnnArbor). Users can submit photos of and documents about Ann Arbor to the library to be included in a collection documenting everyday life in the city. However, the pictureAnnArbor project is on the library's Web site rather than on a third-party server, and the pictures are posted to the gallery by librarians and not the general public. When using any third-party service, read the terms of service carefully. What rights does the service have to your information, how will they protect your privacy, and what happens to your data if they go into bankruptcy or are sold to another company?

The final option is using a combination of community tools. You could use a blog to disseminate information or start conversations, and forums for discussions on nonlibrary topics. You could have an electronic mailing list for discussion, and a wiki for sharing. Whatever medium you use, make sure it will meet the stated goals of your group, would work for your population, and offers the level of control you need to meet the online community's goals.

Once you have chosen the tool or tools you would like to use, think about how you will administer your community. This involves making decisions about how open you want the community to be. Usually, the more freedom you give, the more work you will have to put into administration. A wiki that is completely open to the public will require moderation to remove spam and inappropriate content. A forum that requires a username and password strictly limits who can post, making it possible to identify a person who posts inappropriate content. This makes it easier to moderate that community and ban members who consistently break the rules. Many options exist between these two extremes. A wiki can be password-protected. Community members could be required to e-mail the library to get a username and password. A blog can be moderated by the community the way Slashdot is. Forums can require a username and password to edit, but anyone could be allowed to read the content. The most successful online communities are those that are not strictly controlled, but libraries must be cognizant of their status in their community and their connection to a larger institution. The balance between putting up barriers and creating too much work for yourself is a delicate one. You don't want the online community to require full-time moderation, but you also don't want to make it so hard for people to contribute to the community that they decide it's not worth their effort.

Chrystie Hill on Online Communities

What tools do you think have the greatest potential for building online communities?

I am completely tool agnostic. The major message of my work in online community has been that it's not about the tools we use, but the people we connect with. Seriously, the minute this book is published, the tools that I put down here are going to be "so six months ago!" I'd also say that different tools can serve different purposes; they are each valuable at different times and in different contexts. I don't care how much I personally dislike a certain tech-tool, it may be a godsend to someone else. That said, I think that there are a few qualities shared by the most successful tools.

Good community building tools are easily personalized, so that my personality can come through with images, sound, and/or text. This builds trust between members over time. Ease of use is also important. I don't want to have to think to myself, "how do I ...?" when trying to connect with others online. The most successful tools also let me participate from where I already am on the Web, or they make it easy for me to take a leap into their new space. Bridges between old and new spaces are especially useful. Decentralized management, where governing decisions are collaborative, and distributed responsibility, where I own and control my contributions, is also important. Community members need to feel recognized and valued by other members—and the space needs to be transparent about who's doing what—and why! When communities or collections get quite large, some sort of rating or other metric function may be useful for getting to the good stuff. Finally, the sharing or collaborative aspect has to be clear. When members can see that their contributions add up to a whole lot more than any of us could ever do on our own, it's more compelling and people want to be a part of it.

What are the biggest mistakes people make when trying to build online communities?

They try to control things. Community is not something that can be "created"—it can only be nurtured and facilitated. Librarians are actually really good at this already. Our ethics of anti-censorship and nonjudgment in terms of access to information resources can really come in handy in the online community building space. If we step out of our "I'm the expert" and "I know best" roles, and just allow people to connect with each other and speak their minds (within the guidelines, of course), it helps build trust and foster an environment where people are willing to both own and share their work together. Communities have to have guidelines, and members have to abide by them, but not everyone has to agree. Another mistake is to be in a hurry. Collaboration takes time. That can be frustrating for people who like to just get things done—now! The trick is having a balance of community leadership, appointed by the community and facilitated by trust over time, that can push things along and ensure that the collaboration isn't becoming inefficient. Finally, I think there is a mistake in thinking that a single community or group of any kind can go on forever. Communities form around particular ideas, needs, or content because it makes sense and is useful right now and maybe for a little while after, but certainly not forever.

Chrystie Hill is the online community manager at WebJunction and runs It Girl Consulting (www.itgirlconsulting. com) to help libraries build online communities.

Making Connections Online

Most librarians have been involved in some kind of online community for librarians at some point. Maybe you posted to an electronic mailing list asking for advice on a program you were planning at your library. Or perhaps you wanted support regarding a frustrating exchange with a colleague. Maybe you're a job searcher and joined an electronic mailing list to network and look for job postings. Whatever your involvement, you probably know that, just as online communities can be useful to our patrons, they can be tremendously useful to us as professionals. No matter where you are located, other librarians have shared many of the same experiences. Whether we are working at the reference desk, designing a Web page, cataloging nonbook materials, or teaching a class, we can benefit from the advice of people who have done it before.

Librarians most often use mailing lists as online communities. Librarians get daily e-mails from various lists they subscribe to, including lists about interlibrary loan, cataloging, Web design, reference work, distance-learning librarianship, acquisitions, serials, government documents, and much more. There are communities for new librarians, school librarians, dance librarians, law librarians, medical librarians, prison librarians, and library administrators. There are groups based on ethnicity, geographic location, sexual orientation, and language. Lists exist for users of different technologies in the library, such as the ILS, select databases, and public access computers. Many lists stem from local library associations, consortia, and national professional associations. In all, hundreds of electronic mailing lists exist just for librarians. No matter how esoteric your question, you can find an appropriate space to ask it.

One model online community for libraries is WebJunction (webjunction. org; see Figure 6.4), which was developed in 2003 by OCLC, the Colorado State Library, the Benton Foundation, and TechSoup, with funding from the Bill and Melinda Gates Foundation. WebJunction, whose goal was to create a community portal for small public libraries to share ideas and learn about technology, has succeeded in developing an online community that offers practical information and support to public libraries and a space where librarians can connect and help each other. WebJunction offers free online classes and Webcasts, articles, policy examples, and forums on issues that affect public libraries, including computer security, outreach, grant seeking, dealing with difficult patrons, library services to special groups, and more. Within each broad forum, multiple topics garner

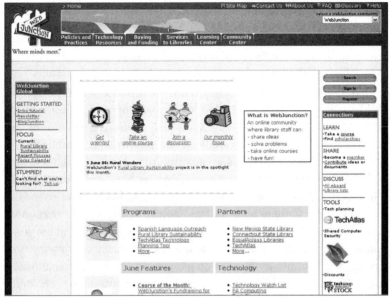

Figure 6.4   WebJunction is a leading community for librarians where members can read articles, take classes, and share ideas with their colleagues. (*Reproduced with permission.*)

active discussion by community members. Each forum is hosted by a moderator who welcomes members, sparks interesting discussions, and keeps everyone talking. These members are more like facilitators than moderators, since they do more than simply enforce community guidelines. WebJunction's forums and content make the community an excellent resource for librarians seeking solutions to common problems.

Other less traditional communities have been developed by and for librarians. Many librarians who blog have developed a distributed community of their own. Bloggers share ideas about the profession and their experiences providing services to patrons, while continuing conversations started on other blogs. Nonbloggers can join the community by posting comments on blog posts they find interesting or controversial. While the conversations do not go on in a single space as in most other online communities, they can be tracked by services like BlogPulse (blog pulse.com/conversation) and Technorati (technorati.com). Wikis are also being used as library communities. The ALA Chicago 2005 Wiki (meredith. wolfwater.com/wiki) included a space where people could ask questions about the conference, and other members of the community would answer those questions. Since a wiki can become anything the community wants it to be, it can flexibly meet the needs of all community members. In most wikis created by librarians, anyone can contribute and ask questions; no one person controls the conversation.

In our increasingly wired society, it is more common and more acceptable to meet people online, whether for mutual support, for sharing ideas, or for initiating in-person contact. Many of our patrons are joining online communities. When we fail to provide our patrons with a public online space, we miss out on a valuable opportunity to connect with them and help them connect with each other. Libraries have a responsibility to improve the communities they inhabit. This responsibility also extends to the online realm, where libraries can "Webify" many of their traditional services. Libraries can market to patrons by getting involved in the communities they are already a part of, and they can actually improve the welfare of their community by providing a valuable and safe online public space. Although building an online community involves many considerations, when done properly, the benefits greatly outweigh the effort.

Endnotes

1. John Horrigan, "Internet: The Mainstreaming of Online Life," Pew Internet and American Life Project, January 25, 2005, www.pewinternet. org/pdfs/PIP_Communities_Report.pdf (accessed December 15, 2005).
2. "Library Lists on WebJunction," WebJunction, November 22, 2005, web junction.org/do/DisplayContent?id=11245 (accessed December 24, 2005).
3. "craigslist Facts and Figures," craigslist,www.craigslist.org/about/pr/ factsheet.html (accessed December 29, 2005).

Chapter 7

Social Networking

Over the past few years, online social networking has received growing media attention. The phenomenon has taken the younger generations by storm—and left many older adults wondering about the appeal of these services. Sites like MySpace and Facebook are more popular than any other online community, although they are almost entirely populated by people under 30. At many high schools and colleges, every student has a profile on at least one of these sites, which are quite different than the online communities discussed in the previous chapter.

Interest groups on most social networking sites are simply peripheral, and people do not specifically use the sites to discuss common interests. People use online social networking sites to display their identity and social network publicly and make new connections. This indicates a change in the way people build identity online and get to know each other. Many library patrons spend almost all their online time on social networking sites so we need to understand the implications of this and how to provide related services. To provide outreach beyond the library walls, librarians can capitalize on these new community sites by building presence and providing services in the online spaces where their younger patrons congregate.

What Is an Online Social Network?

In the mid-1960s, Stanley Milgram experimented to determine the structure of social networks. Milgram, a social psychologist best known for his experiments on obedience to authority (where participants were instructed to administer electric shocks to an unseen subject), also had a tremendous impact on the field of network theory, taking it from the realm of mathematics into the social world. In one of his studies, Milgram sent 160 letters to randomly selected people in Nebraska, asking that they send the letter to a stockbroker in New York. Instead of sending the letter directly to the stockbroker, participants were asked to give it to someone they knew on a first-name basis whom they thought might have a closer connection to the stockbroker. The next person in the chain was asked to do the same, and so on. A full 29 percent of the letters reached the stockbroker, all of them within six steps. Amazingly, the majority of the letters were given to the stockbroker by three of his friends. Milgram repeated the experiment in a later study, asking white individuals in Los Angeles to get a letter to a black individual in New York. In a still largely segregated society, the results were the same as his other "small world" experiments. Milgram concluded that everyone in the world is connected to everyone else by, at most, six people.[1] While Milgram's studies have been criticized, his small world theory has achieved great popularity, and similar subsequent studies have had similar results.

The question most people ask about this experiment is how the world can be so connected when most people have a fairly homogenous social circle based primarily on proximity and shared activities. These connections are made possible by "connectors," or people who are connected to a large and diverse group of people. While most people live in one or just a few social worlds, these connectors link people from many different social worlds. These people seem to know everyone and are always bringing other compatible people together. We can be so closely connected to one another because virtually all of us know a connector. Malcolm Gladwell wrote about this phenomenon in his article "The Six Degrees of Lois Weisberg" in *New Yorker* magazine. Lois Weisberg, a woman in Chicago, seemed to know everyone due to the force of her personality and her various jobs and interests, from celebrities to politicians to housewives. As a person who connected others, she had an important role in the lives of many. Gladwell views social circles as pyramids, where a single person is often responsible for the majority of initial connections made between any two people. These connectors, like the three people who received the majority of letters to the stockbroker, are responsible for connecting various small worlds together.[2]

Social networking software emerged from this research. Social network theory posits the idea that one person's connections to other people are more important than the person's attributes. Following this logic, people can be judged, for better or worse, by their friends and acquaintances. On the same note, people's social networks can help them succeed in life, love, and business. Social networking software publicly and visually displays a person's social network. While online communities

Reasons
behind

enable communication, provide support, and promote action, the goal of social networking software is to allow users to develop an online identity and grow a social network. This can work for establishing business contacts, dating, or simply making new friends. In terms of dating and friendship, the assumption is that you are more likely to find compatible people through friends of your friends. Therefore, by displaying your social network of friends and acquaintances and seeing who they are connected to, you are likely to meet people who interest you.

Online communities center around forums, discussion boards, or other communication mechanisms, but activity in social networking centers around each member's profile. Profiles usually contain a photo and user-submitted biographical information, which might include where you went to school, where you work, and what your interests are. Profiles also list all of the user's "friends" and any testimonials or comments made by these friends. In terms of finding partners for dating, these testimonials are important in gauging how honestly a potential date portrayed himself. Testimonials, which can only be made by friends, are designed to be the online equivalent of pumping your friends for information about a friend of theirs. In addition, friends can only be added if they also add you as a friend, preventing a person from displaying a large group of social connections to which he or she really has no connection. *oh, really?!*

Social networking sites all differ in the level of interaction that occurs outside of profiles, but the profile is the central part of the software in all of them. This is where people can build their online identity and graphically portray their social network. Individuals can carefully control what aspects of themselves they wish to display, making themselves seem more attractive or interesting. They can even choose to display only the friends who make them seem more interesting. While the social aspects of the software give users a better ability to verify the accuracy of the person's portrayal, the possibility for deception still exists. Some people find social networking software attractive for that very reason. While they may have one identity in their offline life, they can very easily develop a different persona online and build a very different network of friends.

Other common features of social networking sites include the ability to create and join groups, allowing people to connect with others who share their interests, but may not be in their social network. Each group usually has its own message boards and lists all the members with their photos. Social networking sites often contain other ways for members to connect with one another, such as forums, synchronous chat, and blogs. While some members may actively seek to communicate with other members this way, others may simply use social networking software to create an online profile of themselves and their connections. People also don't have to belong to any specific groups. Since everyone adds their own friends to their network and everyone has different circles of friends, there are no specific boundaries as in many other online communities. Just as the name implies, these sites are structured more like a network, where people can navigate from node to node to discover new potential contacts. Social networking is more about creating identity within a community than about collaboration toward a specific end.

Types of Social Networking Sites

Social networking software is used for many purposes. Some use it to make new friends or meet new people to date; others use it as a tool to increase business contacts, both to make themselves look good and to capitalize later on the network they build. Some use it to keep in contact with geographically dispersed friends; still others simply use it for voyeuristic entertainment. Social networking software is geared toward different interests and different age groups. Despite the many social networking sites, a few major sites garner the most traffic. This section highlights a few of the most popular social networking sites, how they work, and their user appeal.

Social Networking for Generation X

Social networking started with Generation X, and dozens of social networking sites are geared primarily toward that demographic. Friendster (www.friendster.com), the first site that really made a name for itself, opened to the public in 2002 and attracted 1 million users in less than a year. The site was initially geared toward 25- to 35-year-old urbanites, but as their social networks grew, friends around the globe began to join and network. Anyone can join Friendster; they just need to create an account, create a profile, and add photos. Members can add their friends to their network, but a friend can only be added if that friend adds you as well. This is a measure designed to prevent people from adding hundreds of

Fail!

"friends" to their profile whom they don't really know. Once you have a group of friends, Friendster will show you your "second-degree" friends, or people who are listed as friends of your friends. The assumption is that you are more likely to have something in common with your friends' friends than with a random person you might meet at a traditional dating site or networking event. Friendster lets users post testimonials—things your friends write about you that are in many cases more telling than a profile. Friendster also lets users create individual blogs, share photos and video, post to discussion boards, and chat with other Friendsters. Finally, the site lets people create and join groups where they can meet members outside of their social circle with similar interests. This group membership information is geared to creating a richer profile, which is central to the site.

Social Networking for Millennials

In 2003, social networking was all the rage among those in their 20s and 30s. By 2005, however, the frenzy over social networking among members of Generation X had calmed down significantly. Not only did usage of Friendster decline, but a number of social networking sites shut down because of the lack of a loyal user base. Surprisingly, the trend is quite the opposite among members of Generation Y (Millennials), young people born in 1980–2000. Social networking sites designed specifically for that demographic have flourished. Corporations and bands have also capitalized on this trend, using these sites to connect with potential consumers and fans. Young people see sites like MySpace (www.myspace.com) and Facebook (www.facebook.com) as spaces designed for them, where they can express themselves freely and connect with friends online.

MySpace began in mid-2003 after Friendster had already developed a significant membership base. MySpace quickly rolled out many features that distinguished it from Friendster and made it very attractive to teenagers and young adults. One of its most significant features is the ability to customize profiles. MySpace members can use HTML and CSS to personalize the look of their profiles and can add video and audio clips for visitors. While this can lead to garish and unreadable profiles, it also makes the profile a space where young people can express themselves creatively. Hundreds of outside sites help MySpace users customize their profiles. As in Friendster, a member's friends are displayed in his or her profile. Instead of member testimonials, a comments section attached to each profile works much the same as a bulletin board where users post messages to each other. Blogs are also an integral part of MySpace. Each member has a personal blog with posts displayed on their profile. Because of these features, MySpace attracts those interested in self-expression as well as networking. By mid-2006, about 61 million people were registered MySpace users,[3] and in July 2006, it became the No. 1 Internet site in terms of traffic.[4]

In 2004, MySpace began letting musicians create their own profiles and post streaming clips of their music. Many struggling musicians saw this as an amazing opportunity to connect with potential audiences; bands used their profiles and blogs to create an online presence and develop a loyal following. Young people were excited to connect with band members in the same space that they use to connect with their friends. Bands can add fans as "friends," increasing the sense of personal connection. In November 2005, *Wired* magazine documented the unlikely success of the punk band Hawthorne Heights, active bloggers on MySpace who have almost 300,000 "friends." The author of the article describes the new model of marketing music to the MySpace generation:

> "MySpace bands," as the site's publicist refers to them, keep production and promotion costs as low as possible. They give away their best two or three songs as downloads or streams and use social networking and e-mail blasts to reach an audience hungry for new music. Converts become zealots, more than making up for any lost CD revenue through sales of concert tickets, T-shirts, messenger bags, hoodies, posters, and bumper stickers. With little fanfare, these groups are creating a new middle class of popular music: acts that can make a full-time living selling only a modest number of discs, on the order of 50,000 to 500,000 per release.[5]

By the end of 2005, there were 400,000 bands on MySpace, running the gamut from struggling artists to musicians whose songs have made the Billboard Charts. Television shows have also started using MySpace as a way to connect with audiences and provide a space for fans to discuss the shows. Many companies, especially those that market their products primarily to those under the age of 30, have become increasingly aware of the impact of MySpace. Social networking software such as MySpace provides them with a captive audience they can connect with and elicit feedback from. MySpace makes a tremendous profit from ad revenue from ads placed all over the site. In September 2005, Rupert Murdoch's News Corp. bought MySpace's parent company, a clear recognition of its potential as a marketing vehicle.

Newer social networking sites intend to tap niche markets. Facebook (Figure 7.1) was founded in early 2004 to bring college students together online (though Facebook now includes high schools and some companies). To belong to Facebook, users must have a valid e-mail address from the institution they are registering with, preventing people outside of that institution from joining. When users become members, they become

Figure 7.1   A Facebook profile contains photos, a list of friends, and "The Wall." (*Reproduced with permission. ©2006 Facebook*)

members of their school's particular network on Facebook. Users can only see profiles of people at their own school—unless a friend is added from another school and that friend adds the user as well. This creates a sense of local community and insularity that MySpace, Friendster, and others lack. As with all social networking software, the profile is central to Facebook: It includes photos, a list of friends, and "The Wall," where friends can post messages. People can make new friends by viewing the profiles of friends of their friends, or by searching for people who are taking the same classes. Users can also create groups. Facebook aims to build a local social network within the academic community, so that people can also connect with one another offline. By the end of 2005, the site had attracted more than 9 million users. Facebook, which also earns revenue from companies looking to market to its members, has even allowed companies including Apple and Electronic Arts to create groups within Facebook to communicate directly with their potential consumers.[6]   ↑ outdated, beyond Academic now

Social Networking for Business

More and more people now do business online. Whether companies merely use e-mail to contact clients and maintain contacts, or run an online-only business, the medium has become important to staying connected and making money. For decades, organizations have let business-people network and build valuable lists of contacts. This model easily translates into the online medium. Individuals can meet other business-people around the world who are doing similar or related things. They can network, provide support and advice, and meet potential partners for future ventures. An online profile is also free advertising for a business. Instead of being limited to making connections with people in one field or in a local area, business owners and employees can find like-minded people in different fields all over the world to build business-centered relationships with. Employees who graphically display their network can also benefit their companies; businesses now see the value of publicly articulating their employees' networks in order to capitalize on them in the future.

Ryze (www.ryze.com), the oldest social networking site in existence today, debuted in 2001 with the goal of helping people build their business networks. Users enter information about what they do for a living, schools they've attended, places where they've worked, and their interests. This becomes their profile. Once members have a profile, they can start adding contacts. Some people only add contacts with whom they have an existing relationship. Others add anyone who may be useful to them in the future. The latter group thinks it looks good to potential clients or employers to be connected to as many people as possible—although whether they can depend on these contacts is questionable. Connections made in these business networks, however, can be useful in the future. When looking for a job, new clients, or partners for a business venture, it's good to have a ready list of people to contact in your field. Ryze also has networks, or groups, to join that are usually interest-based, profession-based, or geography-based, and offer additional opportunities to make connections with like-minded people or people in your area. Ryze once offered paid memberships with added features, but it is currently free for anyone to join.

LinkedIn (www.linkedin.com) is another social networking site that lets users keep track of business contacts. The site was originally designed as a social networking space for upper-level management, but it has grown to include people at all levels of business. You can add friends to your LinkedIn profile in two ways: You can find people already using the service, or you can invite people in your e-mail address book. LinkedIn makes it easy to send invitations to everyone in your Microsoft Outlook or other online address book and constantly encourages members to add to their network. The real value of LinkedIn is not simply in seeing who your contacts are, but in seeing who your contacts' contacts are. If a friend of yours knows someone who could be helpful to your career, you can have them arrange an introduction. Sites like LinkedIn and Ryze let users capitalize not only on their personal network, but on their second- and third-degree networks. LinkedIn also allows people to post jobs and to search for people in their network or in their area who provide specific services. For that reason, LinkedIn is geared more toward people interested in marketing their services online or who are looking for a job.

Mobile Social Networking

The social networking sites mentioned so far are useful in making contacts to capitalize on future opportunities in friendship, dating, or business. Other social networking software is designed specifically to encourage people to meet in the physical world. This software, usually designed for mobile devices, is called MoSoSo, or mobile social software. Instead of only letting you look up your friends online, MoSoSo adds location and time elements so that you can find them in the physical world. MoSoSo helps people find friends in their local area while they're on the go. If there is a party in their area or a friend of theirs is at a coffee shop down the street, MoSoSo provides this information on their mobile device. Dodgeball (www.dodgeball.com) is currently the most popular MoSoSo available with users numbering in the tens of thousands; the site was bought by Google in 2005. Dodgeball lets mobile phone users see what their friends (and friends of friends) are doing within a 10-block radius. Members can also tell Dodgeball where they are going to be and have that information sent to their friends. Users can even designate "crushes" and have their location sent to those users as well. Dodgeball, which is currently located in 22 metropolitan areas, is best suited for areas where members live close together.

Unlike Dodgeball, Socialight (socialight.com), another phone-based social networking service, can be used just about anywhere. Users can tell their friends where they are or where they will be in the future with "sticky shadows," which are created by entering information and accompanying text for a given location. When a member's friends visit that location, they will receive the text the member entered about it, be it a story or an invitation. Members can add media as well as text to location coordinates and can also limit who can view their sticky shadows. Socialight can be used to warn friends about a bad restaurant or to set up a dinner party. Rather than reading a guidebook, users can get relevant information about the places they visit on demand from trusted friends in their network.

Capitalizing on Social Networking in Libraries

Businesses are paying more attention to MySpace and Facebook as opportunities to engage in viral marketing. Parents of teenagers are paying more attention to MySpace and Facebook in an effort to protect their children from predators and from putting inappropriate content online. Librarians also should be paying more attention to social networking sites because we can learn from seeing where our patrons hang out online. Just like businesses, libraries can engage in viral marketing, integrating themselves into their patrons' social networks and using that "in" to promote library services. Libraries can also play a valuable role as educators, teaching parents, teens, and young adults how to be safe online. Librarians can sift through the hype and paranoia to give parents solid information about ways to keep their kids safe. While social networking sites have received negative attention over the past few years, libraries can use them in positive ways to provide better services to their patrons.

Market Research

As with any organization, market research is a vital element in providing effective library service. Libraries should constantly conduct both formal and informal research to determine whether they are meeting the needs of their population. Many community populations are constantly changing. Whether that means your library serves more speakers of foreign languages, a growing elderly population, more single parents, or more tech-savvy young people, you will need to adapt to the changing demographics in your area. One way to do market research is to go where your patrons congregate outside of the library. This may involve going to public spaces in your community and casually talking with patrons, or visiting the online communities your patrons are using. If you are a school, public, or academic librarian, it should be easy to find out whether your students or younger patrons primarily use MySpace, Facebook, or one of the other popular social networking sites. Becoming a member of that site will let you gain valuable insights into the interests, needs, and wants of your patrons. From this research, you might be able to determine what other technologies your patrons are using to inform your library's future services. At public and special libraries where populations may be more diverse, patrons may belong to a wide range of online communities geared toward different interests. More than likely, though, some of your patrons will belong to Facebook, MySpace, or Friendster, as well as Flickr and other popular online communities. Many of these communities let you search for members by geographic area or by institution, making it easy to find local people. Observing your patrons' interactions in these spaces will offer insights about your community that you may never get from a survey or other formal research tool. *Spying??*

Building Presence Where Your Patrons Are

An article in *Business Week* called "The MySpace Generation" discusses how businesses are trying to integrate themselves into social networking sites such as MySpace and Facebook in order to market to their members. Instead of marketing from the outside, many companies are actually starting groups within these networking sites to encourage back-and-forth communication.[7] This gives members a sense of the company being within their network and concerned with what young people really care about. If businesses are developing a presence within these communities, why can't libraries? Libraries can develop a profile and build a network to help integrate themselves into patrons' social worlds.

By 2005, a number of college and university libraries were already on Facebook, including the University of Illinois at Urbana-Champaign Undergraduate Library, the Kresge Library at the University of Michigan, and the Perkins Library at Duke University. These libraries had a profile just like any member of their school's community. They also could create groups, where students could ask questions or offer comments about the library. In the fall of 2006, Facebook began closing organizational profiles—including those of libraries—stating that profiles are designed solely for use by individuals. Some librarians reinstated their profiles under their own name, but other libraries' outreach in Facebook was effectively blocked by this new measure. One librarian who resurrected her library's profile under her own name is Oceana Wilson, Director of the Crossett Library at Bennington College in Vermont. In her profile, she asks students to post books and movies they would like the library to purchase in the discussion section of the profile (Figure 7.2). Although acquisitions request forms are usually available on a library's Web site, asking the students within their own online space makes the students feel that their opinions are valued and lets them feel more comfortable making the request. Facebook has advantages over other social networking sites for developing a seamless presence, because students' social world in Facebook is more or less limited to the school they attend.

While it might be more difficult to randomly stumble upon a local library's page in MySpace, creating a presence in MySpace allows for more self-expression and marketing. With MySpace, libraries can design their profiles with CSS to create a consistent look with other library Web pages. They can use the blog feature to market their resources and programs while also putting a human face on the library. Many libraries use IM to

Figure 7.2   Students can post books and movies they would like the library to purchase at the Facebook profile of the Director of the Crossett Library at Bennington College (VT). (*Reproduced with permission. ©2006 Facebook*)

provide reference services to patrons, and MySpace has a built-in instant messaging client right inside users' profiles. Under interests, where people can put books and movies they like, the library can provide links to the catalog or to readers' advisory pages and reviews. Libraries can link to their MySpace profiles on their own home pages, making the connection between the library and MySpace nearly seamless. The Denver Public Library has done an excellent job of integrating their MySpace account (www.myspace.com/denver_evolver; Figure 7.3) with eVolver (teens.

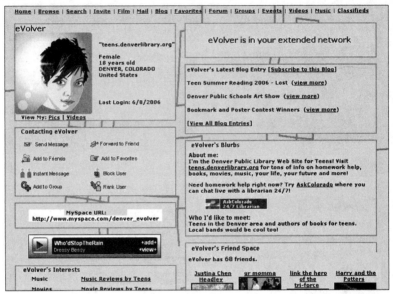

Figure 7.3 The Denver (CO) Public Library integrated its teen site, eVolver, with MySpace. (*Reproduced with permission. ©2006 Intermix Media*)

denverlibrary.org), the library's Web site for teens. The sites have a similar look, and the MySpace account links back to teen reviews of books, movies, and other media on the eVolver site. A number of libraries have made their MySpace page a portal to library services, with links to the catalog, virtual reference services, and remote access instructions for the databases. The Denver Public Library, like many other libraries on MySpace, has a list of friends who have been mutually added and can comment on the library. This also increases exposure of the library's presence, as other people see the library on the lists of their friends' friends.

There are many reasons for a library to have a profile on MySpace and Facebook, but it should involve more than just trying to look cool. Just putting up a profile does not make the library cooler, nor does it make the library more visible. A big difference exists between being where our patrons are and being useful to our patrons where they are. A profile should be designed to offer something to patrons, so they will keep coming back to it. Libraries can create value in MySpace and Facebook by offering a space for patrons to give feedback, by providing news and information, or by providing a portal to library services.

When using community-building services from other companies, consider that when you put content on someone else's server, you may not have as much control over what happens to that information. Look carefully at each site's terms of service to determine what rights you have to your own content and what rights the service provider has to your content. Look at the privacy policy: Will the company sell your personal information or republish it elsewhere? What will happen to all of your personal information if the company running the service goes bankrupt or is sold to another company? If you decide to stop using the service, make sure you can erase your content if necessary.

As information professionals, we also have the responsibility to educate our patrons about online safety. Young people may be more technologically savvy, but they may not be as aware of privacy issues online. Students using Facebook may think that only other students can read their profiles, but faculty and staff with a valid .edu address can register and see what their students have been writing. Young people creating profiles online also need to be aware of the potential dangers of meeting people they communicate with online. Even information that people think is private can sometimes be picked up by search engines. Patrons may not realize how easy it is for a potential employer to do an online search and find things that they've written. It's important to distinguish between what is truly private and protected and what content is freely accessible to anyone with Web access. Some services republish content from other Web sites, and patrons may be shocked to find things they've written published in other places on the Web. Libraries have an important role in educating patrons about the dangers of putting personal information online and the ways they can participate in online communities while protecting themselves.

Social networking sites are a new breed of online community designed to build identity and showcase people's networks of friends and acquaintances. Due to their use and misuse by young people, they have produced a moral panic among some segments of the population. Value judgments aside, librarians should be aware of this phenomenon and should consider the educational role social networking sites can play. Libraries should also find ways to use these sites to provide services to their patrons. The marketing potential is tremendous, as evidenced by the level of business activity within MySpace and Facebook. Some potential library patrons may never visit their library's Web site, but libraries can build presence and services within the online spaces their patrons do use. Creating an online space designed specifically for young people and within their online world can help us build relationships with this demographic.

Endnotes

1. Mark Buchanan, *Small World and the Groundbreaking Theory of Networks*, New York: W. W. Norton and Co., 2002.
2. Malcolm Gladwell, "The Six Degrees of Lois Weisberg," *New Yorker*, January 11, 1999, www.gladwell.com/1999/1999_01_11_a_weisberg.htm (accessed December 20, 2005).
3. Steve Rubel, "MySpace Mania," Micro Persuasion, March 30, 2006, www.micropersuasion.com/2006/03/myspace_mania.html (accessed July 12, 2006).
4. "MySpace is America's Top Site," CNNMoney.com, July 11, 2006, money.cnn.com/2006/07/11/technology/myspace.reut/index.htm (accessed July 12, 2006).
5. Jeff Howe, "The Hit Factory," *Wired* 13.11 (2005), November 15, 2005, www.wired.com/wired/archive/13.11/myspace.html.
6. Jessi Hempel and Paula Lehman, "The MySpace Generation," Business Week Online, December 12, 2005, www.businessweek.com/print/magazine/content/05_50/b3963001.htm?chan=gl (accessed December 18, 2005).
7. Hempel and Lehman.

Chapter 8

Social Bookmarking and Collaborative Filtering

The sheer amount of online information can overwhelm those looking for quality resources, and the increasing ease of publishing to the Web has created so much content that no one search engine can index it all. In 1995, Yahoo! created a Web directory where human catalogers assigned each site to specific hierarchical categories. As the Web grew, however, it soon became obvious that it could not be formally cataloged in a comprehensive fashion by humans. Search engines today use automated Web crawlers to index the Web and algorithms to determine relevance. Google now indexes more than 6 billion items, and even that only represents a portion of online content.

This abundance creates what is commonly known as the tyranny of choice. People confronted with too many choices often have trouble making a decision. How can we find the best Web sites? How can we find the most interesting articles in our areas of interest? How can we know which products will best meet our needs? Search engines can only do so much. Searchers are often bombarded with completely irrelevant Web sites, because relevance is determined by an algorithm not by a person. However, those developing search engines, e-commerce sites, and social software have been working to create systems that capitalize on both the implicit and explicit input of human beings. Rather than professionals formally cataloging the Web, regular people are making sense of it in their own way, adding their own keywords and opinions to the mix. Recommendation systems and social bookmarking can help people to make better decisions online by capitalizing on people's aggregate explicit and implicit impressions.

Reputation and Recommendation Systems

Reputation systems help users make everyday choices on the Web, including which Web sites to pick, which articles and books to read, which hotels to stay at, and which products to buy. The systems use ratings and feedback from users as well as user behavior to offer real people's opinions of a given product or service. Recommendation systems similarly predict preferences based on information collected from users. The main difference between the two is that reputation systems simply collect and display user ratings and reviews, while recommendation systems actually make concrete recommendations for each visitor. Many e-commerce Web sites display characteristics of both systems. Both reputation and recommendation systems predate the World Wide Web, but the Web makes it much easier to collect user feedback.

To collect that feedback, some systems require specific action from users while others analyze user behavior to get implicit feedback. Rating systems require people to evaluate an item, document, or service explicitly. TripAdvisor (www.tripadvisor.com) allows people to rate and write reviews of hotels, attractions, and restaurants. Users are asked to rate each destination on a variety of variables by assigning each between one and five stars. People can then look at these ratings when making their decisions about where to eat, where to stay, and what to do. They can see the overall rating or people's individual ratings with user reviews.

Other systems don't require action from users to generate feedback. Ranking systems measure user behavior to rank items quantitatively. User behavior can include purchasing behavior, membership, how frequently you visit a certain page, how often an article is cited, and how many people link to a particular item or document. Based on the prevalence of certain user behaviors, a computer can generate a rating.

The *New York Times* Bestseller List is an example of a system that uses purchasing behavior to determine rank. Google also uses a ranking system: Its Page Rank algorithm ranks Web pages based upon how many inbound links there are to each particular page. The more links to a page, the more popular it is, and the higher its rank. In essence, the search results that appear at the top of the list in Google are the ones that people implicitly rank as most popular through their linking behavior. Unfortunately, Web developers quickly learned how to manipulate the system to improve the rank of their Web sites. This is why a person searching Google can find a large number of irrelevant commercial Web sites. Systems that use linking behavior, page views, membership, and even ratings as measures of rank can be manipulated, and algorithms have to be frequently improved to prevent false data from affecting the results.

Collaborative Filtering

Collaborative filtering has tremendous potential for both academic and commercial information systems. It harnesses the opinions, recommendations, and behavior of people in order to make recommendations to others. Collaborative filtering systems assume that people who agree on some things will likely agree on others. For example, if two people both like Billie Holiday's music, and one of them likes Duke Ellington as well, the assumption is that the second person will probably also like Duke Ellington. In that case, a collaborative filtering system would recommend Duke Ellington to person No. 2. However, systems such as this one quickly get more complex: They don't depend on a single opinion from one other user, but often on millions of user opinions. Collaborative filtering simply automates something most people already do: ask their friends for opinions. Most people rely on their friends for recommendations of restaurants, movies, music, and other items and services. If I have a friend who recommended a movie to me that I liked, and another friend who recommended a movie to me that I hated, I'm more likely to ask the first friend for advice the next time I go to a movie because our tastes seem to be similar. The more two people have in common, the more likely that one will like what the other one likes.

Although collaborative filtering uses rating and ranking measures, it adds a human element into the mix. TripAdvisor and Google don't know how much a particular person is going to like something, since everyone gets the same results when making the same query. With collaborative filtering, however, instead of generating a single rating or rank for an item, relevance is determined based on the opinions of the specific user and how well his or her opinions match ratings of others. This means that the system needs some information about a user before making recommendations. Some systems ask new users to rate a variety of items, then compare their ratings to those of others. From these initial ratings, they can recommend items that other people with similar ratings liked. Other systems base ratings on prior purchases and items the user has looked at.

Many popular commercial Web sites use both recommendation methods for their users. Amazon.com (amazon.com) keeps a record of everything each user has purchased and bases recommendations on prior purchases. Users are also asked to assign a rating between one and five stars to items that they have previously purchased or already have an opinion of; if the user doesn't rate a purchased item, the system by default assumes that the user liked it. Users are also allowed to publicly rate and write reviews of items, offering additional information about why they liked or did not like an item.

The system also makes recommendations to users based on an item they are looking at. Amazon.com's "Customers who bought this item also bought" feature lists items that correlate strongly with the item being viewed in terms of purchasing behavior. For example, when looking at the Bruce Springsteen *Born to Run: 30th Anniversary 3-Disc Set*, users can see that others who purchased that album also purchased music by Bob Dylan, Neil Young, and the Rolling Stones. Amazon.com tells its users that if they like the music of Bruce Springsteen, they will likely enjoy the music of these other artists. In this case, site visitors aren't giving any information to the system other than visiting a page, but they still benefit from other people's purchasing behavior. In a collaborative filtering system, your ratings and behavior help the system get recommendations for you, and help the system to give recommendations to others. This mutually beneficial system works best with as much data from as many people as possible.

Netflix (netflix.com) is an online subscription-based DVD rental service. For a monthly fee, users can choose DVDs on the Web that are delivered to their home by mail. Netflix has an extensive selection of DVDs and uses collaborative filtering to help its users make decisions about what to rent. Unlike Amazon.com, Netflix does not consider a rental an automatic endorsement of a DVD. Users must explicitly rate movies to get recommendations based on their likes and dislikes; the more movies they rate, the more recommendations they get. As on Amazon.com, users can write public reviews of movies and television shows. Netflix also lets users designate other members as friends. They can share their private ratings with friends and receive recommendations based specifically on their friends' ratings. Rather than trusting the wisdom of crowds, the friends option allows users to choose the people whose recommendations they trust the most.

Peers and Reputation in Recommendation Systems

Trust is an important component of some recommendation systems, especially those that do not rely on collaborative filtering. With collaborative filtering, people who have rated things similarly become part of a user's "neighborhood," from which recommendations are drawn.[1] In regular rating or ranking systems, someone may give an item five stars.

This does not, however, mean that another user will agree with that review. In addition, some people may submit false reviews for items they have a vested interest in seeing succeed or fail. This is where trust plays a part. On Amazon.com and Netflix, users can rate whether a public review was helpful or unhelpful. This will help others determine whether they should trust that review.

The blog community Slashdot (slashdot.org) employs two tiers of trust ratings. Contributors are given a karma rating based on posting frequency and how their posts are rated by moderators, and members choose their personal rating threshold, which determines which posts are displayed. A user who posts frequently has the opportunity to receive a higher rating, but only if they have received a good rating from other users as well. Other Web sites have adopted similar reputation systems to give users more information on which to base their decisions. In peer-based systems, users can choose who they want to receive recommendations from, based on user profiles or on prior knowledge of the individual. Choosing your own recommendation network will ensure that the recommendations are based on trusted sources. Without collaborative filtering, however, just because these sources are trusted doesn't mean that users will have similar opinions.

Problems with Recommendation Systems

Recommendation systems have their flaws: Some are based on the limitations of computers; others are based on the limitations of people. Collaborative filtering systems are based on mathematical algorithms. These algorithms attempt to make recommendations based on people's preferences, which may not be entirely possible. Two people may like the same five books, but one may not like the sixth recommended book on the other one's list. However, the situation is the same when computers aren't involved. My friend and I may have similar taste in movies, but this doesn't mean that we will always agree. Likewise, while purchasing behavior is considered in making recommendations, readers make no explicit recommendation. Just because someone buys a book does not mean that they were actually happy with it or that they bought it for themselves.

Unfortunately, people can also game the system. It's easy for spammers to plaster their Web address all over other Web pages, blogs, and wikis to improve their Google rank. The owner of a hotel can write a bad review

like Imdb

about a competitor, the author of a book can write a glowing review of the book on Amazon.com, and a malicious individual can add fake reviews for an item they know nothing about. Some systems only permit one review from a registered account, but many make it easy to create fake reviews. Sites such as Amazon.com, TripAdvisor, and Netflix allow users to rate the helpfulness of reviews, but people don't always know whether any particular review is legitimate.

User's recommendations can also be skewed when one account is used to choose items for more than one person. Often, an entire family uses a single Netflix account, so the site's recommendations incorporate the viewing behavior of many family members who may have very different tastes. Netflix later improved its system by allowing a single account to contain multiple profiles, each with its own queue and recommendations. On Amazon.com, if a man buys a one-time gift for his newborn niece, he may get recommendations for other baby items. Users can go to their ratings and choose to exclude certain purchases in recommendations, but this requires explicit user action. This kind of purchasing behavior usually has a negligible effect on the "Customers who bought this item also bought" system, since that tends to be based on a significant amount of data. However, other user behaviors can skew the results. School reading lists can have an impact on the Amazon.com recommendations. Certain books are part of virtually every high school and college reading list, and books that commonly show up on these reading lists will likely be recommended together on Amazon.com because they are so often bought together. So, a book like *Animal Farm* may be recommended to those interested in *To Kill a Mockingbird*, even though the books are about completely different topics.

In spite of the potential problems with recommendation systems, they have an undeniable power to help users make decisions. These systems harness user input, both explicit and implicit, and use it to help other users make sense of the choices presented to them.

Social Bookmarking

The proliferation of information makes it difficult for people to keep current on subjects of interest. Searches for a topic of interest in a popular search engine often net a few relevant results that are obscured by thousands of irrelevant results. Journals, blogs, and Web sites often contain more information on a given subject than a single person can read. How can people find the best information in their subjects of interest? One way that people are making sense of the glut of information on the Web is through social bookmarking. Social bookmarking allows people to catalog the Web using terms that are familiar to them, and offers others the opportunity to find out what people with similar tastes are interested in. Just as with recommendation systems, social bookmarking systems capitalize on the actions of people to help others make better decisions. When people bookmark documents for themselves, they then by extension help other people find the items they have "tagged" and implicitly noted as being worthwhile.

The first Web bookmarks were browser-based, and many people still bookmark links this way. Mosaic, the first Web browser, developed Hotlists, which allowed people to place links to sites they liked into a hierarchical system of categories for later use. When Netscape appeared soon afterward, this feature was renamed Bookmarks; Internet Explorer came out with a similar feature called Favorites. When users found a Web page or article they liked and wanted to find it again, they would simply add it to their bookmarks or favorites. Within these bookmarks, users could create hierarchical folders, or they could simply put all of their bookmarks into a single file. The former strategy involved work to develop the categories and then figure out into which single category a link should go. However, the latter strategy often led to lists of links that were so long that it later became hard to find items.

This bookmarking solution was incomplete; the more people's bookmarks grew, the more difficult it became to place links into the predetermined hierarchy or to remember in which folder a link was located. When bookmarking a site, users could put the bookmark into only one folder, even if it might fit equally well into a number of their categories.[2] In addition, these bookmarks were tied to a user's browser. If you decided to switch browsers or use another computer, you could not call up your bookmarks. People using multiple computers (at home, work, school, or other locations) required a more portable solution.

To solve this problem, Joshua Schachter developed his own method of keeping track of his links. He used a text file in which he began assigning "tags" to each of his links. Tags were essentially keywords that described each link. Instead of using defined categories, these tags could be created on the fly when a link was added to the file. This system inspired del.icio.us (del.icio.us; see Figure 8.1), the first social bookmarking system on the Web.[3] del.icio.us lets users store their bookmarks online and share them with others. Instead of creating hierarchical folders in advance, users assign tags, or keywords, to their bookmarks, along with an optional description of each link. Users can choose a single tag to associate with a link, or they can use multiple tags, helping them later find the things they bookmarked.

To use social bookmarking, users place a "bookmarklet" in the toolbar of their browser. A bookmarklet is a JavaScript tool that allows a user to call up a Web page or perform a specific function in a single click. When users find a site they like, they just need to click on the bookmarklet and assign tags to add that link to their social bookmarking software. The user doesn't even need to add tags if he or she is in a hurry, though it helps in later retrieval. People can also look at or search other users' bookmarks, by tags or by specific user. When users bookmarks a link, they can see how many other people bookmarked that same link. They can also see specifically who bookmarked that link, then browse those users' bookmarks to find other links that might be of interest. In this way, social bookmarking can lead to the discovery of other useful resources. Users can easily

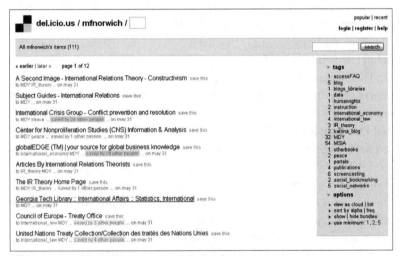

Figure 8.1   del.icio.us was the first social bookmarking system.
(Reproduced with permission. ©2006 Yahoo! Inc. del.icio.us and the del.icio.us logo are trademarks of Yahoo! Inc.)

browse through tags and through specific users' links to find items other people thought were interesting enough to bookmark.

Soon after del.icio.us came onto the scene in late 2003, many other free social bookmarking services were developed. The newer social bookmarking tools offer a variety of features that distinguish them from del.icio.us. Some sites not only bookmark a link, but keep a copy of the Web page itself. If a page changes and the bookmarked article disappears, the cached page can still be viewed. Users can also search their tags and descriptions as well as the full text of the pages they have bookmarked, and some bookmarking tools detect broken or redirected links. For people who are still attached to topical hierarchies, some services allow them to use folders and tags to both categorize their bookmarks hierarchically and describe them. Some social bookmarking tools let people create groups, where people can add topically related bookmarks to a common pot. For people who are working on a project together, this keeps all bookmarks related to that project in a single place. Users of some applications can also subscribe to other people's bookmarks, so if they find someone who shares their interests, they can easily keep track of what that person is bookmarking. By subscribing to other people's bookmarks, you basically use them as a filter for finding information in your field of interest. There are even social bookmarking sites such as Connotea (www.connotea.org) and CiteULike (www.citeu like.org) designed specifically for academics and scientific researchers who want to bookmark and share research papers they are reading.

Social bookmarking gives users a better way to collect links of interest and find them later. Rather than being forced to place links in hierarchical folders, users can assign descriptive tags that are meaningful to them. Web-based bookmark managers can also be accessed on any computer connected to the Internet and from any browser. Social bookmarking also lets people benefit from what others have tagged. It combines collaborative filtering and bookmarking to help people remember and discover useful resources.

Tagging

Social bookmarking is only one of many areas where Internet users are tagging items. On Flickr (flickr.com) and other photo-sharing sites, people tag photos. On many blogs, people now tag their posts so that they can be found more easily. On LibraryThing (www.librarything.com), an online service for people to catalog their books, people tag their books. Users tag items to make it easier to find them later and to collect similar items under a single tag. For example, a user on LibraryThing can find all of her fantasy books by giving them the same "fantasy" tag. A user taking pictures of places in Vermont could assign the tag "Vermont" to all of those photos and then easily find them all when he searches for that tag. Not only does this make it easier for users to find the things they bookmarked, but it also makes it easier for both friends and strangers with similar interests to find what they tagged. This can lead to the development of mini-communities centered around a certain goal or interest.

The tags that people choose to assign often reflect their motivations. People can tag an item in many ways: They can create a tag related to an object, an activity, an idea, a category, a food, a group of people, a person, or a location. Users can even create tags that describe what they want to do with the thing they tagged, such as "to_buy" or "read_later." Many users also tag things with terms that are personally useful to them but would not help anyone else. In LibraryThing, "read" is one of the most common tags, while in del.icio.us, "cool" and "free" are among the most popular; in Flickr, people often tag photos "me" and "people." While the majority of people tag things for themselves, many use tags that others can also understand. People often use familiar topic keywords, such as RSS, wikis, JavaScript, and podcasting when tagging items. Many people use a variety of descriptive tags for each item in the hopes that both they and others will later be able to find the link. While not everyone tagging an article or Web page on RSS will tag it with RSS, it's likely that enough people will use that tag that others will be able to find that item.

This activity of making sense of the Web through tagging is called folksonomy (folk + taxonomy), or classification by the people. Where taxonomies are hierarchical, going from the very general down to the specific, folksonomies are flat. Taxonomies are usually created by large standard-making bodies, such as the National Library of Medicine and the Library of Congress. The process for creating new controlled vocabulary terms or updating old ones can be lengthy, so the terms used for a given subject may not be those now commonly in use. Folksonomies are created from the bottom up by anyone who wishes to tag an object. Taxonomies use a controlled vocabulary where an object or concept is referred to by a single term and each term relates to only one object or concept. Human beings, however, use many words to describe the same thing. Where a controlled vocabulary may use the term "motion pictures," many people may instead think of the terms "cinema," "movies," or "film." Just as people use different words to describe the same phenomenon, users will search for the same concept using different words. Folksonomies are created by everyday people, so they reflect the language that people actually use to refer to concepts. Terms used to describe an article in a taxonomy may not even be words actually used in the document. In a folksonomy, the terms are more likely to reflect the language the author used in his or her own work. Taxonomies were created to disambiguate polysemes (words with multiple potential meanings) and gather similar terms, but folksonomies reflect the terms people actually think of when they are tagging the object.[4]

Using Tags for More Than Remembering

People are already using tagging for more than just remembering links. Social bookmarking sites allow users to browse tags and tagged items in many ways, encouraging them to explore beyond their own bookmarks. They enable serendipity by making it easy to click on a tag or on a username and encounter new items. If a user is interested in wikis, he or she can simply click on that tag to see what other people are tagging on the subject. A user can also browse other users' tags to find people who are interested in the same things. A user's "tag cloud," or weighted distribution of tags, is a good way to determine prime areas of interest. An individual's tag cloud will show all the tags he or she uses, but the ones used more frequently will be larger (Figure 8.2). From this, a user can see what tags another individual uses most frequently, and thus what each person is interested in the most. For sites where users can subscribe to each other's bookmarks or form groups, this is an excellent way to form a community of interest.

People also broadcast their bookmarks to others in an effort to share the best things they find on the Web. Some people post their most recent bookmarks on their blogs or Web sites. Most sites that use tagging also provide RSS feeds for each tag. Social bookmark managers usually create an RSS feed for each individual's bookmarks, an RSS feed for each tag an individual uses, and an RSS feed for each tag used by everyone on the system. Members can use a line of JavaScript, which is often made freely

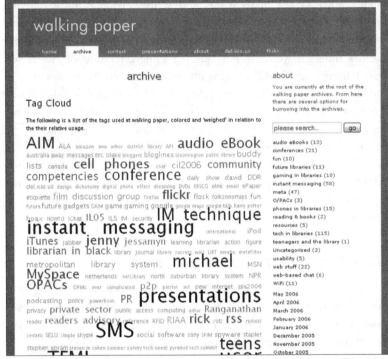

Figure 8.2   The archive for the Walking Paper blog can be viewed as a list
or as a tag cloud. (*Reproduced with permission.*)

available by the bookmark manager, to display a constantly updated feed of what they've bookmarked on their Web site. If people are interested in what a particular individual is tagging, they can subscribe to that user's RSS feed, or they can subscribe to the RSS feed for a particular tag to see what everyone else is tagging with a given term.

Some people also run "linklogs," or blogs made up entirely of links. In most cases, these links are automatically imported from the individual's social bookmarking service; the blogs sometimes include brief descriptions of each link. Bloggers can also tag their posts so that people can more easily find them using blog search engines like Technorati (technorati. com). Bloggers whose software doesn't allow them to create categories can simply bookmark and tag their posts, then provide links to those tags in the place of categories. Bloggers can also assign Technorati tags by adding special links to each blog post. Tagging can help users find things serendipitously, share useful article and sites, and make their own content easier to find.

Problems with Tagging and a Few Solutions

Some Web pundits have declared the death of taxonomies. They argue that because tagging is easy to do and reflects the ways users perceive objects and phenomena, folksonomies are universally preferable. However, folksonomies have some major drawbacks that make them less than ideal in many settings. Taxonomies have one term that refers to each concept because people use different terms to refer to concepts. This is why "synonym control," or pulling together all of the terms referring to a given concept under a single authorized term, is a part of all taxonomies. In a folksonomy, if a user searches under the tag "cinema," he or she will miss out on all of the useful items that are only tagged with "movies" or "films." When the same user searches for "cinema" in a library catalog, he or she will be directed to the authorized term "motion picture." If a user is looking for the best materials on transcendental philosophy, it will be far more difficult to find them in a folksonomy, because there are so many terms people could use to describe the same idea. Folksonomies also don't disambiguate between polysemes, words that can mean more than one thing. For example, a mole could be a spy, a unit in chemistry, a bit of pigmentation on the human body, or a rodent. If someone uses the tag "mole," how do we know which one he's referring to? This is why taxonomies disambiguate polysemous terms by creating different categories for each meaning. Taxonomies are hierarchical, making it easier to understand the relationship between terms. In folksonomies, no explicit relationships exist between tags.

People simply have different ways of conceiving of the same thing. If a person is looking for articles about JavaScript, will they all be found under the JavaScript tag? Or will many of them instead be found under "scripting" or "web_design"? People will tag things at different levels of specificity.[5] People who are only browsing tags to see what is available probably won't care if everything isn't classified under a single term. However, people who are looking for the best articles, or for all articles, on a specific subject will have a difficult time finding them in a folksonomy. Folksonomies will never replace taxonomies; hierarchical taxonomies have distinct advantages that make them necessary in some settings.

However, it simply isn't possible to catalog the entire World Wide Web using a controlled vocabulary, and current search algorithms don't always find the best resources in a user's area of interest. This makes tagging a pragmatic approach to cataloging the Web and encouraging discovery of items that may never have been found by a machine.

improvements

User agreement in tagging could be improved in several ways. First, Web sites that allow users to tag items can suggest popular tags. del.icio.us already does this, providing lists of popular tags for a given item, tags the user has already created, and recommended tags based on both the user's tags and how other users have tagged that item. This encourages users to assign an article or Web site the same tags that others have already used. Another way that tagging could be improved is by suggesting synonymous terms. This way, instead of users tagging a site about movies only with the tag "motion_pictures," they could assign all of the synonymous tags to that item. Users may not think of all the possible synonymous terms when tagging an item, but they might add the synonyms when the bookmark manager makes it easy to do so.

One way to improve the ability to disambiguate terms that have more than one meaning is through "clustering." Clustering uses the additional tags attached to an item to determine which tags are referring to the same thing. For example, a jaguar could be a car, a cat, an aircraft, or an operating system. By using the additional tags that people associate with the term "jaguar," the system can separate the tag into clusters. Flickr has a clustering system that does just that. For each tag, there are clusters that are separated by the additional tags users have used to describe the photos. If I do a search for the animal "jaguar," Flickr has determined that the terms "zoo," "animal," "cat," "animals," and "big cat" separate the cat from the other jaguars. Clustering makes it easier for people to find relevant items and avoid those that are not.

One significant issue in this user-created metadata is how people will discover useful information. This is done through searching, collaborative filtering, or manual browsing. While some social bookmark managers search the full text of each tagged item, the majority only search the tags themselves. This means that when a user is searching for articles about RSS, he or she will only find articles tagged "rss," not articles tagged "rss2.0," "rssarticle," or "aggregator." As Talis' Ian Davis states: "Tagging bulldozes the cost of classification and piles it onto the price of discovery."[6]

The search functionality on social bookmarking sites still has a long way to go before it can be considered sufficient for enabling discovery.

Collaborative filtering is an excellent way to make tagging more useful. Web sites that let users tag items can develop an algorithm to group people together who tag many of the same things, then make recommendations based on what other people in that group have tagged. One social bookmark manager, Furl (www.furl.net), has already done this, and there is no reason why other social bookmark managers couldn't also harness all of this user-created metadata to make recommendations to their users. Users could even subscribe to an RSS feed of their recommendations so that these would be delivered to their aggregator regularly. Instead of having to search for like-minded users to discover new resources, collaborative filtering would automate the process.

Social Bookmarking and Collaborative Filtering in Libraries

Libraries already have plenty of user data right under their noses on which they can capitalize. Every day, our patrons borrow materials. Some come back and tell library staff that "I really didn't see what was so great about this book," or "this was the best book I've read in a long time!" Patrons have opinions about materials they borrow. What if we asked our patrons to rate the books they've read, just like on Amazon.com? Interested users could log into their library account to see a list of books and other materials they've taken out of the library. Users could rate each item (from one to five stars) and submit their ratings to the recommendations engine. Once enough people have rated materials, they then could start receiving recommendations. If two people liked the same four books, then each may like additional books the other recommends. Patrons often come into the library looking for a good book to read, but "good" is very subjective. If they knew they could get recommendations based on their likes and dislikes, patrons may be much more likely to contribute ratings of their borrowed materials.

Libraries could also adopt an Amazon.com-like recommendation system based on implicit behavior. Each item in the library catalog could display a list of other items under a "People who borrowed this item also borrowed …" heading. An algorithm could analyze the materials patrons take out to make these recommendations. Many libraries in the U.S. currently don't save their users' borrowing records to protect patron privacy. If identifying information about patrons could be wiped out and replaced with random ID numbers, the privacy problem would not be an issue; data could then be used to help patrons make decisions without worrying about violating any right to privacy. This could also be done collaboratively by many libraries. By sharing user-generated data among a large number of libraries, recommendations would be based on the behavior of a larger number of patrons and would likely be more precise.

It isn't always easy to know what a book is about by looking at records in most library catalogs. Tagging the catalog is one way library users could offer feedback on the "aboutness" of materials. Patrons searching the catalog could see tags assigned by other patrons, which might give them a better idea of what each item is about. Since subject headings are usually difficult for patrons to use in their searches, they could instead click on a tag to find all the books that match that tag. Patrons looking for information about Alzheimer's, for example, could search for the tag "alzheimers" to find books with that tag. Allowing users to tag the catalog, though, would have to be moderated since it could unfortunately lead to abuse.

Some libraries have started letting patrons annotate catalogs with their opinions of materials. The Hennepin County (MN) Library allows patrons to comment on books and other library materials. Just as on Amazon.com, each item displays a text box where patrons can enter their opinion. These reviews are then added to a listing of all comments on an item that can be accessed from the record for that item. The Ann Arbor (MI) District Library offers a "virtual card catalog" service, where patrons can virtually write on what looks like an old catalog card for each item they view in the online catalog. Whatever brief phrases they write will show up as handwriting in the margins of the card. While this is more of a novelty than the Hennepin County Library's service, it still lets people see other patrons' impressions of a book or other item. These services give patrons more information about library materials than is available from the traditional library catalog, and let patrons offer useful insights to their community.

Libraries could also use social bookmarking to help patrons find articles and Web sites in their areas of interest. To get patrons started, librarians could offer classes on using social bookmarking sites. This could be incredibly useful in academia and business, where keeping up with information in a specific field is paramount. However, learning about social bookmarking would be useful to patrons in any library. Librarians could also recommend social software sites that provide readers' advisory services. Sites such as LibraryThing let users catalog the books they have read; they can then see which users have read similar books and look at others' catalogs to find new titles they might be interested in reading. LibraryThing makes book recommendations by comparing the books you have cataloged with the books cataloged by everyone else in the system (Figure 8.3). Anyone visiting the site can also enter the name of a book they liked and get recommendations on what they should read next. Another site that provides similar readers' advisory functionality is What Should I Read Next (www.whatshouldireadnext.com), which collects lists of readers' favorite books and then uses them to make recommendations based on a book title entered by the user.

Librarians could also tag items for their patrons using a social bookmarking site, creating entire subject guides through social bookmarking. A library could either add an RSS feed of new links to the front page of its Web site, or it could put the entire subject guide on the site using JavaScript and RSS. The Lansing Public Library in Illinois (www.lansing.lib.il.us) uses

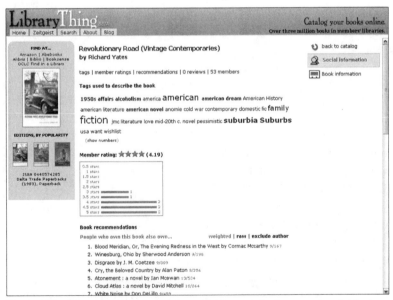

Figure 8.3   LibraryThing is not only useful for cataloging your books, but for getting recommendations based on what you like and what other users have cataloged. (*Reproduced with permission.*)

del.icio.us to bookmark useful links for its patrons (del.icio.us/lansing publiclibrary), then syndicates these links on its Web site. Lansing's users have the option of either subscribing to the RSS feed or visiting the library's Web site to see the new links.

Institutions and libraries are now developing their own social bookmarking sites for members of that institution or patrons of that library. The University of Pennsylvania was the first library to create its own institutional social bookmarking system from scratch. PennTags (tags.library. upenn.edu; see Figure 8.4) is a social bookmark manager for students and faculty. Members of the university can bookmark items from the Web or the library catalog, of which each page has its own "tagit" button. Faculty and students can create annotated bibliographies using PennTags and save them as individual projects. These can include readings for a class or resources for a project. University of Pennsylvania librarians have been creating annotated bibliographies that recommend works on specific topics. Groups can also be formed so users can bookmark items directly into the group.

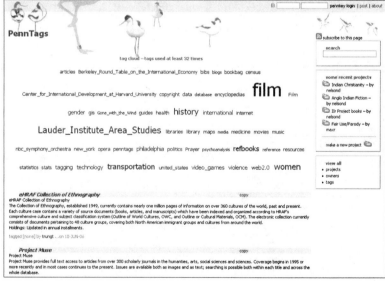

Figure 8.4   PennTags from the University of Pennsylvania was the first institutional social bookmarking system created from scratch. (*Reproduced with permission.*)

Laurie Allen on PennTags

What made you decide to create your own institutional bookmarking service?

Several librarians had been using del.icio.us and other social software systems, and were finding tagging useful for organizing links. However, external systems weren't able to capture links to most library resources, including our OPAC or journal article search engines. Additionally, we recognized that a system of this kind would provide a nice lightweight way to build flexible database-driven applications without designing new data models for each project. So, for example, we can use the backend of the PennTags system as a way for librarians to produce research guides, as the basis of a video reviewing system, and to add user-created content to our catalog.

How does PennTags differ from social bookmarking services like del.icio.us?

Basically, it is designed to work in an academic setting. So there are many ways it differs, but here are a few of them:

- Users can tag local resources that do not have stable URLs, like records from our OPAC and our video catalog. Also, we make it very easy to tag links to articles through our SFX link resolver, proxied e-resources, etc.

- Because users authenticate through the Penn authentication system, we can allow different kinds of tools for different users (e.g., librarians can use PennTags to create Research Guides).

- We have created projects, which function sort of like folders. Using projects, a user can group and reorganize posts outside the tag system. Projects have so far been used to create annotated bibliographies and research guides, and will be used as shared workspaces for groups in the somewhat near future. Projects will also have a set of styles that users can apply, and a number of export options.

How are students and faculty using PennTags?

As of the summer of 2006, we have done no publicity at all for PennTags to the general Penn Community, so its use is quite limited. However, it is used as part of an annotated bibliography assignment in all of the classes of one of the cinema studies professors. The students in his classes get extra credit on their assignments if they use PennTags to collect and annotate resources on a film of their choosing and organize them in a project. We also have a number of students, faculty, and researchers who have found PennTags incidentally, and who use it to organize projects, keep track of citations, or in many of the other ways that people use social bookmarking sites. We've been really pleased to see interesting uses of PennTags even without any publicity. A researcher has collected a list of his most used e-journals and we assume he is using the RSS feed provided by PennTags in a feed reader. Since PennTags only launched in the fall of 2005, many of the uses so far have been by librarians, who have found it really useful in planning for course presentations, constructing research guides, and collecting resources for particular students.

Laurie Allen is the Social Science Data Librarian and liaison to the Urban Studies Department. She has been instrumental in the development of PennTags.

Social bookmarking has also taken off as a way to help employees stay up-to-date in their field. Michael Angeles of Lucent Technologies wrote about how his team developed a social bookmark manager for internal use. Lucent Technologies' system is designed to let employees tag Web sites as well as articles from proprietary databases and to reuse the bookmarked content in portlets on company Web sites.[7] IBM is also developing its own social bookmarking system called dogear. The firm described its reasoning for developing an institutional system in an article for *Social Computing*:

The discovery of shared (or complementary) interests would help to nurture the communities of practice within the enterprise and potentially allow searching and finding experts on specific topics to help solve business problems.[8]

In addition to being a social bookmarking system, dogear also acts as a collaborative filtering engine that recommends other people's bookmarks that may be of interest. Other academic and biotechnology organizations have created their own institutional versions of Connotea (www.connotea. org), a social bookmark manager for scientists, since the company has opened up its source code.[9] This use of social bookmarking for specific groups can help communities discover useful resources targeted to their field and can help institutions share information more easily.

Social Bookmarking to Help Librarians Keep Up

Just as social bookmarking is useful for patrons, it is equally useful as a way for librarians to keep up with what's happening in our field. Social bookmarking lets librarians easily organize and file articles and Web sites for future reference, and browse others' bookmarks to discover resources they may never have found using a search engine. Librarians with common interests can create groups within social bookmarking sites where each can act as a filter for the group, finding interesting material from diverse sources. Groups can also be created to share links for specific projects, such as an article-in-progress or a Web-design project. Each librarian is likely to find at least a few resources that others have not found, so together we can create a collection that represents the best works in our field on many subjects.

When choosing a social bookmark manager, be sure to research its features and choose one for your unique needs and goals. Here are a few things to consider:

- Are the materials you're planning to bookmark primarily academic papers, or are they a mix of Web sites, articles, and blog posts? If you're almost exclusively bookmarking scholarly articles, consider using an academic service such as CiteULike (www.citeulike.org).

- Does the bookmark manager only bookmark the link or save the entire page? Saving an image of each page can be useful in case the content changes or the site vanishes.

- Is it easy to add new bookmarks? The process of bookmarking a page should be quick and easy. If you make a mistake, is it easy to edit your bookmarks? Can they be deleted?

- When you add new bookmarks, does the bookmark manager suggest tags, either popular tags for that Web site or tags you have already used? If not, it's quite easy to accidentally use different tags for describing similar things.

- Is it easy to import and export your bookmarks? If a company goes out of business and you can't export your bookmarks, you will lose all your links. That's why it is a good idea to backup your bookmarks periodically. Some bookmark managers let you export links in a variety of formats, others in only one format. So make sure the format you need is available.

- Does the site search only the assigned tags or the full text of the bookmarked Web pages? It is easier to find things you've tagged if it also searches full text.

- How easy is it to find someone else's bookmarks? Is the site easy to browse? Can you search everyone's bookmarks or just your own?

- Can you create groups and can those groups be made private? If you are planning on using social bookmarking for a collaborative project, is it easy to create a group? This way, you won't have to look at each participant's bookmarks separately.

- Are there RSS feeds for every tag? Are there RSS feeds for searches?

- Does the bookmark manager recommend links that other users have bookmarked? (This is a feature currently seldom offered in social bookmark managers, but it is a natural fit, given the wealth of information collected by tagging.)

- If you're planning on creating a linklog, is it easy to export bookmarks to your blog software?

Some of these considerations may not be important to you, depending on your particular needs, but be sure that your social bookmark manager has all the features you need. Once you've started using a certain service, it can be difficult to switch to another later.

Our ideas about how we make sense of our online world are changing. We have moved from hierarchical categorization through greater search engine development, but everyday users are now making tremendous contributions to the Web by helping to organize it. People are adding their own metadata, their own preferences, and information about their behavior to the Web's collective intelligence. This information is used both to help the individual make sense of available choices and to help others by contributing to the body of online knowledge. Tagging lets people easily organize the online materials they want to find again and helps people keep up with their fields of interest by finding materials others considered valuable enough to tag. People may have inherently selfish motives to contribute to ratings systems and social bookmark managers, but they may end up benefiting others nonetheless.

Libraries need to be aware of the valuable information they can glean from patrons and their behavior. Collecting this sort of information can allow libraries to develop collaborative filtering systems to help patrons make better decisions about what to borrow. Libraries should consider how they can capitalize on this new trend toward user-created metadata and content, and how social bookmarking can benefit librarians, libraries, and our patrons.

Endnotes

1. Mimi M. Recker and Andrew Walker, "Supporting 'Word-of-Mouth' Social Networks Through Collaborative Information Filtering," *Journal of Interactive Learning Research* 14.1 (2003): 79–99.
2. Tony Hammond, Timo Hannay, Ben Lund, and Joanna Scott, "Social Bookmarking Tools (I): A General Review," *D-Lib Magazine* 11.4 (2005), dlib.org/dlib/april05/hammond/04hammond.html (accessed December 29, 2005).

3. David Weinberger, "[berkman] Joshua Schachter," Joho the Blog, October 25, 2005, www.hyperorg.com/blogger/mtarchive/berkman_joshua_schachter.html (accessed January 1, 2006).

4. Ellyssa Kroski, "The Hive Mind: Folksonomies and User-Based Tagging," InfoTangle, December 7, 2005, infotangle.blogsome.com/2005/12/07/the-hive-mind-folksonomies-and-user-based-tagging (accessed January 7, 2006).

5. Scott A. Golder and Bernardo A. Huberman, "The Structure of Collaborative Tagging Systems," Information Dynamics Lab, HP Labs 2005, arxiv.org/abs/cs.DL/0508082 (accessed January 4, 2006).

6. Ian Davis, "Why Tagging is Expensive," Silkworm Blog, September 7, 2005, blogs.talis.com/panlibus/archives/2005/09/why_tagging_is.php (accessed January 4, 2006).

7. Michael Angeles, "Making Libraries More Delicious: Social Bookmarking in the Enterprise," urlgreyhot, June 24, 2005, urlgreyhot.com/personal/node/2463 (accessed January 3, 2006).

8. David Millen, Jonathan Feinberg, and Bernard Kerr, "Social Bookmarking in the Enterprise," *Social Computing* 3:9 (2005), acmqueue.com/modules.php?name=Content&pa=printer_friendly&pid=344&page=2 (accessed January 4, 2006).

9. Timo Hannay, "Tagging for Business and Education," You're It!, November 16, 2005, tagsonomy.com/index.php/tagging-for-business-and-education (accessed December 26, 2005).

Chapter 9

Tools for Synchronous Online Reference

Libraries offer access to a wealth of information on just about any subject imaginable. Just as importantly, libraries provide services to help patrons make sense of that information and find what they're looking for. Librarians have a long and proud tradition of providing reference and instructional services to patrons. These public service functions primarily take place in person, at the reference desk, or in the classroom. However, as new technologies emerge, many libraries now endeavor to provide these services to patrons remotely. First, libraries began offering reference assistance by telephone. Rather than coming to the library, patrons could call the reference desk and ask a question from home or work. This was particularly useful in the decades before the World Wide Web, when ready reference questions could not be answered easily without books.

Since Internet access has become almost ubiquitous, more and more libraries provide virtual reference services. According to the Pew Internet and American Life study, "Generations Online," the majority of U.S. individuals from ages 12 to 70 now use the Internet. Eighty-seven percent of teens use the Internet, as do about 75 percent of those in their forties.[1] For many, the Internet is an integral part of their daily lives, including work, recreation, and socialization. Most students are now likely to do research online rather than going to the reference section of their local library. In recognition of this trend, many libraries have been offering reference assistance by e-mail since the 1990s. Patrons can e-mail a question to the reference desk, which will then be answered via e-mail by a reference librarian. While this offers patrons the ability to ask a question from virtually anyplace and at anytime, it does not guarantee the instant answers patrons would get at the reference desk. While an e-mail message sent on a Monday afternoon may get answered immediately, one sent Friday night may not get answered until Monday, depending on the institution. This asynchronicity makes it difficult to conduct a reference interview, especially if the patron's question is ambiguous.

Some libraries have created Web forms with structured fields to obtain specific information from patrons seeking reference assistance. Even then, librarians often require additional information to answer the question. If a patron's question needs clarification, librarians must send an e-mail message, which may be answered in a few minutes—or in a few days. If more back-and-forth communication is needed, this process could take a significant amount of time. The speed with which a reference question is successfully answered depends on the clarity and availability of both the librarian and the patron.

Young people in their teens and twenties have embraced the Internet as a way to communicate with their friends and those with whom they share common interests. However, instead of using e-mail, which they view "as something you use to talk to 'old people,'" they primarily use instant messaging (IM).[2] Three-quarters of all teens online use IM. Many of them chat online with their friends for hours each day, while they surf the Web, play games, do schoolwork, and talk on the phone. Their IM service is active most of the time they're online. For some, IM is their primary method for keeping in touch with friends.[3] While IM is primarily used by teens, 53 million American adults (42 percent) also use it regularly. As a communications tool, it is used for more than socializing: More than half of IM users also IM at work for business purposes.[4] Online synchronous communication has become an integral part of people's everyday lives.

The problems inherent in e-mail reference and the growth of IM as a communications medium underscore the need for tools that let librarians synchronously communicate with patrons online. Whether they are providing reference services or instruction, the ability to communicate with patrons in real time allows librarians to offer more personalized and timely services. Chatting back and forth allows librarians to conduct a reference interview and get an answer quickly to a patron. It also lets teaching librarians tailor their instruction to participants and answer their specific questions. While screencasts and other online instructional aids are useful, they are somewhat generic and not tailored to the particular person who may be viewing them at that particular time. A variety of ways exist to help users communicate synchronously online, including commercial virtual reference, IM, co-browsing, and Voice over Internet Protocol (VoIP). Each option has its own blend of pros and cons, and your choice of tool should depend on the specific conditions and needs of your library and population.

Commercial Virtual Reference Software

In the late 1990s, as IM use increases, commercial vendors began to see the potential of synchronous virtual reference. Most vendors were already providing software to the technical support sector and saw libraries as a new market for their products. However, repurposing their software often required more customization than anticipated, and many companies in the virtual reference software market disappeared early on.[5] Even now, virtual reference companies are struggling to provide the functionality libraries need to provide good reference services. Few libraries chose to develop their own solutions or use free tools such as IM software; for the first half-decade that libraries offered synchronous virtual reference, the vast majority offered it through a commercial service.

These commercial services contain a variety of attractive features for libraries. One available chat service will place a button on the library's Web site that patrons simply have to click to begin a chat with the librarian: Clicking the button opens a Web-based chat interface where patron and librarian can type messages to each other that are transmitted in real time. In most cases, the patron does not have to download software to chat. In addition to providing a chat interface, most services also allow librarians to "co-browse" and "push" Web sites to patrons. When pushing a Web site, a librarian can have a Web page open up on a patron's computer without any intervention from the patron. Co-browsing lets librarians demonstrate visually what they are trying to explain through chat. In an effort to be an all-encompassing virtual reference solution, many of the services even offer integrated e-mail reference.

The management functions found in commercial software are also popular with libraries, preventing some of the policy issues seen with other forms of online reference. Many commercial products let more than one librarian answer questions from patrons at the same time, and the staff interface indicates whether other librarians are online. When patrons ask a reference question, they are placed in a queue and questions are answered in the order in which they are received. All reference sessions are saved so the library always has a transcript of the session. In many cases, patrons can also receive session transcripts to make sure that they won't forget about the resources the librarian recommended or how to find them. If libraries wish to measure the impact of their service, patrons can automatically be taken to a survey page where they can evaluate their experience. Usage statistics can also be generated. Some products offer a knowledgebase where librarians can see how others have answered similar questions, helping them respond to questions in areas outside their expertise.

The management features of commercial virtual reference services are particularly attractive when many librarians are providing reference services. With features such as easy queuing of patrons and the ability to have multiple librarians staffing a virtual reference desk simultaneously, commercial software has led to the growth of chat reference cooperatives. These groups of libraries, often connected by geography, share the cost of the software and collaboratively staff a virtual reference desk. Some cooperatives pay for outside reference librarians to answer questions during hours their own libraries are closed. When a patron contacts one of these cooperatives, they may be contacting someone from their own library or someone who has never even seen their library. Multiple libraries can be represented by a single online identity. While this may not always be ideal for providing patrons with library-specific information, it does allow libraries to staff their virtual reference desk 24/7 without hiring any new staff. Several statewide cooperatives now exist (for example, Maryland AskUsNow! at www.askusnow.info; see Figure 9.1), as well as national reference cooperatives.

drawbacks   While commercial virtual reference software offers many benefits that other synchronous virtual reference options lack, it still has a number of drawbacks for libraries. First, since the software is often expensive, it may be out of reach at many cash-strapped libraries. The combined purchasing power of reference cooperatives can help make it more affordable, but it still can't compete with IM and VoIP on price. Librarians have also complained about the interface on some of these products, saying it is difficult to use and requires a significant amount of training. (Many vendors offer training but at a price.) Before contracting with any virtual reference vendor, make sure that you and your colleagues are comfortable with their interface. If a good deal on software results in significant time and money spent training staff to use it, your library may end up losing out in the long run. Keeping records of each reference transaction puts useful information at the librarian's fingertips, but it also means that libraries must keep this data secure. When dealing with a third-party vendor, be sure to examine the policies and procedures for dealing with patron data. Protecting the privacy of patrons is integral to libraries' mission, and keeping all this data safe adds an additional burden.

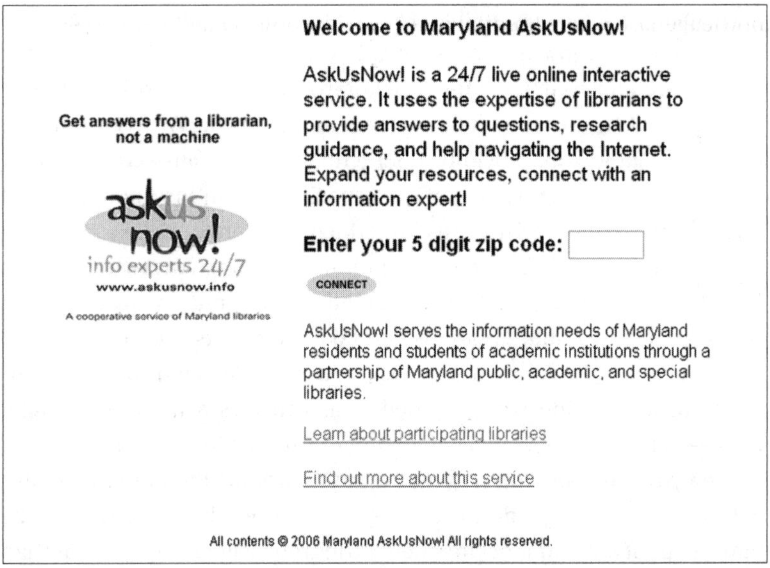
Welcome to Maryland AskUsNow!
Get answers from a librarian, not a machine
AskUsNow! is a 24/7 live online interactive service. It uses the expertise of librarians to provide answers to questions, research guidance, and help navigating the Internet. Expand your resources, connect with an information expert!
ask us now!
info experts 24/7
www.askusnow.info
A cooperative service of Maryland libraries
Enter your 5 digit zip code:
CONNECT
AskUsNow! serves the information needs of Maryland residents and students of academic institutions through a partnership of Maryland public, academic, and special libraries.
Learn about participating libraries
Find out more about this service
All contents © 2006 Maryland AskUsNow! All rights reserved.

Figure 9.1 Maryland AskUsNow! is one example of the many multitype library chat reference cooperatives. (*Reproduced with permission.*)

The most significant complaint about commercial virtual reference software is the one most likely to affect patrons. The complexity of these systems has led to strict system requirements and instability in some cases. Virtual reference software may require patrons to have a specific browser type and version; disable pop-up blockers; disable, enable, or download Java; and/or disable their firewall. With the number of browsers and security software packages in existence, it is unrealistic to expect patrons' computers to be perfectly compatible with such strict requirements. Sometimes the patron will meet all of the requirements, and the software will still fail for some reason. If patrons have a bad experience with their library's virtual reference software, they will be unlikely to try it again. If given a choice, many patrons would likely select software with fewer features, but that works properly more often. Patrons are simply looking for an answer to their question.

Co-browsing is the most potentially beneficial—yet problematic—feature of online virtual reference. Co-browsing involves two or more people browsing the Web together using separate computers; the users share the same connection and see the same things. If one user clicks on a link, all participants will be taken to that page. With some software, users can even view where the librarian is scrolling and what she or he is highlighting or entering into forms in real time. The librarian can control co-browsing, or the librarian and patron(s) can take turns navigating the Web. Co-browsing is an excellent tool for providing instruction as well as answering patrons' questions. If a patron wants to find a specific patent, the librarian could merely retrieve the information about the patent, or he or she can use co-browsing to actually show the patron how to do a patent search online. Instead of describing how to do something in words or just showing patrons the end result, librarians can take their users into the resource. Librarians can also let their patrons control the search, providing feedback and redirection when needed. This provides a more meaningful hands-on learning experience than other forms of virtual reference.

However, co-browsing may not always work for the patron. Failures with co-browsing include freezing up the patron's browser, kicking the patron out of chat, or blocking the patron from seeing what the librarian is seeing. Any of these problems could sour a patron on virtual reference forever. Certain products also require users to install MS Java (as opposed to Sun Java, which is already on most users' computers) for co-browsing to work. Some of these failures can be avoided. A few chat reference products will scan the patron's computer to determine if their setup will support co-browsing. The librarian should also ask the patron questions to ensure that they are on the same page and seeing the same thing; this should never be taken for granted.

One other issue involves the inability to co-browse licensed databases reliably. In many cases, the person authenticating into the database will be able to see the database, and the other person will be left behind at the authentication screen. This is a significant issue, especially for academic libraries, where much reference assistance involves using licensed databases. Some products have come closer than others to solving this problem, but none have been successful with every database. Pushing licensed content to people who did not authenticate themselves can violate some licensing agreements. While the problem of co-browsing licensed content may be solved in the future, it does not work reliably now.

Undoubtedly, co-browsing has tremendous potential for instructing library patrons, but no company has yet created a stable product that doesn't require a download or specific system requirements and that can successfully browse all licensed databases. While most studies have found a

co-browsing failure rate of only about 20 percent, is it acceptable to potentially alienate 20 percent of your patrons?[6]

Commercial virtual reference software offers many features that no
other virtual reference technology currently provides. Especially for virtual reference cooperatives, the management and queuing features are
essential. Currently, it is the only option that lets multiple librarians simultaneously provide reference services using a single identity. However, this
is a costly option for an individual library, and its added features may not
be worth the investment. If only one librarian staffs the virtual reference
desk at a time, management features become less important. Managing
queues and offering transcripts make librarians' lives easier, but it's easier
to keep track of patrons and statistics when a single library is providing
the service. The most important feature of commercial virtual reference
software for all libraries is that patrons generally do not have to download
anything to use the service. However, if the system tells patrons they need
to disable their firewall, disable Java, or shut off their pop-up blocker to
join a chat, this may be just enough of a barrier to prevent its use.
Commercial virtual reference software, which has been used by libraries
for less than a decade, is still being developed and improved. Librarians
are likely to begin seeing more homegrown solutions developed by
libraries themselves; these systems will be better designed to meet the
needs of individual libraries. Homegrown and open-source solutions may
give software vendors the impetus to design more lightweight, modular
solutions that can meet the needs of both the big cooperatives and the
small libraries.

Instant Messaging (IM)

Instant messaging (IM) is the primary way that people all over the
world communicate synchronously online. Once thought as frivolous, it is
now being used in many businesses for both internal and external communications. Given the number of people who have adopted IM as a communications vehicle, it makes sense for librarians to consider using the
medium to provide reference services. IM lets you interact over the
Internet with anyone in the world. You type a message to another user and
the user receives it instantly; simply sending a message opens up a small
window where users can type messages that each of them can see. E-mail

is more like a letter since you write a narrative to someone and send it for later perusal; IM is more like back-and-forth conversations we are accustomed to having over the phone. IM previously required users to download an IM client, but newer Web-based clients let users access IM from any computer. To start IM, users just need to register with one of the popular IM services.

Online chat has been going on for more than 20 years. The precursor to IM was the "talk" command in UNIX. In the 1980s and early 1990s, before the graphical Web, a user could type in the word "talk," followed by the username of the individual they wanted to contact. They then could type messages back and forth that would show up instantly on the other person's computer screen. While early on this could only be done with people on the same network, by the 1990s, networks were better connected and people could chat with users on other networks as well. In 1996, ICQ (www.icq.com) was released as the first IM client. Downloaded as a separate program, it let people chat with more than one individual at the same time and create "buddy lists." A buddy list is a list of people a user sends messages to regularly that the user can contact with a single click. The list contains not only the name but also the status of each buddy. This way, people can easily tell if the person they want to contact is online or offline, and if they are available to chat. People can create and use "away messages," which show up under users' icons in a buddy list to tell others exactly what they are doing and whether they currently want to communicate with others.

In 1997, America Online (AOL) came out with AOL Instant Messenger (AIM), which is still the most popular IM service. Users do not need to be AOL members to use AIM (www.aim.com); they can simply register and set up a free account. Registered users can IM via AOL Instant Messenger (a proprietary client), from a multi-protocol IM client that lets users use accounts from different services from a single interface or by using AIM Express on the Web. With a multi-protocol client, people can sign up for accounts on multiple IM services and manage all their accounts from a single client. This is useful for IM users who have some friends who use AIM and other friends who use different services, or for libraries providing virtual reference services via IM. Other major IM services include MSN Messenger (join.msn.com/messenger), Yahoo! Messenger (messenger.yahoo.com), and Google Talk (www.google.com/talk).

Over the past few years, libraries have increasingly started exploring ways of using IM for reference services. The number of libraries using IM has grown significantly in a very short time, likely due to the ease with which libraries can begin providing the service. While IM only recently became a popular option for providing reference services, some libraries have been using it for reference since the late 1990s. In his article "Give Them What They Already Use—AOL Instant Messenger" in *Chat Reference: A Guide to Live Virtual Reference Services*, Bill Drew describes the IM reference program he and his colleagues at Morrisville State College in New York set up in 1998. For their "Talk to a Librarian Live" project (library. morrisville.edu/talk.html), they surveyed their students to see what they used to communicate online. Survey results led them to decide to use AIM to provide virtual reference service. Almost a decade later, the college is still providing reference services using AIM.

Many libraries that have started their services more recently create screen names on multiple services and monitor them all using a multi-protocol client. This means that patrons using a different service such as Yahoo! Messenger or MSN Messenger can contact the library without having to create an account on a new service. IM reference is now being used by libraries of all kinds, from the Massachusetts Trial Court Law Libraries (www.lawlib.state.ma.us/chat.html) to the New Castle-Henry County Public Library in Indiana (www.nchcpl.org/ask_librarian.htm) to the University of North Carolina at Chapel Hill libraries (www.lib.unc.edu/house/im_a_librarian.html). Each library staffs its own virtual reference desk; there is no requirement as to how many hours the service must be available. At small public libraries, a reference librarian may be available via IM only a few hours per week. At large academic institutions, librarians may staff IM reference more than 100 hours per week. Patrons can see if their library is online by checking its status on their buddy lists. You can also place a simple piece of JavaScript on your library's Web site that will indicate whether a librarian is available to chat. This indicator, available through some of the major IM clients, will change based on whether a librarian is logged into the IM client.

One tool that has become popular with libraries providing IM reference services is Meebo (meebo.com), a Web-based multi-protocol IM client. Because Meebo is Web-based, it requires no download, meaning that it can be used from any computer that is connected to the Internet. Some technology staff block the downloading of software, but since a Web client doesn't need to be downloaded, patrons can use it in the library. In 2006, Meebo introduced MeeboMe, a customizable chat interface that people can embed in a Web page. Patrons can chat with librarians directly through the tool, so long as the librarian is logged into Meebo. This means that patrons no longer need to sign up for an account with AOL or MSN, nor do they need to bother with a desktop or Web client. They can simply come to the library's Web site and immediately start chatting with the librarian via MeeboMe.

IM can be used in other ways to provide instant information to patrons. A "bot" is a software agent that can interact with people through IM and other media. It takes information submitted by a human and uses that information to generate a response based on the data in its knowledge-base. For example, the Moviefone bot allows users to use IM to search for a specific movie and see if and when it is playing in their local area. Bots could be programmed to provide library hours or information about upcoming events at the library. It may even be possible to engineer a bot that allows patrons to search the library catalog from the IM interface.

IM's best feature is that it is so easy to implement. Libraries don't need to spend any money to get started; the only cost is the time it takes staff to learn how to use it and then actually use it. It is easy to sign up for an account with one of the IM services, easy to download an IM client, and easy to learn how to IM. Essentially, to IM someone, click on that person's icon in your buddy list, type a message into the chat window that appears, and hit Enter. When you receive a message, it will appear in the same window instantly. IM clients now let you chat with several people at the same time, customize away messages, encrypt communications, send files, and even use video (if both computers are equipped with Web cameras). Some IM clients also allow you to keep a transcript of every chat session you conduct. The training necessary to learn IM is minimal; new users usually just require a bit of practice chatting with other people. Users don't need to master many software functions, so it's a very lightweight and intuitive solution.

Most importantly, IM is a technology that many of your patrons already use daily. If your patrons are already using IM, then they already have accounts and probably have their client up most of the time they're on their computers. If the library is on their buddy list, it just takes a single click to contact the library. This puts the library into the patron's world rather than requiring the patron to go to the library's Web site and use an unfamiliar service. For patrons who have never used IM before, it is so easy to set up and use that most people would just need simple instructions on the library's Web site to get started.

If you look at a list of libraries providing IM reference services, such as the one on the Library Success Wiki (libsuccess.org/index.php?title= Libraries_Using_IM_Reference), you may notice there are no virtual reference cooperatives using IM. There are a couple of reasons for this. First, libraries have only recently begun to use IM for reference services; it usually takes time for a group of libraries to organize themselves into a cooperative. Secondly, and most importantly, IM lacks the sort of management tools that enable multiple libraries to provide virtual collaborative reference. With IM, only one librarian can use a screen name at a time. For more than one librarian to provide services at the same time, the service would need to use multiple screen names, requiring users to know which screen name to contact at which time of day. Since IM does not offer a formal queuing feature, when a patron IMs a question to a specific screen name, the question will appear only to that librarian. If 10 people send messages to one screen name at the same time, the librarian must message each patron, either letting them know that she will answer their question soon or giving them the IM screen name of another available librarian. This can be complicated both for patrons and the librarians staffing the service. There may be ways to make this easier using bots that can route messages to available librarians, but, at this point, no one has developed the necessary technology. While it may be possible to develop a virtual reference cooperative service using IM, this is a less-than-ideal solution. Commercial virtual reference software is designed for groups; IM is designed for one person to use at a time.

Several other reasons exist as to why IM may not be ideal in every library setting. If most of your patrons do not use IM, the library has little incentive to adopt its use. IM is also primarily a textual medium where users send text messages back and forth. It can sometimes be difficult to explain concepts that would better be demonstrated via co-browsing. IM is better designed for reference assistance than for instruction, and while some clients keep a log of conversations, specific statistics must be kept manually just as for phone or in-person reference.

Security is also a significant issue. When unencrypted data is sent back and forth on a network, hackers can easily capture the entire conversation. Keeping transcripts of every IM conversation means that the library needs to ensure the privacy of that data. (If this is a concern, you can easily turn off the automatic logging function.) Just as with e-mail, librarians must be aware of IM viruses, hoaxes, and spam. If security becomes a significant concern, you can investigate enterprise-level IM services designed for businesses to communicate securely online. While these are costly, many are less costly than commercial virtual reference products. The biggest barrier to using IM in libraries, though, is often the attitude of administrators and IT staff. Many libraries block IM access for both patrons and staff. This stems from security concerns and the belief that IM is a frivolous distraction. In institutions with these policies, it may take considerable lobbying to change these attitudes.

Once you've decided that you want to provide IM reference services at your library, you first need to sign up for an account on one or more of the major IM services, then determine the software you need to monitor reference questions. Libraries can choose from a variety of free multi-protocol clients, such as Gaim (gaim.sourceforge.net; see Figure 9.2), Trillian (www.ceruleanstudios.com), Meebo (meebo.com), and Fire (fire.sourceforge.net). When choosing a client, you may want to try each piece of software to see which one has the features you need. If you only plan to offer IM reference through one service (such as AIM or MSN Messenger), you can simply use the client that service offers. However, since it is so easy to offer IM reference through all of the popular services, there is little reason not to offer IM through more than one service. Its availability through multiple services means that patrons using each service can easily contact you without having to register for anything new.

Training staff to use IM is usually a simple process, and the best way for librarians to get familiar with IM is to practice using it with their colleagues. The staff should also learn how to set an away message, how to respond when multiple patrons contact you at the same time, and how to understand chat lingo. Young people IM in their own shorthand, and librarians who learn key phrases ahead of time will help avoid confusion. People are usually more informal on IM, so librarians should be prepared to see plenty of abbreviations and misspellings. Users frequently go offline without saying goodbye, and librarians might not know a patron is gone until they try to send them another message. It is also important that librarians who staff IM reference keep patrons frequently apprised of what they are doing. If you go to look something up for a patron, let them know what you're going to do. If it takes a while, pop in to tell them that you're

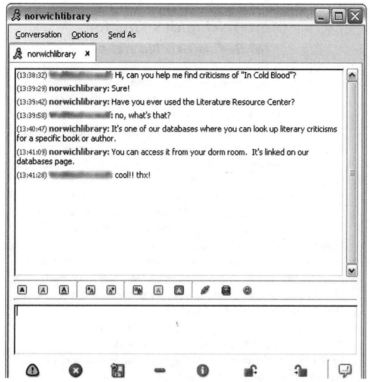

Figure 9.2   Gaim is a free instant messaging (IM) service used by libraries.

continuing to do research for them. If you think it's going to take a long time to find the answer, ask the patron for an e-mail address and get back to him asynchronously later. Every library will need to develop its own procedures for dealing with these issues.

IM has been around for more than a decade, but libraries have only recently begun to view it as a viable way of providing reference services to patrons. IM's low cost and ease of use makes it ideal for cash-strapped libraries and librarians who don't have the time to learn something complicated. In addition, if many of your patrons already use IM, you are essentially bringing reference services to them; you can put your service into their world instead of expecting them to come to you. This is a very user-centered approach to providing virtual reference services. While there are many reasons to adopt IM, it isn't the best solution for every library. Librarians should examine the needs and behavior of their patrons as well as the needs of their library to determine if it's the appropriate choice.

162 Social Software in Libraries

Aaron Schmidt's Tips for IM Reference Novices

1. *Instant messaging is free, except for staff training time.* You can register screen names on the major services (AOL Instant Messenger, Yahoo! Messenger, MSN Messenger) for free. Since there is no capital outlay, starting an IM program has an extremely high return on investment.

2. *Millions of our patrons are already IMing.* By adopting IM, libraries provide a user-centered service instead of a librarian-designed service.

3. *Don't alienate potential IMers by only using one service.* Use a multi-network IM client like the Web-based Meebo or the client Trillian.

4. *For some of your potential users, not being available via IM is like not having a telephone.* IM is the main method of communication for many young people. Some have even skipped getting an e-mail address.

5. *Having in-house practice sessions is a good way to get librarians comfortable with IM.* Spending a bit of time familiarizing librarians with the technology will quell fears and illustrate the power of IM.

6. *Don't panic.* Remember, the "instant" in IM refers to how fast the messages go back and forth, not necessarily how quickly you must respond. The quality of reference work should not be affected by the medium.

7. *Libraries can choose to have one IM point of contact or they can divide it departmentally.* This decision depends on the size and culture of your institution. Giving patrons too many options can lead to confusion, but some libraries have had success with assigning specific screen names to the Reference, Audio/Visual, Youth Services, and Circulation departments.

Aaron Schmidt is a Reference Librarian at the Thomas Ford Memorial Library in Western Springs, Illinois. He is the author of the blog Walking Paper (walkingpaper.org) and frequently gives talks on implementing IM reference services in libraries.

Voice over Internet Protocol (VoIP)

For most of the products discussed so far, the one missing element is interaction with patrons via the human voice. IM and co-browsing are excellent tools, but it can be more difficult for people to express their information needs in a small chat window than if they were speaking to someone. The ability to talk to a librarian remotely makes it easier to conduct a reference interview and clarify points. It humanizes the interaction: The patron is talking to a real librarian. It also provides a valuable service to those who have visual impairments and cannot be served by other types of virtual reference services. Offered in combination with visual elements such as co-browsing or page pushing, Voice over IP (VoIP) is an ideal tool for providing reference assistance and instruction.

VoIP, also known as Internet telephony, has been around for many years. But until recently, it lacked the reliability and sound quality necessary to become a mainstream social tool. VoIP means that a conversation is routed over an IP network rather than over phone lines. With VoIP, you can talk to people over the Internet just as you would on the telephone, with similar sound quality, either using a headset or a phone that connects into a computer's USB port. People often use VoIP to communicate with long-distance friends or colleagues, since it doesn't usually cost anything to make calls to other people using the same VoIP service. For-pay VoIP phone service was introduced a few years ago, allowing users to make and receive calls as they would with a normal telephone. The only major difference is that the calls are being routed through their broadband connection. For-pay VoIP services allow users to make calls through an IP network and also choose options such as call waiting and voicemail. The cost of VoIP phone service is significantly less than that of service through traditional telecommunication companies, which is why it has quickly become so attractive to consumers.

VoIP is a part of many expensive Web conferencing and co-browsing products, but it is also provided as a primary feature in a number of free applications. Skype (www.skype.com) is a popular peer-to-peer VoIP network that offers free Internet telephony and IM. The service is proprietary, so users can only make calls to other Skype members. Skype also has for-pay services, SkypeOut and SkypeIn, which allow people to make VoIP calls to real telephones and to have a regular telephone number for receiving calls. Google Talk (www.google.com/talk) is another system that allows users to talk and IM for free using VoIP. Unlike Skype, it uses open standards and is compatible with a number of other VoIP services, meaning that people on different services can speak to each other for free. There are a variety of VoIP products—some open source and some proprietary—that could easily be integrated into a library's virtual reference offerings.

Many libraries, even those that offer services to distance learners, do not provide a 1-800 number for their patrons; those who need immediate assistance must call the reference desk at their own expense. This is a barrier preventing many patrons from taking advantage of library services. Offering reference assistance through a VoIP service enables patrons to connect to the library for free, whether they're down the street or on the other side of the world. While it is likely that patrons will have to download a program or plug-in, they will only have to do so once and then will have free voice access to a librarian through their computer. Most VoIP software is easy to install and use, and only requires an inexpensive headset or USB phone. If the patron does not have the necessary equipment, he or she can instead use the chat function available in most VoIP products. The librarian can then either use VoIP to answer the student or engage in chat as well. Like IM, many VoIP products allow users to send files, which lets librarians send patrons materials on their subjects of interest. Due to its minimal cost and ease of use, the number of people using VoIP is growing rapidly. In the future, it's likely that many of our patrons will be using VoIP every day just as they now use IM.

At the moment, VoIP has been adopted by few North American libraries for use in reference service, but many librarians do use it to communicate with colleagues. It's an easy way to contact a colleague in another state or country with whom you're working on a project without incurring a large phone bill. The popularity of VoIP is also growing in Europe, Asia, and Australia. VoIP is being used by Macquarie University and Murdoch University libraries in Australia to provide reference assistance to patrons. Using Microsoft NetMeeting (www.microsoft.com/windows/netmeeting), librarians are able to talk to patrons over VoIP while also co-browsing the Web. If a patron doesn't want to interact through voice, he or she has the option to use text chat instead.[7]

VoIP is also being used to provide reference services for people with visual impairments. InfoEyes (www.infoeyes.org) is a national project that uses iVocalize software (www.ivocalize.com) to provide reference assistance to those with visual impairments. iVocalize includes co-browsing and chat as well as VoIP. With this service, the patron sets up an appointment to receive assistance from a reference librarian, and they then meet in a chat room to conduct the reference interview. It's interesting to note that these services use Web-conferencing software rather than straight VoIP technology. (Conferencing products include co-browsing and text chat as well as voice.) While some people may prefer interacting through voice, others may benefit more from the visual elements where they can go back later and see what was said or look at a Web site the librarian recommended. Offering virtual reference services in as many formats as possible appeals to the widest audience.

VoIP adds a vocal element that most online reference services lack. It is an affordable and easy-to-use tool, but some factors prevent its use as a stand-alone virtual reference product. With most VoIP applications, users have to download something before entering a session. While most libraries may regularly communicate via VoIP in the future, it currently lacks IM's market share. In addition, VoIP services such as Skype are proprietary, so if a library uses Skype and a patron uses Google Talk, they will not be able to communicate (without one party registering with the other service and downloading that service's application). Over time, users will likely gravitate toward a single standard or a few specific services as they have with IM. Other applications that use VoIP, including Web-conferencing software and some commercial virtual reference software, are expensive and are only a reasonable option for large libraries and chat cooperatives. VoIP is an excellent tool for communicating with our patrons online, but at present, it is not the most practical tool.

Individuals have diverse learning styles. Some learn better by doing, others by reading text, and still others through auditory input. In a traditional in-person reference transaction, patrons have the benefit of a variety of sensory input. They can hear what the librarian is saying, see what is happening on the librarian's computer monitor, and usually even try what they've learned. We should strive to make our virtual reference services as close to a face-to-face experience as possible through integrating a variety of technologies. The combination of co-browsing, chat, and audio comes very close to offering the sort of interaction one can have in a face-to-face reference transaction. However, even when the integration of all these tools isn't feasible, libraries still need to provide some form of synchronous virtual reference for the increasing number of patrons using our libraries remotely. Our Web presence can and should be considered a separate branch with its own collection and its own public services department. Our younger patrons already expect services to be available at their point of need, and this expectation is only going to grow in the future. Whatever libraries can provide—from IM reference three hours per day to 24/7 virtual reference as part of a cooperative—will be welcomed by their patrons.

Endnotes

1. Susannah Fox and Mary Madden, "Generations Online," Pew Internet and American Life Project, December 2005, www.pewinternet.org/pdfs/PIP_Generations_Memo.pdf (accessed February 12, 2006).

2. Amanda Lenhart, Mary Madden, and Paul Hitlin, "Teens and Technology," Pew Internet and American Life Project, July 27, 2005, 207.21.232.103/pdfs/PIP_Teens_Tech_July2005web.pdf (accessed February 12, 2006).

3. Eulynn Shiu and Amanda Lenhart, "How Americans Use Instant Messaging," Pew Internet and American Life Project, September 1, 2004, www.pewinternet.org/pdfs/PIP_Instantmessage_Report.pdf (accessed February 10, 2006).

4. AOL's Third Annual Instant Messenger Trends Survey, November 10, 2005, www.aim.com/survey (accessed February 10, 2006).

5. Buff Hirko, "Live, Digital Reference Marketplace," *School Library Journal*, October 15, 2002, www.schoollibraryjournal.com/index.asp?layout=article&articleid=CA251679 (accessed February 17, 2006).

6. Caleb Tucker-Raymond, "Is Co-Browsing Dead? 3 Out of 5 Librarians Agree," L-net Staff Information Blog, December 16, 2005, www.oregonlibraries.net/staff/?p=243 (accessed February 14, 2006).

7. Janet Fletcher, Philippa Hair, and Jean McKay, "Online Librarian—Real Time/Real Talk: An Innovative Collaboration Between Two University Libraries," VALA Conference, 2004, February 20, 2006, www.vala.org.au/vala2004/2004pdfs/20FlHaMc.PDF.

Chapter 10

The Mobile Revolution

Not only does the Internet let geographically dispersed people connect with one another more easily, but handheld devices have made it easier for people to connect to the Internet no matter where they are. People are no longer tied to their home or work computers; they can use handheld devices to do many tasks that used to require a desktop machine, including sending e-mails, text messages, and instant messages, surfing the Web, reading books, and creating videos, photos, and documents. No matter where a person is, Internet access is available as long as he or she has a signal from a wireless cellular service. The number of people purchasing handheld devices, especially cell phones, is growing exponentially. Many library patrons probably already use handheld devices for surfing the Web or communicating with friends and family. Librarians should be aware of this trend and consider how we can serve an increasingly mobile Internet population.

Users can choose from many handheld devices, including iPods. However, this chapter is about those that connect us to the Internet, and by extension, to other people. Internet-enabled mobile devices include cell phones, e-book readers, personal digital assistants (PDAs), mini-PCs, and some handheld gaming devices. In parts of the world with a high penetration of cell phone service, handhelds equal ubiquitous connectivity.

Mobile devices can do more than send and receive e-mails. They can send text messages and enable IM conversations. Mobile users can surf the Web, download movies, and watch them on their handhelds. They can take photos and movies with their handhelds and send them to their server, to a media-sharing site, or even straight to their blog. "Moblogging," or blogging from mobile devices, has become popular as handheld ownership has increased. Moblogging can include sending text, photos, and video from a phone or PDA. Mobile users have access to a variety of cellular-related moblogging services, such as Nokia Life Blog (europe.nokia.com/lifeblog) and Textamerica (www.textamerica.com), as well as blog software plug-ins that let people blog directly from their handhelds without having first to upload content to their PCs. In 2005, moblogging gained significant attention when people around London snapped photos of the terrorist bombings on trains and buses with their handhelds and quickly uploaded them to their blogs. In many cases, mobloggers offered views of the scene before the traditional media. Moblogging offers people the unique ability to blog events as they happen and to document their lives in real time.

Handheld devices also are used for e-learning. The mobile revolution has enabled students to access online course materials and do research anywhere anytime. Embedded Flash players in handhelds have made it easier for content creators to develop multimedia tutorials for the mobile set. Many issues must be considered when designing for mobile devices; it takes a different approach than when designing for a PC. Keep in mind, though, that by 2007, there will likely be 60 million PDA users worldwide. Many of these handheld users will be your students or your patrons.[1]

Making the Web Accessible to Handheld Users

When the World Wide Web was developed in the early 1990s, sites were designed to be accessed by a desktop or laptop computer, which made perfect sense at the time. The biggest early compatibility problems arose from differences in how browsers rendered Web developers' code, but everyone accessed the Web from devices with a given range of screen-size dimensions and graphic capabilities. Starting in the mid-1990s, other devices began to offer Internet connectivity. More and more people are accessing the Web through mobile devices, and this number is likely to grow exponentially during the next few years as the technology becomes more affordable. Currently, most Web sites are designed to be displayed on a traditional computer screen and to be manipulated by a mouse or pointer device. While this is fine for a PC, it makes Web surfing impossible for people using some handheld devices, such as cell phones, because they won't be able to click on links for average pages. Screen sizes and the ability to view colors and graphics also vary from device to device. On the whole, it is currently quite difficult to navigate most Web sites using non-traditional devices. More Web developers are focusing on technologies and authoring techniques for creating Web sites that can be viewed by all Web-capable devices.

If you are keeping up with your patrons, you will know whether they are using handheld devices to access the Internet. If they are, it may be wise to design some of your content and services for mobile users. This can be accomplished in several ways: by designing a Web site with device independence in mind, purchasing content that is accessible to those with handheld devices, and providing an educational role in the selection of handheld-accessible content.

Library Web Content

Device independence requires that Web sites be viewable by any type of device, including personal computers, televisions, mobile phones, and PDAs. This involves ensuring that Web pages can be viewed and navigated as easily with a telephone or a television as with a computer. Designing for device independence does not mean developing a single Web page that will look the same on a PC as it does on a cell phone; it also doesn't mean that you need to develop 10 different versions of your Web site. Device independence involves the separation of content from presentation. This can be done through the use of CSS (cascading style sheets) that change depending on the device accessing a Web page. A style sheet determines the look of a page and is completely separate from that page's content information. This can be a completely separate file that can be used for more than one page; changes made to one style sheet will cascade to all the pages to which it applies. A Web page can have multiple style sheets that are used in different contexts. If a cell phone accesses the page, for example, the Web server will present the style sheet designed specifically for that type of device. First, the device accessing a Web page sends its profile, including information about its capabilities. The Web application then applies a style or displays only certain parts of the page design based on its understanding of that device. There are several ways to accomplish this device independence using different markup and programming languages.

The Lane Medical Library at Stanford School of Medicine (lane. stanford.edu) has a PDA-friendly version of most of its Web site. The Virginia Commonwealth University Libraries (www.library.vcu.edu/pda; Figure 10.1) also provide basic library information, library news, and health science-related resources in a PDA-friendly format. Many other libraries make some of their online content accessible via AvantGo (avantgo.com), which receives content from multiple providers and puts

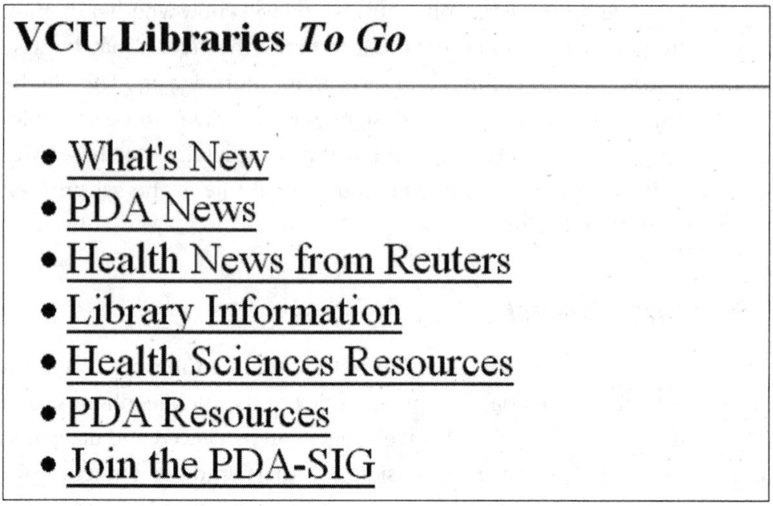

VCU Libraries *To Go*

- ## What's New
- ## PDA News
- ## Health News from Reuters
- ## Library Information
- ## Health Sciences Resources
- ## PDA Resources
- ## Join the PDA-SIG

Figure 10.1 The Virginia Commonwealth University Libraries offer basic library information in a PDA format. (*Reproduced with permission.*)

it into a format accessible to PDAs. Libraries that provide information via RSS feeds—which already separate presentation from content—can encourage their handheld users to subscribe to these feeds through an aggregator designed for handhelds. Two aggregators that work with PDAs and mobile phones are Feedalot (www.feedalot.com) and NewsMob (newsmob.com).

If one of your patrons is at a bookstore and wants to know whether a book is available at your library, what can she do? If she has the library's phone number, she could call and ask a librarian to look up the book in the catalog. If she has a wireless mobile device, wouldn't it be even better if she could go to your Web site and search the catalog herself? Mobile search lets users search an online catalog from anywhere with Internet connectivity. How often do students at your library spend time looking for a book in the stacks only to find that they wrote down the wrong call number? Having this sort of information in the palm of their hands would save them a trip back to the OPAC, or perhaps let them find a similar book nearby if the item they want is not available. Innovative Interfaces offers a mobile version of its Millennium catalog called AirPAC (www.iii.com/mill/webopac.shtml#airpac), which can be viewed by most mobile phones and PDAs (Figure 10.2). A growing number of public and academic

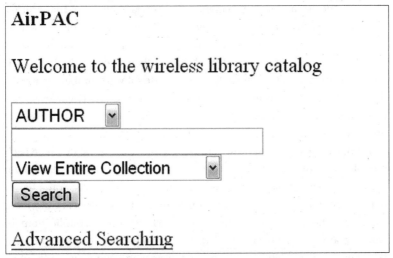

Figure 10.2   Innovative Interfaces' AirPAC allows PDA users to search the
library catalog. (*Reproduced with permission. ©2006
Innovative Interfaces*)

libraries are using AirPAC, including Wayne State University in Michigan
and the Minneapolis (MN) Public Library.

Collections

Library Web sites now usually have more than their own Web content
and catalog; much online content for libraries is leased from content
providers. This means that libraries must lobby their database vendors to
provide a handheld-friendly version of their search interfaces and/or a
version of their content that can be downloaded to a mobile device, so
users can read reference works and scholarly journal articles directly from
their handheld.

Some database vendors are beginning to provide handheld-friendly
versions of their content. This is especially true in the health sciences
field, because PDAs are widely used in hospitals for research and accessing medical records on demand. The National Library of Medicine offers
the freely accessible PubMed for Handhelds (pubmedhh.nlm.nih.gov/
nlm), which lets users search or browse PubMed and read article
abstracts. Ovid@Hand (www.ovid.com/site/products/tools/ovidhand/
ovidhand.jsp) helps medical field professionals make evidence-based

treatment decisions for their patients. The interface offers journal articles, drug information, and other useful clinical decision-making tools in an interface designed for PocketPC and Palm handhelds. Many free and fee-based downloadable programs are designed for handheld users in the health sciences, and many health sciences libraries license software for their patrons to download. For business and government, both LexisNexis (www.lexisnexis. com/handheld) and Factiva (www.factiva.com/factivafeedback/wireless.asp) offer accessible versions of their databases for BlackBerrys.

E-book content and handheld devices are also a natural fit. Since each e-book is a distinct entity, e-books can easily be made downloadable for a handheld device, making them as portable as regular books. Some handheld devices are even designed only for reading e-books. Project Gutenberg (www.gutenberg.org) has more than 17,000 free online public domain works, many in very basic text formats, making them readable on most handheld devices. NetLibrary (www.netlibrary.com) is making more of its e-books downloadable to Palm handhelds. OverDrive's Digital Library Reserve (www.dlrinc.com) lets libraries offer their patrons downloadable e-books that are accessible from a number of handheld devices. Reading e-books on a handheld device comes much closer to reading a physical book, because you can take them with you and read them anywhere.

Education and Support for Handheld Users

Health science libraries have long recognized the value of handhelds in providing on-demand research for clinical decision making. The Healy Library at the University of Massachusetts at Boston (www.lib.umb.edu/ pda/nursing) loans PDAs to nursing students for up to one week. The PDAs are preloaded with useful reference works in the health sciences. The Harvey Cushing/John Hay Whitney Medical Library at Yale (info.med.yale.edu/library/technology/PDA) has a PDA Software Workstation where patrons can install medical software onto their Palm handhelds. The Frederick L. Ehrman Medical Library at NYU (library.med. nyu.edu/library/eresources/toolkits/pda.html) offers infrared ports, where patrons can sync their Palm handhelds to get updates from networked content. Many medical libraries also offer classes on using PDAs in the health sciences with instructions on downloading content and using software.

An abundance of clinical decision-making software can be downloaded to handheld devices. Librarians at health science libraries have capitalized on their traditional role as selectors to guide patrons in choosing the best resources in the field. The Edward G. Miner Library at the University of Rochester Medical Center (www.urmc.rochester.edu/hslt/miner/selected_topics/pda/pda_resources.cfm) offers a list of recommended software products for PDAs, including descriptions of each product, what devices it can be installed on, and whether it is free to download. This list gives patrons a way to choose the best software products in a saturated market, and many other libraries provide similar guides. Just as librarians hand-pick the best books, databases, and Web sites for their patrons, it is important that they also ensure their patrons are using the best academic and clinical software.

Staff Uses

Handheld devices could streamline much library-related work and free library staff from being tied to their workstations. By using wireless mobile devices, librarians can provide reference assistance anywhere in the library without needing computer access. Librarians can use catalogs and other PDA-accessible library content to help patrons with research anywhere a wireless connection exists, even outside the library. This can free librarians from the reference desk, which may make them seem more approachable to patrons. Handhelds can also allow circulation staff to come out from behind the circulation desk. Handhelds can be used to check books in and out and update the status of a book anywhere in the library. If a librarian finds that an item is missing, he or she can update its status in the stacks rather than trying to remember to do it later. Handhelds can also be an excellent tool for inventory-related functions. When weeding, a handheld device could scan each book to offer information about past use. This allows librarians to do work related to library collections anywhere in the library.

Communicating with Patrons via SMS

Cell phones are becoming nearly ubiquitous in our society and are on track to become the most common electronic device in the world. The

Gartner research firm projects that by 2009, 2.6 billion cell phones will be used regularly and 1 billion phones will be sold.[2] In many places even now, most people own a cell phone, including young people. In early 2005, NOP World Technology reported that 44 percent of 10- to 18-year-olds in the U.S. have a cell phone, and the percentage is even higher for older teens: Three-quarters of 15- to 17-year-olds own a cell phone.[3] Teens use their cell phones for more than just talking. Many use their phones to take pictures and communicate with friends through SMS (Short Message Service), or text messaging, which lets users send text messages to other cell phone users. With SMS, a user can enter a brief message into a cell phone and type in the cell phone number of the person who is to receive the message. The other person usually receives the message on his or her own cell phone a few seconds later. While messages are not received instantaneously as with instant messaging, many young people use SMS to chat. However, SMS is used more often to send small, discrete bits of information. Text messages can be sent by cell phone or by a number of computer applications. Text messaging is a quiet and unobtrusive way to communicate, especially in settings when making or taking a call is not possible.

What *is* obtrusive is the cost of text messaging. Unlike computer-based IM, there is a charge for each text message, and messages can also sometimes be delayed. Depending on the cell plan, a single text message can cost between 5 and 25 cents. This may not seem expensive, but it can add up for users who send and receive dozens of messages a day and are billed both for sending and receiving text. In 2005, about 5 billion text messages were sent each month in the U.S.,[4] while in January 2006, cell phone users in the U.K. also sent 5 billion text messages in a single month.[5]

While some cell phone plans offer unlimited text messaging, these can be expensive and are usually only cost-effective for heavy SMS users. In addition, each individual message is limited to 160 characters in length. While the users can send longer messages, each of these "concatenated" messages will be separated into several distinct messages, and users will be billed accordingly.

While SMS is popular with teens, many adult users are also finding a use for text messaging. They can communicate via SMS for both work and recreation, which is an ideal communications tool when users are too busy to make a call or when they just want to send out a brief message. It is also a method of pushing content to subscribers. People can subscribe to receive weather forecasts, financial information, news, and other content that appears as a text message on their cell phones. Information delivered via cell phone is ideal for an increasingly mobile population who may need information far from a computer.

The number of patrons who own cell phones is growing exponentially. While many libraries currently provide some form of virtual reference service, many of these services require users to be in front of a computer. A few cell phone plans let people send IMs, but sending IMs by cell phone can become even more expensive than text messaging. Some libraries have started capitalizing on the text messaging feature of cell phones to offer virtual reference services. One commercial virtual reference company, Altarama (www.altarama.com.au), already offers reference services via SMS. Its service allows patrons to send a text message to a phone number, which is then routed to an e-mail account at the reference desk. The reference librarian can then answer by e-mail, which will be converted to a text message that goes to the patron's cell phone. SMS reference lets patrons access a librarian from wherever they happen to be.

Megan Fox on Mobile Devices

What are the most important ways that libraries can be serving users with mobile devices?

Libraries need to determine what information their particular users will need on the go, in the moment, when they will be relying on their mobile device for advice or an answer. They need to figure out how to deliver this themselves, or otherwise connect users to the content. Libraries could provide local information, such as hours, or connect patrons to resources, such as ready reference answers accessed out of an encyclopedia that is mobile-optimized to be readable on a small screen. Librarians must take responsibility for helping to keep their patrons informed about existing and developing mobile resources. In addition to connecting our patrons with the growing selection of mobile accessible or optimized information, we need to be incorporating communication through a mobile device. Just as adding an e-mail address to business cards seemed novel and extraneous 10 years ago, but now is absolutely essential, we are at a similar crossroads with the adoption of texting to cell phones, IM handles, and text addresses.

Do you think SMS is a viable option for providing reference services? Why or why not?

I certainly don't see the norm becoming librarians using their thumbs to triple click on a mobile phone's numeric keypad, while negotiating a 2-inch screen, to provide reference assistance to users! However, there are a growing number of intermediaries that will translate an SMS message into a regular e-mail and vice versa. Integrated Library System vendors, such as SirsiDynix, Innovative Interfaces, and Talis, are also developing the ability to communicate with users via text, providing features such as SMS hold and overdue notices. Since texting is rapidly becoming such a standard mode of communication, especially among Millennials and corporate users, I definitely think librarians will need to "go to where their users are" and communicate and provide quick assistance via SMS. SMS will never replace the traditional face-to-face, hands-on, one-hour reference appointment for an in-depth research project, but it will likely become one of the methods of choice for getting quick answers at the point of need.

What types of libraries absolutely should be providing services to handheld users?

Actually, all kinds of libraries need to be evaluating ways to incorporate these services, since the patrons expecting this method of communication spread across the spectrum. The younger generations, who use our public and school libraries, are among the heaviest adopters—texting on their phone feels as natural as a video game controller in their agile hands. College and university libraries are being greatly affected by handheld users. Even if older faculty may be slower in adopting this form of mobile communication, the traditional undergraduate is a heavy texter, never without their iPod, and almost always plugged in. Libraries in higher education need to incorporate this mode of communication if they are to retain their place as authorities in information seeking, retrieval, and evaluation. Special and corporate libraries are dealing with a workforce that is likely to own and use a handheld such as a BlackBerry or Treo. If they are conducting business on the road, business users are now able to access not just voicemail or e-mail, but Web search, intranets, documents, internal databases, and more. Corporate librarians should strive to keep library resources on that list. No library can afford to ignore the provision of services to handheld users, since information tools used anywhere, anytime, will soon far surpass those used via fixed desktop workstations.

Megan Fox is the Web and Electronic Resources Librarian at the Simmons College Library. She frequently writes and speaks about handheld devices in libraries and maintains a resource page on the subject (web.simmons.edu/~fox/pda).

Curtin University of Technology (library.curtin.edu.au/contact/sms.html), located in Sydney and Perth, Australia, has been offering reference services by SMS since 2004. In a study of its service, the university found that patrons primarily asked questions with easy answers through text messaging, such as "What time does the library close?" Only 9 percent were actual reference questions. Out of all of the questions asked, only 13 percent required more than 160 characters to answer and had to be answered with a concatenated message. The majority of queries (87 percent) were received during the normal library hours, and the average turnaround time was 74 minutes. Most of the surveyed respondents found the service easy to use and indicated that they would use it again.[6] While SMS clearly does allow students to easily ask questions from wherever they are, the answers may not always be sent as quickly they would like, especially if a reference librarian is busy or if the query comes in after hours.

Southeastern Louisiana University in Hammond has the largest population of distance learners in the state of Louisiana. As a result, its library (www2.selu.edu/Library/ServicesDept/referenc/textalibrarian.html) has often been on the leading edge of providing virtual reference services to its patrons. With national statistics reporting that 89 percent of college students have a cell phone and two-thirds of them use their phones for text messaging—a subsequent on-campus survey found very similar usage results—the library realized the potential of the medium for providing reference services. In 2005, the library began offering virtual reference via Altarama's Reference by SMS. Since the library is working with an Australian company, patrons' text messages must first go to a server in Australia, where the messages are converted to e-mail and then sent to the library. This process is reversed on the way back to the patron. Because they are texting to Australia, it costs 25 cents per 160-character message. The software notifies librarians when a message the library is going to send is more than 160 characters, so they can try and make the message shorter. In a report in late 2005, the library found that during the short time the SMS Reference was offered, it had been underutilized compared to chat reference and e-mail. This may be attributed to the fact that the service was new or because of the limitations of SMS for answering complicated questions.[7]

SMS could also be used to push information to patrons who have requested it. Many people subscribe to services that regularly send information to their cell phones, and some library users may appreciate receiving information via SMS. Free online services like TeleFlip (www.teleflip.com) allow users to send text messages via e-mail without needing to know the patron's cell phone provider. While this will not work for two-way conversations necessary in providing reference assistance, it is useful for broadcasting messages. Patrons could sign up to receive text messages about the type of library events they are interested in or lists of the new bestsellers.[8] Libraries could also send alerts to patrons when their books on hold come in. In academic libraries, users could be messaged when a requested reserve reading is returned. Since reserve readings can sometimes be in high demand and students are highly mobile, sending a message to a device the student keeps with them at all times makes more sense than leaving a phone message or sending an e-mail. It is important, however, that these services be opt-in only; otherwise, what you're sending is tantamount to expensive spam. Libraries could also set up automated services by which patrons entering a particular code will have information delivered to them on demand, including library hours, directions to the library, or event information.

SMS helps patrons no matter where they are and right at the point of need. It lets patrons who are away from a computer send a message to the library. In addition, this is a technology many of your patrons are probably already familiar with. Given the large number of young people who have cell phones and use text messaging, SMS is an ideal tool for academic libraries. However, SMS has some serious drawbacks. Text messaging back and forth costs money for both the student and the library. Patrons who are perfectly happy with communications via the phone, e-mail, or IM may not wish to spend the extra money to text the library. For information pushed to the patron, it is important to allow patrons to easily opt-in to the service and opt-out if they decide they no longer want the messages; patrons who have not requested such communications from the library should not receive them. Unlike IM, text messaging is not synchronous. It is similar to an e-mail where the user will get a quick response only if someone happens to be there to respond quickly.

Another major limitation is the length of the text messages. If libraries send messages longer than 160 characters, the messages will be split into two or more messages and both parties will be charged accordingly. Be careful to send short, succinct messages. Librarians may have to use the same shorthand that young people use when they text message their friends. In such a restricted medium, no reference interview can be done, so answers must be based only on what the patron asked. This means that SMS is not appropriate for many of the questions libraries receive at the reference desk; it is more suited for brief, factual, ready-reference questions. While SMS does offer patrons a way to get information from the library wherever they happen to be, with all of the limitations of SMS, librarians will need training on ways to make this an effective communication tool.

We are becoming an increasingly mobile society, where people are able to access the Web and communicate virtually no matter where they are. This mobility will require changes in many institutions, including libraries. We will need to rethink the services we provide, in light of the fact that patrons may be accessing the library from anywhere and from a device with a small screen. Libraries can also fill a role in providing education about and support for these devices. Libraries will also need to realize that as text messaging becomes more routine, patrons may wish to contact them using SMS. Libraries responded quickly to the invention of the telephone, the birth of the personal computer, and the development of the World Wide Web. The mobile revolution is just another step on the road to technological progress, requiring libraries to be agile and innovative.

Endnotes

1. Ellen D. Wagner, "Enabling Mobile Learning," *EDUCAUSE Review* 40.3 (2005): 41–52.
2. "Mobiles Head for Sales Milestone," BBC News, July 19, 2005, news.bbc.co.uk/1/hi/technology/4697405.stm (accessed February 10, 2006).
3. "Backpacks, Lunch Boxes and Cells? ... Nearly Half of U.S. Teens and Tweens Have Cell Phones, According to NOP World mKids Study," GfK NOP, March 9, 2005, www.gfkamerica.com/news/mkidspressrelease. htm (accessed February 10, 2006).
4. "Text Messaging Statistics," SMS.ac, corporate.sms.ac/industry resources/text_messaging.htm (accessed July 12, 2006).
5. Mike Grenville, "Stats & Research: SMS Hits January Growth Forecast," 160 Characters Association, February 27, 2006, www.160characters. org/news.php?action=view&nid=1960 (accessed July 12, 2006).
6. Nicola Giles and Sue Grey-Smith, "Txting Librarians @ Curtin," Information Online 2005, conferences.alia.org.au/online2005/papers/ a12.pdf (accessed February 10, 2006).
7. J. B. Hill, Text a Librarian: Integrating Reference by SMS into Digital Reference, 7th Annual Virtual Reference Desk Conference, November 14, 2005, data.webjunction.org/wj/documents/12542.pdf (accessed February 20, 2006).
8. Michael Casey, "Easily Pushing Info via Text Message," LibraryCrunch, January 13, 2006, www.librarycrunch.com/2006/01/easily_pushing_ info_via_text_m.htm (accessed February 10, 2006).

Chapter 11

Podcasting

Libraries have been looking for new ways to communicate with their patrons online. Blogs, which are an excellent means of disseminating information, lack the personal feel that comes from talking to a human being. With blogging, you can't hear the inflections in a person's voice, so it's difficult to get to know the person who is writing the posts; further, not every user enjoys reading—or is able to read—on a computer screen. Podcasting offers libraries a way to speak directly to their patrons to provide news and educational content. Podcasts, a term that combines "iPod" and "broadcast," are syndicated audio broadcasts that can be played on any MP3 player. Anyone can easily create a podcast, and libraries are starting to use the technology to empower young patrons and encourage their creativity. Podcasting is the one of the newest social software tools, but podcasting applications have already been developed to help libraries provide better services to their patrons.

What Is a Podcast?

While blogs were the most referenced social software tool in 2004, podcasts made their way onto people's radar in 2005, when "podcast" was named Word of the Year by the *New Oxford American Dictionary*.[1] That year, many mainstream media outlets began podcasting, such as CNN, the BBC, NPR, and the *New York Times*. CEOs, educators, musicians, comedians, and people from all walks of life adopted podcasting. Unlike radio where only certain people have the ability to broadcast, anyone can create a podcast. This puts the executives at GM on equal footing with car enthusiasts in rural Maine. Podcasts exist for just about every interest, from wine to cars and from technology to art—and more. As with blogs, people can broadcast their ideas to the world, and anyone who wants to listen can subscribe. Because podcasts are an audio medium, however, they allow people to express more of themselves in their own voice.

Podcasts can also be taken anywhere using a portable MP3 player, accompanying daily activities in a much different way than blogs.

A podcast is a syndicated audio broadcast; users can subscribe to the content and play it on any media player capable of playing MP3s. People have been making audio files available online for more than a decade in portable formats or streaming media. With streaming media, video or audio files are downloaded as they play and cannot be copied to a more portable device. People often posted audio as streaming media because they did not want it duplicated and distributed to others. Even files that were made available for downloading and copying prior to the late 1990s were less portable because they predated digital audio players or MP3 players. These files were usually played only on a user's computer (while laptops are portable, they are certainly too large to carry around while on the treadmill or while buying groceries). The lack of available high-speed Internet connections at the time also made downloading audio files a time-consuming process. The growing availability of broadband and the birth of the MP3 player made digital audio exponentially more popular.

MP3 players let users take their music and other audio content with them anywhere—to the gym, on their commute, or while doing housework. An MP3 player is similar to a Walkman or a Discman, except the device plays digital audio files that users download onto it. The first MP3 player was introduced in 1997, but it wasn't until the introduction of the iPod in 2001 that their popularity grew with consumers. Whether it was the marketing blitz, the slick styling, or the improvements in usability, the iPod became the "must have" tech accessory, especially for young people. By mid-2006, 77 percent of teens who owned MP3 players owned iPods.[2] In the technology industry and on campuses across the country, the iPod's little white earbuds have become almost ubiquitous. While the iPod is the most popular MP3 player, the market for all MP3 players has grown tremendously. In June 2006, an Ipsos Insight survey found that one in five Americans over age 12 owned a portable MP3 player, and that MP3 sales made up 85 percent of all portable audio sales.[3]

With the tremendous growth of the MP3 player market, the market for online audio content has also grown—and no other form of audio content has grown as rapidly as the podcast. Podcasts are distinguished from other audio content in MP3 format because they are syndicated. While the term "podcast" wasn't coined until 2004, the idea of syndicating audio content is not new. In 2000, people began experimenting with RSS feeds containing audio enclosures as well as text. In 2003, "audioblogging" gained in popularity, though few blog services included the ability to syndicate audio. Then, in late 2003, former MTV VJ Adam Curry and Kevin Marks developed an easy way to download RSS enclosures and transfer them directly to an iPod. By mid-2004, the term podcast was being used (although most software can transfer RSS enclosures to any kind of MP3 player, not only the iPod). The label, certainly a misnomer, is simply a testament to the popularity of the iPod.

How does a podcast work? On the production side, the podcaster first records the audio using a small digital audio recorder, a computer with a microphone or headset and some recording software, or a high-tech recording studio with a mixing board and all the trimmings. Most people use one of the first two options. After recording the audio, they can either edit it using digital audio editing software or use their work as is. The edited audio file needs to be saved into MP3 format and loaded onto a Web server. Then the audio is syndicated, which can be done manually or by using a free service. (See more on creating podcasts later in this chapter.) Individuals then subscribe to the podcaster's feed in their aggregator to receive new audio content automatically. Some services will also physically download podcasts to a computer; users can set theirs up to do this at convenient times. Once the MP3 file is on your computer, you can listen to it there, burn it to a CD, or download it to any device that plays MP3s.

Podcasting, which has many advantages, can be an excellent alternative or addition to text. It makes sense to offer content in various formats to accommodate people's diverse needs. People driving, walking, or exercising often find that podcasts are a good way to use that time to get information about topics of interest. Since podcasts are portable, users can take audio content with them wherever they go and integrate it into other activities. For busy people, this makes podcasts a convenient solution for getting daily news and entertainment.

Many people learn better when listening rather than reading, and these auditory learners may prefer listening to podcasts to reading blog posts or newspaper articles. Podcasts are also useful for people who are blind, have low vision, or a reading disability. Unlike radio, podcasts are on-demand: You can listen to a podcast anytime you want.

Podcasts, however, may not be the best format for every situation. Some content simply isn't engaging in audio form. Podcasting is not a *disadvantage — harder To scan* [handwritten annotation]

great option for people who are more likely to scan content than read it in its entirety. For example, most people would rather not listen to an entire podcast of upcoming library events when they're only looking for one specific program. For this type of content, it is easier to scan a Web page than to download and listen to a podcast. Further, for those who still access the Internet using dialup, MP3 files can take a very long time to download. "Podcatchers" that download files automatically can help, but lack of broadband is still a significant barrier to use. For those without MP3 players or CD burners, podcasts are still tied to a user's computer, lacking the very portability component that makes podcasts so attractive.

While some people are auditory learners, many learn visually, absorbing information better by reading and looking at visual aids. Text has advantages for people who like to skim content and fast readers who can get through the content at their own pace. With a podcast, everyone must use the media at the same speed, which can become tedious. Busy people who prefer to read and scan are unlikely to prefer podcasting, so podcasts depend on the needs, preferences, and level of technology adoption of the users.

How Libraries Can Use Podcasting

Podcasting has been used by people and organizations to entertain, disseminate news, educate, and promote services. Libraries can create podcasts for these same purposes, offering their patrons an alternative to traditional library content. Libraries provide a lot of text content on their Web sites, which is great for those who prefer that format. Auditory learners and those unable to read text on a computer may find this content either difficult or impossible to use. Broadcasting some of this information in audio format can be useful. The Decatur campus at Georgia Perimeter College has been podcasting since early 2005, offering students and faculty library-related news and information. Each Listen Up! (gpc libraryradio.blogspot.com) podcast includes library news, a description of new and notable books, and musical selections. Originally lasting from 20 to 35 minutes, the podcasts were long and required a significant commitment from listeners. The podcasts are now a much more manageable five to 12 minutes. Omnibus (www.dowling.edu/library/newsblog/podcasts. asp), the monthly podcast from the Dowling College Library on Long

Island (NY), provides a potpourri of library information and content of local interest. In the library's December 2005 podcast, the archivist discussed the history of an unusual local traffic intersection, the director of IT was interviewed about computer security, and a librarian read the library news. The librarians even provide notes telling users exactly when certain topics are discussed in the podcast so that those who only want to listen to a specific feature can skip ahead. Podcasts can be a great way to market library services to the community, but it's important to keep them engaging and succinct. It's a good idea to include interviews and stories with local flavor to make the podcast more engaging; listening to a single voice for 20 minutes can be tedious. If students or patrons can get the same information from the library's Web site, they need a reason to listen.

Podcasting can be an excellent way to educate patrons about useful resources and offer readers' advisory. Since people can take podcasts anywhere, they can learn how to use PubMed while driving to work, or they can find out about interesting books while on the treadmill. Audio tutorials are also very useful to auditory learners who may have difficulty understanding a list of instructions in text form. These educational podcasts can be used to inform patrons about resources or to actually teach patrons how to use the resources. The George C. Gordon Library at Worcester Polytechnic Institute in Massachusetts offers Audio to Go podcasts (www.wpi.edu/Academics/Library/Borrowing/Podcasts), which provide brief practical information about databases, Web sites, and other research tools. Each podcast is between one and three minutes long and describes a resource, how to use it, and what it is useful for. The library periodically offers a raffle in conjunction with the podcast, asking students to use the resource to do a specific search and then send their answers to the library. This encourages students to actually use the resource, which may help them see its usefulness.

Almost every public and elementary school library offers storytime for their youngest patrons. At storytime, a librarian will read children a story, and sometimes may discuss it afterward. Children who don't visit public libraries and whose parents don't read to them miss out on an important part of childhood. Children need to listen to words being read aloud to build vocabulary and learn how to read. Podcasting stories gives children the opportunity to listen to a story any time. This is especially useful for parents who do not speak English and whose children need to learn the language. Children learning to read could read along with the podcast to get a better

idea of how certain words are pronounced. Children having difficulty learning how to read could play the podcasts over again to learn the words.

A storytime podcast could simply record a librarian reading a book, but
it could also contain discussion questions for parents and children to talk
about together. If your library has a large population of non-English
speakers, you may want to podcast bilingual stories. The Thomas Ford
Memorial Library in Western Springs, Illinois, offers Click-A-Story
(www.fordlibrary.org/clickastory), recordings of stories in the public
domain. Each story is read by members of the youth services department
and made into a podcast. At the Grandview Elementary School Library in
Monsey, New York (www.grandviewlibrary.org), media specialist Sarah
Chauncey has used recorded stories to encourage parents to help their
children build a good vocabulary. On the library's blog, Chauncey includes
lists of books appropriate for each child's grade, along with a brief MP3
clip of each. Students can also take home a CD of all the stories read aloud,
with discussion questions about each story.[4] While this isn't a podcast in
the strictest sense since there is no RSS feed, it illustrates some possibilities of podcasting for children. Librarians can create podcasts of entire
books in the public domain, and include discussion questions for children. Since reading aloud is such an integral part of early childhood, podcasts for this demographic are a perfect fit.

Storytime isn't just for children; many adults enjoy attending author
readings and listening to audiobooks. Librarians could record themselves
reading from works in the public domain. Making public domain titles
available as free audiobooks offers a great service to all patrons, particularly those who are blind or have low vision. The Public Domain Podcast
(publicdomainpodcast.blogspot.com) contains the work of one woman
who reads from classic stories and novels by such authors as O. Henry,
Lewis Carroll, and Jules Verne. Similarly, LibriVox (librivox.org) is a collaborative volunteer effort to record entire public domain works. Volunteers
already have recorded many classic works, such as *Call of the Wild*, *Notes
from the Underground*, and *The Secret Agent*.

Libraries that often have authors visit, read from their books, and
answer questions from patrons may, with the permission of the authors,
record these events for the public and make them available online as a
podcast. The Tattered Cover Book Store in Colorado offers Authors On Tour
(www.authorsontourlive.com), podcast recordings of authors' appearances at their bookstores. Some great contemporary authors visit the

Tattered Cover; these podcasts offer people in remote areas the opportunity to listen to their favorite authors. Beyond author readings, libraries could record any of their programs and offer them online as podcasts. The Lansing Public Library in Illinois (www.lansing.lib.il.us/podcast.htm) records its technology and resource classes and makes them publicly available to those who can't attend. This makes them useful not only to patrons of the Lansing Public Library but to people around the world who happen to run across them. For librarians, sessions at library conferences can be recorded and made into podcasts for those who are not able to attend.

Museums often offer audio tours of their collections that take the visitor through the museum, offering background information on items of interest and the opportunity to learn more about the collection than they would by simply looking at it. Audio tours can replace the traditional group tour, which can be noisy and forces all participants to go at the same pace. Some libraries have also started creating podcast library tours that serve as a self-guided introduction to their layout, collections, and services. The Alden Library at Ohio University offers a podcast tour (www.library.ohiou.edu/vtour/podcast) to supplement its traditional tours. The tour introduces the student to the library and can be downloaded either in its entirety or by specific areas of the library. The University of Sheffield in England (www.lbasg.group.shef.ac.uk/downloads/index.html) has created animated iPod Induction Tours, narrated by campus radio personalities. Rather than going on a tour with a large group of other students, students can go at their own pace using these audio tours, pausing the podcast when they decide to look around. Library tour podcasts could be recorded in many languages for those students whose first language is not English. The main drawback of an audio tour is the lack of a tour guide to answer students' questions, but this can be dealt with by guiding students to the reference desk at the end of the tour and suggesting they direct any questions to the librarians there. This may even help some students overcome their reference desk phobia!

Some libraries have begun to lend out iPods for recreational and educational use. The South Huntington Public Library in New York (shpl.suffolk.lib.ny.us) received publicity when it started lending out iPod Shuffles (iPods with smaller Flash memory) in 2005, each preloaded with a requested audiobook or album. Patrons can select from a list of available audiobooks, and staff members load their selections onto the iPod for them. Patrons can keep the iPod for two weeks, at which point librarians load a new audiobook for another patron. By offering mediated down-loadable audiobooks, the library avoids the copyright issues involved in letting patrons download audiobooks themselves. College and university libraries have started to lend iPods holding reserve materials in such subjects as music and foreign languages. At Brown University in 2005, students in two music classes were given iPods for the semester so they could

Greg Schwartz on Podcasting

What is it about the podcasting medium that appeals to you?
Podcasting appeals to me primarily as a consumer. I'm really compelled by the idea of building my own audio newspaper. I started podcasting because my audio newspaper lacked a "library" section and I imagined that there were others who were searching for that type of content.

What are some of the barriers to podcasting in libraries?
The main barrier to podcasting is time and staff resources. It takes time to plan. It takes time to record. It takes time to edit. You can spend three to four times as long producing a program as you spend in the real-time recording of it.

What are three of the best potential applications of podcasting in libraries?
Selecting the best potential applications for podcasting depends entirely on the context, but three that immediately come to mind are: distributing in-house programming to a wider audience; disseminating news or service updates to the visually impaired community; and promoting new materials, upcoming events, and other happenings at the library.

Greg Schwartz is the supervisor of electronic services at the Louisville Free Public Library and has been instrumental in promoting the use of podcasting in libraries. He is the author of the blog and podcast series Open Stacks (open stacks.net/os).

listen to podcast lectures and required music in the course.[5] This allows students to listen to course materials at their convenience wherever they want and as many times as they want (which is advantageous for students who may have difficulty absorbing information). While libraries and academic institutions can loan any type of MP3 player, the iPod is an attractive choice, since so many people are familiar with it.

Patrons as Content Producers

Learning is a two-way street. People learn not only by listening to someone tell them what to do, but by actually doing it themselves. Education should be a dialogue, and librarians can promote lasting learning by encouraging patrons to create content through podcasting. For young people, podcasting can promote creativity and encourage self-expression. It gives people the opportunity to share their passions with others. Podcasting can get children excited about educational activities, because the process allows them to put a little bit of themselves into the assignment.[6]

Public libraries can help students think critically by encouraging them to create podcast reviews. Whether they review a book, a movie, or a new album, the process of reviewing forces students to think critically. Students will want to create good reviews if they know they will be recorded. This also encourages them to analyze whatever it is they are reviewing. Two Illinois libraries, Thomas Ford Memorial Library in Western Springs (www.fordlibrary.org/yareviews) and the Bloomington Public Library (feeds.feedburner.com/bplpodcast), help local teens create podcast reviews of books, movies, music, and Web sites. It's interesting to hear the students' enthusiasm and listen to their descriptions. Podcasts in which teens recommend library items could also encourage other teens to borrow those items—who better to recommend materials for teens than their peers?

For younger patrons, creating podcasts of their early reading efforts can help them improve. If librarians record children reading a book and help them with the pronunciation of difficult words, the child could then listen to the podcast over and over again while reading the book for practice. This helps children connect words and sounds. Children could also be recorded periodically during the learning process to show them how far they have progressed. If children see that they already have made positive progress, this could reduce the frustration that often comes when learning to read. These approaches could also be used with people learning English as a second language.

Podcasting in Education

Some librarians provide instruction, and many librarians work to support instructors. Podcasting has wonderful educational applications for these librarians. While libraries can create podcasts of their own, they can also provide a valuable service by teaching educators about podcasting and encouraging its use in the classroom. More people are learning over the Web, via a single class or an entire program. However, the Web is a medium in which instructional techniques are still being developed. Podcasts can be used to supplement online and face-to-face classes, allowing students to personalize their learning and freeing faculty to try more interactive teaching methods in the classroom.

Over the past year, more faculty at colleges and universities have begun podcasting lectures. Stanford University has its own page at iTunes (itunes.stanford.edu) that includes publicly available podcast lectures as well as a private section for students of specific classes. Perdue has developed its own service called BoilerCast (boilercast.itap.purdue.edu:1013/Boilercast/), which lets users record and upload lectures. Recording equipment is permanently mounted in each classroom for optimum sound quality. Podcasting has received rave reviews from students, who find it makes learning more accessible and prevents them from missing important material when they can't make it to class.[7]

While some faculty fear that class attendance will drop to zero if they podcast their lectures, others have seen it as an opportunity to change the focus of their classes. Jean-Claude Bradley, a chemistry professor at Drexel University, lets his students listen to podcast lectures as homework and now uses class time to run workshops and help students one-on-one with problems. In certain classes, he can even reuse lectures from previous semesters, giving him more time to develop in-class activities. Having students listen to lectures outside of class gives faculty a chance to make their in-person classes more interactive and provide more attention to students' needs. Bradley makes the important point that, "as educators, we should be focusing on education, not counting bodies."[8]

Podcasting can enrich the educational experience while making learning easier for nontraditional learners. Allowing users to play back lectures at their leisure recognizes the diversity of learning styles and abilities. Students with learning disabilities might learn better through repetition, and with podcasting, they could replay lectures as needed. Those who are not auditory learners may also benefit from the ability to replay parts of lectures; podcasts allow them to do this easily. Educators could even offer extra lectures or audio content for interested students, personalizing education to individual interests and abilities.

Finally, podcasting lets professors incorporate guest speakers. They can interview speakers over the phone, recording the conversation so that the guest doesn't even have to leave home. This way, professors can interview great guest speakers who might otherwise not be able to make the trip, which is often the case for busy and successful individuals. A professor could also use the recording in later classes, letting students benefit for years from one guest's recording. As with podcasting lectures, podcasting guest speakers can also free up classroom time for other activities. Professors could have students listen to these podcasts before class, then spend class time discussing what they learned from the speaker.

Many grade school teachers are creating podcasts with their students. Since this is a technology many young people use in their personal lives, podcasting is a great choice for use in the classroom. Students can create weekly podcast shows where they can talk about what they're learning in class; they can do book reviews, report on a field trip, and talk about assignments. The third and fourth grade students in Room 208 at the Wells Elementary School in Wells, Maine, create weekly broadcast-quality podcasts (bobsprankle.com/blog) about what they learned during the week, including interviews, book reviews, background music, and regular segments. Podcasting helps the children review what they're learning and be creative; it also gives them experience expressing themselves verbally. Students at Mabry Middle School in Marietta, Georgia, (mabryonline.org/podcasts) recite poetry and prose in French as podcasts to improve their language skills. The school's principal often interviews students and records podcasts based on those interviews. Podcasting offers a unique way to highlight a school's successes, help students know what's going on in other classes, and let parents hear what their children are learning.

Many classes require individual or group oral presentations. This offers educators a perfect opportunity to encourage students to podcast.

In creating a podcast presentation, students can be more creative with their presentations, as well as edit their presentations, which can lead to a more polished product. Rather than spending class time on oral presentations, students can listen to the audio broadcast before class and use class time for questions about the presentations. It's also far easier for people with stage fright to record a podcast than give a presentation in front of their class; podcasts help them practice without the same pressure. Podcasting also gives parents an opportunity to listen to the work their children are doing in class, helping them feel more involved in their child's education.

As with other social software applications, podcasting is revolutionizing the way people teach and how students learn. Podcasting lectures allow faculty to create a dialogue in the classroom, as opposed to the monologue of a lecture. It also lets students repeat lectures as needed to learn the material well. Making podcasting a part of student assignments gives them a chance to express themselves creatively and may make them more enthusiastic about their work. Teachers and students developing podcasts together makes students feel more a part of their own learning process. In addition to creating their own content, librarians can play an important role by teaching educators about podcasting and the role it can play in their classroom.

Podcasting: Practical Considerations

Podcasts are becoming easier to create with the introduction of automated podcasting sites. The only equipment you need is a computer and a microphone or headset. You could also use a digital audio recorder to record your audio, then upload its output to your computer. For software, you will need a program that lets you record and edit sound. Audacity (audacity.sourceforge.net), which is open source, is the most popular free sound recording and editing software. However, if you create a recording using Audacity, you will also need to download a free piece of software called the LAME Encoder (lame.sourceforge.net) to transform the file to an MP3. Other for-pay recording software options are designed specifically for creating podcasts.

Once you have an MP3 file, you need to put it on a server. You can use your own server space, or use a service that will store your podcasts and

generate an appropriate RSS feed. OurMedia (ourmedia.org), run by the
Internet Archive, provides free storage and bandwidth for all kinds of media
files. An RSS feed is automatically generated for any uploaded MP3 file.
Several for-pay options will store your podcasts and generate an RSS feed. If
you don't use a service, you will need to create an audio enclosure in an RSS
feed so that it can be syndicated. The easiest way to do this is to post an MP3
file into a blog and then run the feed through FeedBurner (www.feed
burner.com); FeedBurner's SmartCast service will create a podcast with the
podcast enclosure tag. This allows podcast aggregators to find and download your podcast for subscribers. Several newer Web sites automate the
podcast process completely, though most of them only offer limited functionality for free. Their sites allow you to record audio and turn it into a podcast all in one place. Some sites also let users find and subscribe to podcasts,
essentially making them one-stop-shops for podcasting.

Knowing how to record a podcast is only half of the equation. Just as
important is knowing how to create a quality podcast. Length is probably
the most important consideration; most people will not want to sit
through 30 minutes of a librarian discussing library news. Podcasts
absolutely must be brief and concise, or listeners will stop focusing on
your words. If a podcast is long, it needs to include diverse elements that
keep the user interested. Library information could be interspersed with
interviews, snippets of music, local interest stories, or anecdotes from different people.

Listening to the same voice the entire time can also become tedious. If
there is only one person talking throughout, make sure that the narrator
sounds really enthusiastic about what he or she is discussing. Background
music can often help here, but remember that only music that is not protected under copyright can be used in podcasts. The podsafe music network (music.podshow.com) offers a directory of music that can be used in
podcasts. It is very important to consider your audience and your material
when creating a podcast and to keep the user engaged. Otherwise your listeners will start daydreaming or give up on your podcasts altogether.

Finding Podcasts: Practical Considerations

Librarians and their patrons have thousands of useful podcasts to
choose from. Librarians can listen to podcasts such as Talking with Talis

(talk.talis.com), Online Programming for All Libraries (OPAL; www.opal-online.org), Teen Librarian (www.teenlibrarian.com), and IT Conversations (www.itconversations.com). All of these offer content about libraries and technology. Although patrons can choose from podcasts for just about any hobby or interest, the trouble is finding them. Since podcasts are audio, they cannot be searched as easily as text-based Web sites.

When people were just getting started with podcasting in early 2005, podcasts were collected in directories. These usually incorporated a rating system so that the most popular podcasts were easier to find. Podcast Alley (podcastalley.com), iTunes (www.apple.com/itunes/podcasts), and Yahoo! Podcasts (podcasts.yahoo.com) are popular directories still in existence. These sites let users browse by category or search for a specific podcast. However, category browsing usually leaves users poring through thousands of podcast shows, and searching only searches podcast titles and descriptions. Podcast directories still help users find the most popular podcasts, but they are not very useful in finding podcasts with small audiences or on obscure topics. When only a few hundred podcasts existed, browsing through the directories was easy. Now, with thousands of podcasts, people want to search rather than browse.

Right now, podcast search is still in its infancy. While Google can index all of the words on a Web page, a podcast search engine cannot easily index all of the words in a podcast. Most of the older podcast search engines only search the title, description, and any other text that is included in the podcast feed. Other sites encourage podcast creators or consumers to add relevant metadata, or tags, which convey meaning about the podcast. However, as discussed in Chapter 8 on social bookmarking, users often tag items with terms that have personal meaning but do not help others to find the item. Some newer podcast search engines use voice recognition technology to turn speech into text, and then index the text. Both PodZinger (www.podzinger.com) and Podscope (www.podscope.com) find where the search term was mentioned in the specific episode and can play only that portion of the podcast. This method is probably the most promising for the future of podcast search, but it still has a high failure rate.

Once you have found some interesting podcasts, you have three choices for obtaining them. First, you can visit each podcast's Web site to download them manually, which is a time-consuming and labor-intensive process, especially if the podcasts are not created on a regular basis.

Second, you can subscribe to a podcast feed in a regular aggregator to get the MP3 of each podcast in your aggregator as soon as it is created. With most aggregators, you will still have to manually download the MP3 file. And third, you can use an aggregator designed for podcasts, or a "pod-catcher," to download the podcasts you've subscribed to automatically. For those who want to receive podcasts on a regular basis, this is the sim-plest option. Developed by Adam Curry, Juice (juicereceiver.source forge.net), formerly known as iPodder, was the first aggregator for pod-casts. It was the most popular podcatcher until mid-2005, when Apple made iTunes into both a podcast directory and podcatcher. Yahoo! Podcasts lets users download podcasts to their own Yahoo! account and either listen to them there or download them to their computer. Once the podcasts have been downloaded, users can listen to them on the com-puter, burn them to CD, or load them onto an MP3 player.

Before 2004, blogs were the primary social software tool in libraries and education. While blogs are still the preferred medium in many settings and for many subjects, podcasts encourage creativity in teaching, learn-ing, and information sharing. Their value in education as a tool for educa-tors disseminating information and for students creating content has been proven in many different settings. With improvements in audio-recording technologies, podcasts are easy to create and share with others. They are also easy to obtain by anyone with a high-speed Internet con-nection. However, libraries shouldn't start podcasting simply because it's the hot, new thing. Librarians should create podcasts only when the sub-ject translates well into audio and it benefits their patrons. When done badly, podcasts can be monotonous and dull. When developed with care and with an effort to engage, podcasts can make information come alive.

Endnotes

1. "Podcast is the Word of the Year," Oxford University Press, December 2005, www.oup.com/us/brochure/NOAD_podcast/?view=usa (accessed January 21, 2006).
2. Brad Cook, "Piper Jaffray's Latest Teen Survey Shows Continued iPod Domination," The iPod Observer, April 5, 2006, www.ipodobserver. com/story/26229 (accessed July 12, 2006).

3. "Portable MP3 Player Ownership Reaches New High," Ipsos Insight, June 29, 2006, www.ipsosinsight.com/pressrelease.aspx?id=3124 (accessed July 12, 2006).

4. Kathy Ishizuka, "Tell Me a Story," *School Library Journal*, September 1, 2005, www.schoollibraryjournal.com/article/CA6253062.html (accessed January 10, 2006).

5. Simmi Auijla, "iPods on Loan to Students for Coursework in Music," *Brown Daily Herald*, October 5, 2005, www.browndailyherald.com/media/paper472/news/2005/10/05/CampusNews/Ipods.On.Loan.To.Students.For.Coursework.In.Music-1009716.shtml?norewrite&source domain=www.browndailyherald.com (accessed January 15, 2006).

6. Gardner Campbell, "There's Something in the Air: Podcasting in Education," *EDUCAUSE Review* 40.6 (2005), www.educause.edu/ir/library/pdf/erm0561.pdf (accessed January 15, 2006).

7. Jodi S. Cohen, "Missed Class? Try a Podcast," *Chicago Tribune*, October 20, 2005, www.cs.duke.edu/dept_info/news/index.php?article=167 (accessed January 13, 2006).

8. Jean-Claude Bradley, "Beyond Lecture Podcasting," Drexel CoAS E-Learning, October 28, 2005, drexel-coas-elearning.blogspot.com/2005/10/beyond-lecture-podcasting.html (accessed January 15, 2006).

Chapter 12

Screencasting and Vodcasting

Although educational theorists and psychologists have different theories about how people learn, all of them agree that people absorb information in different ways. When it comes to learning styles or multiple intelligences, it is widely acknowledged that each person has different educational needs and will thrive in different educational environments.

In most cases, though, both educational and informational content is offered in only one medium. Text- or audio-based media are only truly effective for a certain segment of the population they intend to serve. So, educational institutions and libraries are beginning to incorporate video into their online offerings. Video content offers patrons both visual and audio channels, increasing the likelihood of lasting learning. "Vodcasts," or syndicated video broadcasts, let viewers come as close to being physically present as possible in an asynchronous online environment. Vodcasts also can be the best way of engaging young people who expect multimedia on the Web. Screencasts allow librarians to provide educational content that appeals to the widest range of learning styles. As video content has become easier to create and make available online, libraries have started using it as another way to educate and connect with their patrons.

Screencasting

Since the early days of the World Wide Web, librarians saw its potential as an educational medium. Most libraries have been developing online tutorials since they first developed a Web presence. Many started out as simple text-based HTML pages or PDFs that offered step-by-step instructions on how to research or use databases and other online tools. While these tutorials offer valuable instructional content to patrons, many people have difficulty learning from a plain-text list of step-by-step instructions.

Next, librarians incorporated more multimedia and interactivity into their tutorials. Patrons could click on different options or had to answer quiz questions. Motion and interactivity captured the attention of some users, but these tutorials were still largely textual. Some people just don't learn well by reading material on a screen. They require audio components, and are more comfortable in the lecture hall than at their desk reading a book. Some people need to learn by seeing how something is done. Still others need to be able to practice what they've learned to understand it fully.

Many library tutorials lack concrete demonstrations of how to carry out a given task. Online tutorials can't compare to face-to-face instruction where users are actually taken through the steps of a real database search, and in many cases, are able to practice what they're learning while learning it. "Screencasting," by contrast, uses many of the elements of a face-to-face class. By incorporating audio, video, captioning, demonstrations, and interactive components, screencasting is the closest to hands-on instruction that can be offered at a distance.

At their most basic, screencasts are video recordings of action taking place on a computer screen. Screencasting software allows users to record computer action, including mouse movement, text entry, scrolling, and movement from page to page. The software either captures individual screen images and interpolates movement from screen to screen, or it fluidly films all movement on the desktop. It lets users create a movie of every action on their desktop. They then can edit this output in several ways, though some software offers more editing control than others. Users can erase erratic movements, mistakes, and unnecessary visuals. Beyond simple screen captures, most screencasting software also allows users to add audio to narrate what they're doing while the screencast shows the action. Users can insert captions, highlight text, and use other tools to call attention to certain elements on the screen.

Some of the sophisticated software packages also enable interactive components, making patrons active participants in a screencast. Libraries, for example, can create situations where patrons must actually initiate a search, click on the right button, or take some other specific action before advancing to the next screen. They can also create interactive quizzes, where patrons receive immediate feedback about their answers. Captioning will appeal to those who learn best by reading text; audio will appeal to those who are auditory learners; and concrete video demonstrations will appeal to those who learn visually or through example. Finally, interactive components will appeal to users who need to practice what they've learned, engaging everyone by requiring action. Screencasting may be the online tool with the most potential for educating users with diverse learning styles.

The term screencasting was coined in late 2004 when technology columnist Jon Udell started using screen capture technology to demonstrate various Web-based tools and techniques. Udell appealed to his readers to suggest a term for "the idea of making movies of software."[1] Among the suggestions he received, screencast was the most appealing. His support of the software helped to increase its popularity as a tool for demonstrating technology and providing online education.

While the term screencasting is relatively new, screen capture software has been around for a decade, since Lotus ScreenCam became the first product to hit the market in the mid-1990s. However, Lotus ScreenCam was difficult to use and its output required a special player to view. By late 1999, TechSmith introduced Camtasia (www.techsmith.com/camtasia. asp), and Qarbon unveiled ViewletBuilder (www.qarbon.com/presentation-soft ware/viewletbuilder). Both applications let users output their movies to standard formats.

Even before screen capture software let users create online tutorials easily, developers used a number of products to create tutorials manually in formats like Flash and QuickTime. Back then, because of the time, skill, and expensive software required, only experts could create professional-looking tutorials. Now, software such as Camtasia, ViewletBuilder, and Adobe Captivate (www.adobe.com/products/captivate) makes it easy for novices to create professional-looking screencasts. Since the software has become more affordable and easier to use, people in a variety of fields have adopted it.

Currently, screencasts are primarily used in the technology and education fields. In the software field, screencasts are a great way to demonstrate a product. Instead of posting a simple list of features, screencasts can actually show users what these features are and how the software works. At help desks, screencasts can be used to demonstrate ways to solve common technology problems, an excellent alternative to traditional FAQs. They can also be used for software reviews or to compare the features of two different products. What better way is there to review software than to demonstrate it for your viewers?

In education, screencasts are being used to create online lectures. Professors can use a mix of PowerPoint slides, Web sites, and audio narration to offer a video lecture. Scott Warnock, an English professor at Drexel University, uses screencasting to create videos of his comments on students' papers. This allows him to offer more in-depth comments that students will be more likely to learn from them.[2] Screencasting is an excellent tool in any situation where audio and visuals would help to explain ideas or when you are demonstrating concrete activities.

Libraries and Screencasting

Since the software has only recently become affordable and easy to use, screencasting is just starting to catch on in libraries. Most screencasting librarians have been developing screencasts for a few years at most. More and more patrons, however, access library services online—from international distance learners to those who just prefer accessing library resources from home. These users increasingly depend on library Web sites for instruction and support. To provide this support, libraries must either provide 24/7 reference services or must develop tutorials that offer the instruction needed for patrons. Many libraries are now turning to screencasting to provide asynchronous instruction on their Web sites. Currently, the primary users of screencasting are academic institutions that offer distance education programs, but several public libraries use screencasting to provide instruction for their patrons as well.

Screencasting in libraries is primarily used to demonstrate how library resources are used. Since you can record every mouse movement and every keystroke on your desktop, it is easy to show students exactly how to use a database or the library catalog by following every step in the process. The Blake Library at the University of Maine at Fort Kent (www.umfk. maine.edu/infoserv/library/resources/tutorials) offers brief screencasts on using its library catalog. Each screencast, which is just a few minutes long, demonstrates a specific action in the catalog such as keyword searching or subject searching. Splitting the lessons into brief discrete screencasts decreases the risk of losing the attention of the patrons. These screencasts do not include audio narration, but captions can be included. Each screencast also offers a PDF version of the slides for those who don't want to watch the screencast or who want a printout. The University of

Calgary Library (library.ucalgary.ca/services/libraryconnection/tutorials. php) offers screencast tutorials specifically designed to help its distance learners use the online library. Tutorials include how to use link resolver software, how to authenticate remotely for database access, and how distance learners can use document delivery forms. Some tutorials include audio narration, and some only offer captions. The UCLA College Library's multimedia tutorial, Road to Research (www.sscnet.ucla.edu/library/ tutorial.php), contains a series of screencasts on using library resources. Some are available in several different languages to serve UCLA's diverse population. Since these screencasts do not include text captions, the library only needs to change the narration in order to offer them in different languages.

Beyond training patrons on using library resources, screencasts can also be used to teach other valuable skills. The Calgary Public Library (calgary publiclibrary.com/library/tutorials.htm) has created a series of screencasts that teach basic computer and Internet skills. Each screencast is between two and 12 minutes in length, covering skills from using a mouse to searching the Web to setting up an e-mail account. The screencasts include interactive components; the narrator asks viewers to take a specific action before the screencast will continue. If the user does the task incorrectly, he or she will receive feedback. This lets patrons practice skills while they're learning. To reach patrons with diverse learning styles, the screencast includes text captions as well as audio narration.

While these examples demonstrate concrete tasks, screencasts can also be used to teach students broader information literacy skills, such as developing a research topic or evaluating sources. In information literacy classes, librarians often teach students how to evaluate sources by showing them examples of materials from different sources, such as peer-reviewed journals, the World Wide Web, and government sites. They then show students what to look for in each document to determine the quality and trustworthiness of a resource. Screencasts could easily demonstrate such examples. To teach students how to develop a research topic, librarians could create a screencast demonstrating a sample case that takes students through the process of developing and refining a topic. While teaching students how to do research presents more of a challenge in the online medium, librarians can create screencasts that teach information literacy skills through concrete examples.

Benefits of Screencasting

In a world where our patrons access more of our services online, screencasting is an excellent choice for instruction. Patrons access our resources 24/7. Most libraries cannot provide 24-hour live assistance, but online tutorials are an achievable and reasonable alternative. Unlike other types of tutorials, screencasts show users exactly what an interface looks like and how to use it. Most provide a set of controls on the screen to pause and rewind tutorials; this enables self-paced learning, so novices can replay confusing sections and advanced users can fast-forward over redundant information. Screencasts are a good tool for providing instruction to distance learners and other patrons who are unable to attend a physical class. Every library also has patrons who are embarrassed to ask for help and wouldn't attend a workshop voluntarily; they may be more willing to watch a Flash tutorial from the comfort of their own home.

Most screencasting software is easy to use and requires little staff training. Its price ranges from free to several hundred dollars, which makes it possible to create screencasts at a very low cost. However, the more money you invest, the more features the software will offer. Screencasts allow librarians to speak to our patrons online while visually demonstrating some program, action, or idea, making it the closest thing to a synchronous class. It is designed to appeal to the widest variety of learning styles, so patrons can read, see, hear, and practice what they learned. While you may originally create a screencast for a specific class, many also can be used in multiple situations. Reusable screencasts can save a tremendous amount of staff time and make instruction available to anyone online.

Drawbacks of Screencasting

While there are many reasons why libraries should start screencasting, some significant drawbacks should give librarians pause. No matter how much you try to compress your screencasts, video files are inherently large. The number of patrons with broadband connections at home and work is growing, but many people still only have dial-up Internet connections and may have to invest a significant amount of time waiting for a three-minute screencast. This creates a major barrier for some patrons. This issue is currently the greatest drawback to libraries using screencasting, but it will become less important as the availability of broadband

Paul Pival on Screencasting

What do you see as the best uses of screencasting on library Web sites?

Point-of-need instruction is one of the best uses, in my opinion. For example, when a student is having trouble with remote authentication, offering a link on the error page to a screencast showing exactly how to do it can save both the student and the library a lot of time.

What are the most important things to consider when creating a screencast?

The length of the production is important, as is letting the user know going in how much time they're going to be asked to invest. Try to keep it short—under three minutes—or most people won't bother watching. Along the same lines, be sure to inform the user ahead of time if there's audio (recommended) included, or they may miss important information without realizing it.

What are some of the barriers to using video on library Web sites?

Bandwidth is a potential barrier. Here in Canada, the majority of users are on broadband, but that's not the case everywhere, and it's important to try to keep the file size down and to choose a streaming delivery option like Flash to help the users who are on dial-up. Another barrier is the visually impaired user who may have difficulty seeing the information presented in a screencast. Ideally, you should provide the same information in text as well.

Paul Pival is the Distance Education Librarian at the University of Calgary in Alberta, Canada. He is also the author of The Distant Librarian blog (distlib.blogs.com), which covers technologies and techniques for providing services to online learners.

expands and its price decreases. These large files also consume server space and require a lot of bandwidth as users download them. If you develop multiple screencasts, this may require additional server space, which will come at a price. (While some free online file storage options exist, these generally lack the speed and reliability that most patrons expect.)

Another screencasting issue concerns frequent changes in Web interfaces, especially those in third-party products. If you create a screencast to teach Academic Search Premiere but then EBSCO redesigns its interface, the tutorial will have to be scrapped and an entirely new one created. While basic screencasts are easy to create, a polished product with audio, video, and captioning requires a significant investment of time.

So You Want to Start Screencasting: Practical Considerations

Once you have decided to begin screencasting at your library, you need to choose your screencasting software. No two products are alike and each has its pluses and minuses. Fortunately, many products offer free trials so you can compare several options at once. Here are some considerations in choosing screencasting software:

- *Capture method* – If the software only takes screen captures, you may need to specify when to capture the screen. This means that you might miss important actions and have to film the entire screencast again.

- *Screen size* – Do you have to film your entire screen, or can you make your filming area smaller? The smaller the area you're filming, the smaller the file.

- *Editing* – How sophisticated is the editing interface? Can you slow down specific parts of the screencast, or get rid of the cursor in other sections? The more sophisticated the editing interface, the less you'll have to worry about getting your initial filming exactly right.

- *Audio* – Can you add audio narration? Can it be added both during and after filming? What is the audio-editing interface like? Is it easy to sync the audio with the video?

- *Annotations* – Can you add captions, links, and highlighting? Can you focus on certain parts of the screen? Can you create menus and indexes for longer presentations?

- *Interactivity* – Can you create places in the screencast where the user needs to perform an action before the screencast continues? Can you create interactive quizzes?

- *Ease of use* – Is the program easy to learn? Does it react quickly? Many older screen-capture products were slow because of the resources necessary to create a screencast, but this has improved overall.

- *Compression* – How small can you make your screencasts' file sizes?

- *Output format(s)* – Which format(s) does your program output to? Are these open or proprietary formats? Do they require a player your patrons might not have?

- *Finished product issues* – Does the user have controls to pause the movie and move to other sections? Do the audio and video sync up? (In some cases, the audio and video do not properly synchronize when the user plays the movie, which can lead to confusion.)

- *Price* – How much does it cost? You can create screencasts for free, but if you can afford the better products, they're well worth the money.

The next step in the process is to create the screencast. Taking time to plan will lead to a more polished product. Once you have chosen your topic, you will need to break it down into small distinct modules. People have short attention spans, so keep your screencast to less than three to five minutes. Plan what you want to film in the screencast before you start to record; you even may want to write step-by-step instructions outlining exactly what you want to show the viewer and in what order. If you're recording simultaneous narration, create a script so you know what you are going to say. Planning ahead can save time in the long run. After all, one mistake, and you may have to start all over again.

Once you've filmed the screencast, the next step will be editing. Some screencasts may not require any editing, but many people add captions and other elements after filming. You may be tempted to add a lot of extra elements, but realize that each adds to the size of the finished file. Focus on the elements that are important to the screencast, like captions and highlighting. Add interactive components where necessary but be careful not to over do it or you may annoy the viewer by forcing him or her to take action constantly. You have to find a happy medium between engaging users and asking too much of them. Finally, make your screencast as small as possible through compression and other means. Making the display size smaller, while still considering the needs of people with low vision, can help decrease the file size.

Vodcasting

More server space, the availability of higher bandwidth, and easy-to-use video editing tools all encourage people to create online video content. Whether users create a full-length film, post a "vlog" (video blog), record a show, or film their baby's first steps, more people now use video to entertain, educate, and communicate with others online. Just as with blogs and podcasts, what was once the domain of a small group of dedicated and skilled hobbyists has opened up to anyone with a digital video camera or Webcam. The amount of amateur online video has grown tremendously over the past couple of years; viewers now can easily find thousands of one-time video experiments among the well-produced "vodcasts," or video podcasts. Video captures people's attention more than audio content or text alone. According to dual coding theory, "learning is better or more memorable if information is referentially processed through both [verbal and visual] channels."[3] Unlike blogs or podcasts, video content puts a human face on the information being transmitted, making it more personal. While video has not been used much on library Web sites, it has potential as a powerful marketing and educational tool.

A vodcast is a video broadcast that is syndicated so that users can subscribe to the content and play it on a portable or computer media player. People have posted video online for some time, but it's been only recently that they have started to create and syndicate episodic videos. In 2004, Steve Garfield began experimenting with video blogging, attracting attention to the medium, both through his vlog (stevegarfield.blogs.com/videoblog) and the Carol and Steve Show, the episodic "real reality show" he produced with his wife. Since the Carol and Steve Show debuted, many other video blogs have come onto the scene, and vloggers have formed a strong online community. Not long after Garfield launched his vlog, Rocketboom (www.rocketboom.com/vlog) premiered as the first vodcast to reach a mainstream audience. Produced in New York by Joanne Colan and Andrew Baron, Rocketboom is a three-minute daily vlog produced as a news show and distinguished by its high-production values and offbeat humor. Rocketboom's popularity increased the visibility of vodcasting, and many humorous television-style vodcasts have sprung up since 2004.

In 2005, Apple released the first video iPod, which gave vodcasting a definite boost. Now consumers can download video content to their iPods, and video content is listed in the iTunes store right along with the audio content. Over the past few years, a number of Web sites have sprung up offering free hosting for video content, the most famous being YouTube (www.youtube.com). YouTube is more than a storage space; it has become a social phenomenon where people can chronicle their lives, become amateur journalists, or share their creative vision. People can find almost anything on YouTube, from hilarious skits, to celebrities caught doing foolish things, to blog-like confessions, to kids doing stunts in their back-yard. YouTube has even created Internet celebrities, such as a 79-year-old Englishman who tells his life story on the site and a rock band that uploaded their creative music video. There are many hosted video sharing sites, but none that have developed the community and following of YouTube. In late 2006, YouTube was bought by Google, which already offers its own video-sharing service, Google Video (video.google.com).

Colleges and universities have started using vodcasting and other video broadcast methods for education and marketing. The Savannah College of Art and Design (SCAD) launched SCAD On Demand (www.scadon demand.com), a site with streaming video content about college life. In each weekly video segment, SCAD On Demand offers glimpses of student life, such as talks with visiting artists and campus activities. Academic institutions have been creating marketing DVDs for some time, but now can offer the content for free to a larger online audience. Schools have also been using vodcasting to offer online access to lectures and events. The Princeton University Channel (uc.princeton.edu) offers audio and video content of lectures and special panel discussions at the university.

Vodcasting in Libraries

Libraries haven't caught onto the vodcasting revolution yet. While a number of libraries are podcasting, only a few are experimenting with online video content. However, of all the social technologies discussed in this book, vodcasts are the newest and have not yet become as popular. Video can be used in libraries to market the library, and to educate and connect with patrons. Libraries can accomplish many of the same things with vodcasting as with podcasting; they just need to add the visual component. Libraries could record speakers, events, and classes using a digital video camera and make those videos available online. Anyone who missed the program could view it online, and people from around the world could benefit from library programming. Videotaping information literacy or technology classes would let distance learners and other patrons benefit from the experience as much as those attending in person. Videos of story-time would not only let kids hear the story but also see the illustrations.

Web-based video can also be used to promote libraries and their services. If colleges and universities can create marketing videos, so can libraries. Libraries could use clips from some of their filmed events and footage of everyday life at the library to portray their institutions as a welcoming place to potential patrons. Libraries can even create vlogs, where the staff can produce regular features about the library, its services, staff, events, and collections. Just as libraries can create podcast tours, they can also create video tours so patrons can become more familiar with the library from their own homes.

Teen librarians could develop programs where young patrons gather and create entertaining video content, such as news shows, music videos, video reviews, or skits. Creating content such as this is empowering and lets young people use their creativity in a constructive manner. Since they have more expertise with online video content, teens could even be enlisted to help create the library's promotional videos. The library could start any of these projects with just a digital video recorder and video editing software. Video speaks to people in a different way than audio or text, offering libraries the opportunity to show patrons a human face.

Vodcasting shares many drawbacks with screencasting. Video files tend to be quite large, even when compressed. Users without broadband will have difficulty downloading video, although a video file can be more accessible by streaming rather than asking users to download the entire file before viewing it. If your library makes a commitment to creating videos, additional server space may be required to accommodate increased bandwidth and storage requirements. Editing video can be quite time-consuming, especially when trying to create a quality product. Video editors estimate that it can take an hour or more of editing to create a minute of quality edited video. Vodcasting also requires a digital video camera, which can cost nearly $1,000 for a good-quality model, and may not be practical for libraries with tight budgets.

So You Want to Start Vodcasting: Practical Considerations

First, shoot your video footage. If you plan on editing it, you don't have to worry as much about what you're shooting. If you make a mistake, just keep shooting and edit out the mistakes later. The next step is editing. You can choose from many different kinds of editing software, ranging from open-source applications for amateurs to expensive applications for professional video editors. Windows Movie Maker and iMovie are good entry-level video-making software applications that come installed on new PCs and Macs respectively. iMovie can also be purchased as part of the iLife suite. If you plan on editing a lot of videos and want to create polished movies with added visual elements, such as titles, credits, transitions, and background audio, you may end up spending between $60 and $130 for decent editing software. Popular entry-level video editing software packages include Ulead VideoStudio (www.ulead.com/vs), Pinnacle Studio Plus (www.pinnaclesys.com), and Muvee autoProducer (www.muvee. com). Video editing software also offers ways to cut your video and put clips together that were taken at different times.

Once you have edited the movie, you will need to compress and save it. (Your editing software may have built-in compression, or you can use a third-party utility.) Determine the format for your movie. If you save your movie in Windows Media Format (.wmv), QuickTime (.mov), or Flash (.swf), users will need a plug-in or player to watch the video. However, most new computers now come with a preinstalled Flash plug-in, making Flash more universal. MPEG4 (.mp4) is an open format that can be played on any video player, making it the most popular format.

Once the video is compressed into the proper format, you will need to put it up on the Web. If you have your own server space, you can upload it to the server. If not, some companies offer free online storage, but download speeds may be slow and sites like YouTube display movies in a very small box. After you upload your video, link to it from your Web site or blog. If you want to create an RSS feed with the proper enclosure tag, run it through FeedBurner (www.feedburner.com). FeedBurner's SmartCast service will create a vodcast with the enclosure tag, allowing video aggregators to find and download your vodcast for subscribers. Some new services more or less automate the entire editing, compression, and syndication process. These companies offer one-click vlogging to your blog or to their own Web site.[4] Before deciding to use one of these services, look at cost, features, storage space, reliability, download speed, and other factors. But for novice vodcasters, using a service may be a good option.

Formerly, only professional designers and video producers created video content for the Web. A decade ago, screencasting required hiring third-party developers, which pushed instructional technologies out of reach for most libraries. There was no easy or automated way to edit digital camcorder footage, compress it, and put it up online. Further, so few people had broadband that it made little sense to make video content available on the Web. Now, the number of people with broadband Internet connections grows every year, making it easier to download video content. The applications for creating screencasts and editing and compressing vodcasts have become more affordable and easier to use. The types of applications once aimed at professionals are now specifically designed for amateurs. With fewer barriers to creating video content, libraries are starting to think about how they can use video to communicate with their patrons, promote the library, and provide educational materials. While some drawbacks still exist to using video, most will become less of a consideration as broadband access becomes more common and online storage more affordable. Video as a medium can quickly capture people's attention and reach patrons with diverse learning styles.

Endnotes

1. Jon Udell, "Name That Genre," InfoWorld, November 15, 2004, weblog.infoworld.com/udell/2004/11/15.html#a1114 (accessed February 3, 2006).
2. Laura Blankenship, "Technology as a Liberal Art," Inside Higher Ed., December 29, 2005, insidehighered.com/views/2005/12/29/Blankenship (accessed February 4, 2006).
3. Daniel Yi Xiao, Barbara A. Pietraszewski and Susan P. Goodwin, "Full Stream Ahead: Database Instruction Through Online Videos," *Library Hi Tech* 22.4 (2004): 366–374.
4. Michael Arrington, "Comparing the Flickrs of Video," TechCrunch, November 6, 2005, www.techcrunch.com/2005/11/06/the-flickrs-of-video (accessed February 4, 2006).

Chapter 13

Gaming

The library is a major institution in many children's lives: Parents often take them to the library to find books and to take part in storytime activities. Most public libraries have terrific programs for young children, making a concerted effort to turn their younger patrons into lifelong readers. Libraries also used to be the first stop for children and adolescents who needed to write a report for class. Before the birth of the Web, the library's place in students' lives was assured since the library was just about the only place to do research. Now, things have changed. Young people can do research online, bypassing the library altogether. According to Perceptions of Libraries and Information Resources, a study conducted by OCLC, 50 percent of young people between the ages 14 and 17 see search engines as the best information resource. Only 17 percent of them consider libraries the best place to find information.[1] When teens can search for information on Google from the comfort of their own home, why would they want to visit the library?

Most teens see libraries as having little to offer, and in many cases, they're right. Many libraries provide neither programming for teens nor a dedicated space where they can congregate. A significant gap in library services begins at the start of adolescence and ends at adulthood. No wonder 16 percent of teens never visit their public or school libraries, and few use the library on a frequent basis.[2] Libraries are losing this population at a rapid rate, raising the question of whether these teens will ever come back to the library when they are adults.

Within a decade, most of today's teens will be tax-paying citizens with a say in the future of their libraries. If their experiences as teens lead them to view libraries as irrelevant and obsolete, they may not see them later as a valuable service to spend their tax dollars on. This is but one of many reasons that libraries need to attract teenage patrons. Research resources used to be the hook for getting young people into the library. Now, libraries need a new angle. What can they do to attract teens?

Of all teenage activities, none is as pervasive as gaming. Ninety-five percent of teenage boys and 67 percent of teenage girls play videogames.[3]

Teens often spend more time playing computer or console games than doing other leisure-time activities. Although gaming was once considered harmful, research now reports that games have educational value and can teach valuable problem-solving skills. While many people once saw gaming as something that introverted teenage boys did alone in their basements, its demographics have changed significantly: The average age of gamers is near 30, and 40 percent of all gamers are female. Many newer games are designed for multiple players or can be played online with participants around the world, so they often are quite social. Since gaming is an $11 billion industry, it is time that libraries took notice.

For more than a century, libraries have struggled with the high-culture versus low-culture debate in building collections and programs. Librarians used to develop collections based on the intellectual value of books; their mission was to provide books based on quality, not demand. However, attitudes changed; libraries now have a mission to serve both the intellectual and recreational needs of their patrons. In the 1970s, many libraries struggled with the idea of circulating videos. Some libraries took years to begin circulating videos, which were seen only as having entertainment value. Now, with the widespread use of gaming among members of Generations X and Y, it makes sense that libraries consider how to provide services to gamers. Through targeted collection development, programming, or education, gaming could be just the hook that libraries need to attract teens and young adults into the library. And, if we can get them into the library at that difficult age, we may just be able to create lifelong library users.

Gaming: What's It All About?

While gaming includes many activities—from poker and hopscotch to Monopoly—this chapter focuses on electronic games. These games, which can be played on a personal computer, a game console that hooks up to a television, or a handheld device, can be broadly separated into computer games and videogames. Games can be played by an individual against the computer or by multiple users against each other. Despite the belief that computer games are a new phenomenon, they have actually been around for more than 40 years. In 1962, to better understand the capabilities of a new computer at MIT, graduate student Steve Russell developed the first computer game. In Spacewar, two spaceships were controlled by switches on the computer; the spaceships could only fire torpedoes and spin around. Some of his colleagues improved the game by adding a star map and forces of gravity.[4] While it was quite simple compared to today's games, Spacewar was interactive, competitive, and worked from a specific premise, much the same as modern games. Back in the 1960s, computer games were primarily used by academics, since they tended to be the only people with computer access.

In 1972, Pong debuted as the first arcade game. A two-player simulated ping-pong game, Pong was such a hit in bars and other entertainment venues that it started the videogame craze. Later that year, the Magnavox Odyssey, the first videogame console, was released for home use. (A game console is a device that plays individual games and plugs into a television for display.) While the original Odyssey quickly flopped because of its high price and limited selection of games, other consoles, such as Atari 2600, the ColecoVision, and the Intellivision, became quite popular in the 1980s. These systems represented the first wave of videogame consoles, giving users hundreds of different games to choose from.

Console gaming took a quantum leap forward in 1985 with the birth of the Nintendo Entertainment System. Nintendo offered better graphics and sound, and the cartridges had a greater storage capacity than the previous generation. This led to more complex games with imaginative storylines and action. Nintendo brought us perennial favorites such as Donkey Kong, Super Mario Brothers, and the Legend of Zelda. Since then, videogame systems have continued to improve at a dizzying pace, and games have become more complex and graphically intense. Handheld gaming systems such as the Nintendo DS Lite and the Sony PSP now allow gamers to take games with them wherever they go.

Computer games have also seen amazing development since the 1960s. When computers made the leap from academia to the home in the mid-1970s with such innovative machines as the Apple II, games became one of the machine's most popular uses. Early personal computers had more memory and computing power than their console counterparts and a more expressive user interface, which triggered the development of games that were more complex than those for console systems of the same era. By the mid-1990s, however, the gap between consoles and personal computers had closed. As the decade drew to a close, many consoles soon were built with features once normally associated with personal computers, such as hard drives, keyboards, and network access. Companies frequently released identical game titles for both dedicated consoles and PCs.

Electronic games have spawned an industry that sells a range of products, including strategy guides and magazines to improve gaming skills. Gaming enthusiasts take part in Web forums and develop fan sites. Many gamers have developed online fan fiction, wikis, and their own user guides. Popular games such as Tomb Raider, Doom, Super Mario Brothers, and Mega Man have branched off into books, cartoons, and movies. Many comic books and films also have been turned into videogames. Gaming is a culture that, for many people, goes beyond the specific games they are playing.

Types of Games

Gaming appeals to a diverse population because of the many different types of games. This first group tends to be most popular with men:

- *Fighting games,* such as Mortal Kombat and Street Fighter II, usually involve combat against one opponent at a time, either the computer or a second player. Players fight against increasingly challenging opponents until they are defeated. These types of games are normally short on plot and long on action.

- *First-person shooter games* are all about using weapons to wipe out the bad guys. To create a first-person perspective, only the weapon and the character's hands are usually seen, such as in Half-Life and Unreal Tournament.

- *Third-person shooter games* let players see the character they are controlling, as in such games as Tomb Raider and Grand Theft Auto. As with first-person shooters, these games can have more involved plots (typically science-fiction or fantasy-based) and can take days or weeks to finish.

- *Strategy games,* which usually focus on wars, let players plan battles strategically, using military tactical maneuvers. These games, including Warcraft and Rome: Total War, frequently take weeks to finish, and can be nearly as complex as the history they're based upon.

- *Flight simulators* allow players to simulate flying an airplane and sometimes involve in-flight combat. Examples include Microsoft Flight Simulator and F-16 Fighting Falcon. Flight simulators have become increasingly realistic over the past two decades. Some, such as X-plane, have even received Federal Aviation Administration (FAA) approval to train pilots working toward their commercial flight certificates.

- *Racing games*, such as Mario Kart and Pole Position, let players simulate race car driving and compete against other drivers. The popularity of the game Gran Turismo with American audiences actually led Subaru and Mitsubishi to import models not previously sold in America but that had developed a cult following after they appeared in the game.[5]

- *Sports games* allow players to compete in various kinds of sports and to develop strategies to win the game. The sports genre, including games such as NBA Jam and Madden NFL, used to be more diverse but has recently seen a shake-up, as games have become more expensive to make and high-priced licensing deals with different sports leagues have edged smaller software houses out of the market.

The following games are usually played by a more diverse segment of the population; you will often see a 40-year-old woman playing side-by-side with a 15-year-old boy. The first three genres include many of the most popular current games:

- *Role playing games* often follow a storyline in a fantasy genre. Players usually need to develop skills incrementally and collect currency to purchase magic or weapons. They are best thought of as the digital equivalent to paper games such as Dungeons & Dragons. Examples include Baldur's Gate and The Bard's Tale.

- *Massively Multiplayer Online Games (MMOGs)* are role-playing games played online with other individuals around the world. Most MMOGs are fantasy-based, although shooter games, sims (simulation games), and science fiction games have also been developed. Typically, players enter a shared virtual world, and work to develop their character's attributes. Examples include

Lineage, The Sims, Second Life, and World of Warcraft. These games frequently have no set end-point; the point of the game is to evolve the characters and the world that they inhabit.

- *Simulations (sims)* include God games, economic simulation games, and city-building games, where players build and control people, cities, or businesses to become as successful as possible. Examples include Railroad Tycoon and Sim City. Because simulation games tend to model real-world systems, they can also be highly educational.

- *Adventure games* are similar to role-playing games, but the focus is on solving a specific problem or a mystery, such as in Myst and Monkey Island.

- *Platform games* are action games where the main character has to run, jump, and climb to get from level to level. These games were very popular in the 1980s, but lost prominence as games with more intricate storylines and 3-D graphics were developed. Super Mario Brothers and Donkey Kong are two examples.

- *Pinball games* are the computer and console versions of the arcade pinball machines.

- *Party games* are designed for multiple players and usually include several types of competitions to keep game play interesting. One popular example is the Mario Party series.

These games are designed for younger audiences:

- *Educational games* teach specific educational competencies during the game. Examples include Where in the World is Carmen Sandiego and the Oregon Trail.

- *Dancing games* require players to move in a specific sequence based on the instructions given on the screen. One popular example is Dance Dance Revolution.

The following games are often played by those who aren't traditionally thought of as gamers; they tend to be played more by women and older individuals than other genres. These games, which are usually offered for PCs, can be played online against competitors around the world. One thing that they have in common is a very low "twitch factor" (that is, they do not require fast reflexes).

- *Puzzle games,* such as Tetris and Minesweeper, don't usually have a plot, and instead involve the player solving logic problems

- *Board games and card games* are simply computerized versions of traditional games including chess, poker, and mah-jongg. The Internet has given these classic games new life; it is now easier to find similarly skilled people online around the globe who are willing to play at any hour of the day.

Benefits of Gaming

The idea that gaming can be beneficial has begun to gain credence only over the past few years. Previously, electronic games were considered nothing but detrimental. Games have been attacked for their violent content; some researchers argue that violent videogames make individuals more aggressive and desensitized to violence. Many groups have blamed videogames for the increasing violence in our society, leading to ratings systems and outright censorship of certain games. Game play has even been blamed for specific crimes, such as the Columbine school shootings. Gaming has further been criticized for impeding young people's normal social development; the argument here is that gaming is isolating and escapist, and young people should be interacting with other young people rather than with a computer. While much research has been done on the detrimental effects of gaming, many of these studies ignore the culture of gaming and the positive effects gaming has on learning and socialization. As with television, gaming will continue to be a popular entertainment medium for young people. We can censor, or we can use gaming to produce positive outcomes for young people.

Gaming can be educational in spite of all of the negative attention. Gaming itself is a learning medium, in that the gamer must learn how to play to win a game. Games like pinball might only require learning how to work the controllers, but in strategy and role playing games, learning is integral throughout. Users acquire new skills and need to find different strategies to solve problems. Being successful in most games requires patience and problem-solving skills. According to Young Adult Librarian

Catherine Delneo, "gamers typically have a focused approach to playing and solve problems through trial and error."[6] In his book, *What Video Games Have to Teach us About Learning and Literacy*, James Paul Gee describes how important learning principles are built into videogames. To get students to want to learn, there must be a reward. The learner must be persuaded to put forth effort to solve the problem and must be rewarded after doing the work. Games often adapt challenges to the skill level of the user, making it possible for students at various skill levels to be successful. As in any type of learning, games build on previously learned skills. Gamers will usually only be successful later in a game if they pay attention to the skills they are learning early on.[7]

Many parents bemoan their children's gaming habits, saying, "I wish she was as focused on schoolwork as she is on computer games." What if learning was a game? As the original gamer generation ages and become teachers or game developers, educators have increasingly explored the use of games in educational settings. Educational games have existed for more than two decades and these teach specific learning outcomes in the course of a game. In an effort to win and in the course of having fun, children are actually learning valuable skills. Children pore over the *World Almanac* to discover where in the world Carmen Sandiego is, and answer math questions while searching for ancient treasures in the Himalayas in Cluefinders Math Adventure 9–12. Even games such as Railroad Tycoon and Civilization that are not necessarily intended to be educational can teach important lessons by teaching players about history, economics, and imperialism. War games about specific battles can make those battles come to life for students. Students in a gaming environment can immerse themselves in history while gaining a richer perspective of the time period. If they enjoy the game, it may lead to curiosity and enthusiasm for learning more about history.

Games can also make excellent educational tools because they promote active learning. When young people play a videogame, they are immersed in the game and practicing new skills. Interactivity is important to learning. The 1960s classic "Learning Pyramid" study found that a person listening to a lecture would retain only 5 percent of what he or she was hearing, while someone who was reading would retain 10 percent. The number increases to 20 percent when both audio and visual components are present, 30 percent when viewing a demonstration, and 50 percent when discussing what they're learning in a group. However, learners can retain 75 percent of what they learned when they practice what they've learned.[8] According to James Paul Gee, "[I]f learning is to be active, it must involve experiencing the world in new ways ... Active learning must also involve forming new affiliations."[9] Gaming allows people to practice what they've learned in a unique immersive environment, increasing the probability that they will retain what they've learned.

Gaming can also have important physical benefits. Since the early Nintendo system, some games have required the use of game pads for running, jumping, and dancing. Modern games such as Dance Dance Revolution require people to compete against each another in a fast-paced game requiring rhythm and fitness. Players must move their feet on a game pad according to instructions on the screen, leading to fast motion and an elevated heart rate. Young people may not realize that while they're competing and having fun, they're also exercising. At a time when childhood obesity is on the rise, anything that makes exercise fun is valuable. In 2006, West Virginia began a program to use Dance Dance Revolution in all of their middle-school gym classes. A study to determine the effects of Dance Dance Revolution on fitness found that one participant actually lost 20 pounds playing the game.[10]

The original electronic games were primarily a solitary pursuit. When arcade games and gaming consoles were created, though, more multiplayer games appeared. In the 1980s, young people would often go to their friends' houses or to the arcades to play videogames together; it was a social activity. Now, some games can be played with four or more players, and computers or consoles can be connected together in a Local Area Network (LAN) configuration to allow more than a dozen people to play games together. "LAN parties" have become very popular with teenage and adult gamers alike. At a LAN party, anywhere from a few to several hundred people can connect their computers into a LAN configuration to play multiplayer action games together. People like to go to LAN parties because graphically intensive games play better over a LAN than over the Internet, due to low latency (or delay). LAN parties also let serious computer gamers show off their skills and their modified computers. LAN parties are about more than computer games; they are parties where people can meet and socialize. Attendees' enthusiasm for gaming is the common thread that unites them. While gaming certainly can be a solitary activity, it also can be used as a tool to develop and nurture social ties, especially among teenage boys.

Gaming can also be social when gamers play on the Internet where they can interact with other gamers. Many people play board games, card games, and puzzle games against others online. Sites such as Pogo (www.pogo.com), EA Nation (www.ea.com/nation.jsp), Yahoo! Games (games.yahoo.com), and MSN Games (zone.msn.com) allow users to play interactive games. Users can play chess, poker, or even Wheel of Fortune. Most of these sites have separate chat rooms for socializing and also let users chat during game play so people with common interests can get to know each other. Communities form around specific games, incorporating tournaments and other online social activities.

Another way that people build gaming communities online is through Massively Multiplayer Online Games (MMOGs). These games allow thousands of people to interact online in a virtual world. Unlike console games, the virtual world doesn't go into hibernation when a user goes offline; it continues evolving through the actions taken by other participants around the world. In an MMOG, players design their own "avatar," or online representation of each player. Players will use their avatars throughout game play, which could last for months—or years. (Many games do not have a specific end point, so play can continue indefinitely.) Some of these games involve individual quests that players must go on, or are "good vs. evil" games where one group fights another. These games are usually collaborative, as characters band together in groups to fight a common enemy. Group membership, however, is not automatic; a person must have needed skills and fit in socially to be welcomed into a group. As players gain experience in the game, their point level goes up, allowing them to do more things. These types of games are true meritocracies. To succeed in these games, users need to obtain certain items by buying or trading for them. In some games, items are purchased with real-world money, giving the game its own economy. The game Lineage, for example, has 4 million players and an economy larger than some small countries!

Communication and community-building exists inside and outside the virtual world. Within the virtual world, players use public and private chat and VoIP to communicate and plan their next moves. Outside of the game world, people also use many of the social software tools previously discussed in this book:

> Players determine roles in groups, recruit new pledge members, negotiate through conflicts (such as competitions over the rights to hunt in territories), establish norms for collaborative

events (such as hunts and sieges), theorize game play dynamics (such as where are the best places to hunt), and debrief. Outside of the game world, they tell stories, post screen shots, write poetry, search databases, post hints and walkthroughs and generally "cuss and discuss" all aspects of game play.[11]

good Term

With some games, activity outside the virtual world is just as lively as the activity inside. The game Second Life (secondlife.com), which is more of an open-ended virtual world than a traditional game, has online newspapers, a wiki, blogs, forums, and Web sites for virtual people selling virtual things (Figure 13.1). Civilization, a game where people can build an entire civilization, has Apolyton University (apolyton.net/civgroups/news.php?civgroupid=56), a virtual university with courses that teach different approaches to the game. Using saved game files and screencasts, many players of MMOGs analyze past game play and plan their next moves. A lot of reflection, strategizing, and debate goes on in these game

Figure 13.1   Users can socialize in the virtual world of Second Life.
(*Reproduced with permission. ©2006 Linden Research, Inc. All rights reserved.*)

communities, where players are judged less by their age, gender, or other factors and more by their ability in the virtual world. As a result, everyone, from teenagers to retirees, is welcome to join the community, both in the virtual world and offline.

How Libraries Can Use Gaming

Over the past 50 years, many towns and cities have lost their "third places." A third place is a space where community members can go to socialize outside of work and home. It's basically a hangout, like the bar in *Cheers* or the coffee shop around the corner in *Friends*. Third places create a sense of place and offer a space where all members of a diverse community can go to unwind and be social. The lack of third place holds especially true for teenagers. In most areas, few public places exist where teens can hang out. Instead, many teens have turned to online communities like MySpace and Facebook where they can chat with friends and be themselves. Libraries are the ideal community institution to fill the vacuum and create a physical third place for Millennials. This is a population that has abandoned libraries, and that libraries have largely abandoned as well. Gaming may be the way to lure them back to libraries. Libraries need to show young people that they have something to offer through their collections and programming.

Programming: LAN Parties and Game Nights

Gaming programs are a surefire way to get younger patrons into the library. Most young people in your area are probably already gamers, and a free program where they can congregate with their friends and play games may just be too much for them to resist. Few places are left where large groups of teenagers can hang out and play videogames; this is a perfect niche for libraries to fill. Many public libraries have started offering game nights and LAN parties for their younger patrons, all of which have been wildly successful.

Libraries must make a few preliminary decisions when developing a gaming program. First, think about whether to offer console gaming or computer gaming. One benefit of computers is that they can be used for other purposes when the gaming program is not going on. The benefit of consoles is that they cost a lot less money—as low as $99 vs. potentially more than $1,000—and they don't take up as much space. If space is at a premium, your library might be better off purchasing consoles and small televisions for display. If you already have a networked computer lab, you can save money by using it for gaming. However, it's important that these computers have good video cards and are fast enough for gaming.

The next decisions involve structuring the gaming nights. Will the program feature open play or tournaments? Open play gives less-skilled players more time to play. Tournaments, which are more structured, are often better for a teenage audience with short attention spans. Competition helps keep them focused. The perfect solution is a blend of both open play and tournament play. However, tournaments require prizes, particularly those that are attractive to teens. Since people of all ages are gamers, libraries need to consider limiting gaming programs. Opening gaming to both young children and teens will lead to conflict because most 7-year-olds will not be able to compete with 17-year-olds. If possible, libraries should offer separate game nights for children and teens.

The Ann Arbor District Library (AADL) Game Tournament is probably the best-known gaming success story. Funding and technological know-how helped the library create a gaming tournament that has become a model for other libraries. The program started as a series of five monthly videogame tournaments where teens competed in Mario Kart: Double Dash, a racing and shooting game rated E for everyone. It was chosen for the tournament primarily for its ability to be played by 16 individuals simultaneously. In LAN mode, eight Nintendo GameCubes can easily be networked together, which allows AADL to get as many people playing at one time as possible. A variety of events were offered in the tournaments, including single player and team competition, and structured tournaments to let people of all skill levels have optimum time at the controls. To make the game more exciting, a feed of the action was projected onto a big screen with software that displayed the results of each round. The fifth event of the gaming season was a tournament of champions with prizes including iPods and gaming systems.[12]

AADL also develops brand recognition and a sense of cohesiveness with its blog. As described in Chapter 3, the AXIS Blog (www.aadl.org/axis) creates a separate space for teens to discuss upcoming tournaments and other teen programming (Figure 13.2). It helps create community online and gives teens a place to socialize between tournaments. AADL

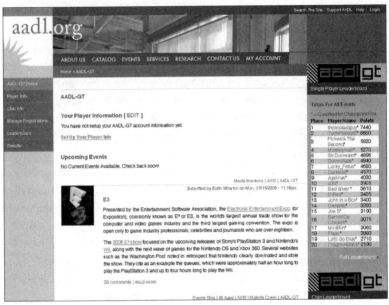

Figure 13.2   The AADL-GT blog lets Ann Arbor (MI) District Library gamers communicate between tournaments. (*Reproduced with permission.*)

encourages teens to have a voice in tournament planning, which makes them feel more invested in the library. Since the first tournament in 2004, the library has expanded its game programming significantly. AADL now also offers tournaments for grades one through five, as well as all-ages Dance Dance Revolution and Karaoke Revolution tournaments. The library has also started offering more games based on teen interests, such as Super Smash Brothers Melee and Duck Hunt. AADL's program has been a major success because the library gave teens a voice, empowering them to get involved in their library.

Libraries can also offer gaming programs by hosting LAN parties. LAN parties require a large number of networked computers, which many libraries already have available in their computer labs. If that is the case, the only major expense for the party is the game software, which must be purchased and installed on each computer. The Santa Monica Public Library in California (www.smpl.org) was one of the first libraries to host a LAN party, in response to a suggestion from its Teen Advisory Council. For the party, the library networked 30 computers together and set them up to play Counterstrike, a popular team-based first-person shooter game.

Unlike any of its previous teen programs, the LAN party was wildly successful, with teens lining up outside hours in advance.[13] The library has been able to capitalize on the success of its LAN parties to start many other teen programs, including talks by game programmers. Due to the nature of the game, the event was attended almost exclusively by teenage boys; similar results have been reported by many libraries offering game nights with shooting or fighting games—which may not be a bad thing. Teenage boys are the most difficult group to attract to the library and get interested in reading. If participants start to see the library as a place they want to be, librarians may be able to turn gamers into readers. Just as at AADL, letting teens have a voice in the library programming led to tremendous success and enabled the Santa Monica Public Library to market itself as a third place for young people.

The Bloomington Public Library (BPL) in Illinois has tried a variety of approaches to gaming programs to find the perfect fit for its community. Initially, its Gamefest (now called the Bloomington-Normal Gamefest; www.bngamefest.com) consisted of a LAN party where participants played Battlefield 1942, a World War II shooter game. BPL decided to host a LAN party because the library had just built a new computer lab with 17 networked computers. The game software, prizes, and food were the only expenses for the participants. The library later purchased Nintendo GameCubes and game pads for Dance Dance Revolution to offer games that appealed to a more diverse population, and now offers Dance Dance Revolution, Mario Kart Double Dash, and Battlefield 1942. Librarians also have board games for kids to play while they are waiting for access to the electronic games. Matt Gullett, former Technology Services Manager at the Bloomington Public Library, explains: "We just like things that can keep over 50 kids active while they are playing or waiting to play."[14] BPL listened to gamers' suggestions and made changes accordingly. This flexibility has made the program so successful that parents from more than 20 miles away have been driving their children to the game nights. To fund the program, the librarians have reached out to the community for sponsorship and support from businesses that depend on the teen gamer demographic. The library, which started working with the Normal Public Library in 2006, also is working with schools and other community institutions that occasionally host the program outside the library.

The major barrier to offering gaming programs is the cost of the equipment. Depending on the gaming a library wants and the equipment it already owns, start-up costs can range up to several thousand dollars. At AADL, the initial cost of eight consoles, televisions, broadband adapters, and memory cards was $3,000. For a library system with a healthy budget, this may be a reasonable expenditure, but it's not for every library. Libraries can still find options to cut costs and fund such a project. They can seek sponsorships from game, electronics, and comic book stores, which depend on the purchasing behavior of teens to survive. A captive audience of local teens is a perfect time to advertise. Libraries can leverage this to get discounted merchandise and free gift certificates to use as awards for game winners. Libraries can also partner with other local community institutions or organizations working with young people to fund the program. With the growing popularity of gaming in libraries, it may be possible to secure grant funding. Finally, instead of having the gaming setup seen at some better-funded libraries, librarians could ask patrons to bring in their own consoles—or computers—and games, then network them together to host a LAN party. The North Hunterdon and Voorhees Regional high schools in New Jersey offer a gaming tournament where the teens bring their own laptops and game systems, and the school provides equipment on which to display the game play. Not having to purchase game systems will cut costs drastically.[15]

Depending on your institution, it may be difficult to convince your library board and administration that gaming programs are something libraries should offer. Come into meetings with hard data. Find studies about teenagers' use of libraries, the pervasive use of electronic games, and the positive effects of gaming. Illustrate what you want to do at your library with success stories from other libraries. Survey parents of teenagers in the community and see how they feel about their teens having a safe place to go and socialize with other teens. The more concrete data you produce to support your plan, the better chance of a successful outcome. Many libraries complain about the difficulty of getting teens involved in Teen Advisory Committees and getting them into the library for programs. Gaming is a fantastic way to attract teens to the library and get them interested in having a voice in their library's future.

Second Life Library 2.0

While many libraries use gaming to draw community members into the library, one group actually works to provide library services within a gaming environment. In early 2006, the Alliance Library System (ALS) in Illinois (www.alliancelibrarysystem.com) spearheaded a project to build a library in Second Life, the massive multiplayer online virtual world. Director of innovation Lori Bell, working with OPAL (www.opal-online.org) and a group of dedicated librarian volunteers, purchased an island (with real money), built a library, and began to provide services to the residents of Second Life.

Since its creation, the Second Life Library has offered a number of programs, including book discussions, classes on achieving success in Second Life, and library research classes. People can actually attend the classes with their avatars and participate as in a regular library program. ALS and its partners are also developing classes for librarians and have partnered with a number of nonprofits interested in providing educational services in the virtual world. The library collection—set up in stacks to look like a regular collection—consists of links to free Internet resources. Reference assistance is even being offered to residents who visit the library.

Second Life, with more than 200,000 participants, is growing every day. The services provided by ALS and its partners are challenging notions about the library's place in the online world and giving new meaning to the word outreach. They have shown that services and education can be provided in virtual worlds, and many libraries in the future will probably explore using gaming environments to provide services to patrons. If our patrons are spending their time in online virtual worlds, libraries should consider how they can provide library services in that environment.

Space: Creating a Gaming Area

A gaming program can attract young people to the library, but a permanent gaming area can keep them coming back. Teens with a friendly library space of their own are more likely to visit and hang out with their friends and do their homework. They might even realize the library has materials they're interested in borrowing. Most libraries have an adult section and a children's section, but lack a specific space for teens. Some libraries, though, have been making an effort to carve out a space for teens where they can enjoy themselves without disturbing other patrons. An ideal teen space should have comfortable chairs, computers, outlets for laptops, books and magazines teens like to read, stations for listening to music and audiobooks, and gaming systems. Gaming systems could be permanently affixed to the building similarly to the demo systems at electronic stores so that no pieces could be stolen. Patrons could use headphones to listen to games, so that the noise level doesn't get out of control.

For a teen space to be successful, it must be physically separate from the quiet areas in the library. When teens are gaming and hanging out in groups, it's likely that they will get loud. If a teen area is open to the rest of the library, chances are they will disturb other patrons and librarians will spend a lot of time asking teens to be quiet. This again makes the library seem to be a teen-unfriendly space. Unfortunately, many libraries simply don't have the space to accommodate a completely separate teen space, and instead must work with what's available. Libraries that want to create a teen-friendly space need to think about incorporating what teens enjoy using the most.

Collection Development and Readers' Advisory: Turning Gamers into Readers

It can be difficult to turn gamers into regular library users. Gaming programs may get teens into the library, but they're not suddenly going to become interested in the contents of the shelves. For these teens, the library can be a third place, even if they never borrow a book. Once librarians have attracted younger patrons into the library, clever marketing and a good collection can help entice them to leave with a book.

Since many children and teens are interested in gaming, it makes sense to collect books related to gaming. First, and most obviously, libraries can collect strategy guides, which offer tips, tricks, and cheats to help readers become better at playing a specific game. Teens love to read these books so that they can play a given game better—and beat their friends. While not exactly great literature, these guides still require a good deal of reading. Considering how difficult it can be to get teenage boys to read, libraries should stock anything they might be interested in. Many popular games, such as Doom, Halo, and Myst, have also been produced into popular book series; comic books based on videogames are also very popular. Many fiction titles feature gamers as main characters. If teen patrons identify with these characters, the book may hold their attention. Young people who are interested in game development will enjoy books about the making of popular games. Many books feature interviews with game creators and follow a specific game from the earliest stages of development until the game hits the shelves. Libraries could also purchase books about game design, especially those specifically written for a teenage audience. A collection that includes gaming-related reading material might be just the ticket to turn passionate young gamers into passionate readers.

To attract young people to the shelves, libraries can also circulate games. Many libraries have been circulating educational CD-ROMs for years, but very few collect games for recreational use, perhaps due to the ongoing high-culture vs. low-culture conflict. Librarians need to ask themselves if they should be making collection development decisions based on their opinion of materials' intrinsic value or on the needs and wants of their patrons. If it's the latter, then it will make sense for some public libraries to consider circulating games. Adding games into the library's collection development priorities is more complicated than adding media such as DVDs and CDs. A number of gaming platforms exist, including PCs, Playstation 2, Nintendo GameCube, and Microsoft X-Box, and each can only play games specifically designed for that system. Libraries that decide to start purchasing games for their collections need to decide whether to collect in just one or multiple formats. Both options have drawbacks. Collecting in only one format prevents people with other systems from taking out games from the library. However, if the library collects several formats, either more money has to be put into the collection or a much smaller number of titles per format can be collected. As John Scalzo, author of the Video Game Librarian column, writes: "More complications arise because libraries love a single unified format."[16] Many libraries have chosen to collect games in a single format, but a few are collecting in all popular formats.

Some libraries have decided against circulating games for several reasons. Games can be expensive (from $20 to $60 each), and the newest and most popular games (those most in demand by patrons) usually cost about $50. If libraries wait several months to purchase them, the price is likely to drop. With this approach, libraries will always be several months behind their patrons, but they will also be able to buy two older games for the price of one new one. By the time they get a game, however, patrons might have moved on to something else. The other issue is that gaming platforms change every few years. Unless newer systems are compatible with games from older platforms, the release of a new system will mean that the library has to scramble to collect titles in the new format. Other arguments against collecting games include the probability of the games getting scratched and stolen. The same arguments, though, were made against circulating DVDs, yet most libraries currently do so. The biggest barrier is simply the price of adding games to the collection; librarians at cash-strapped libraries may have to find creative ways to fund the project. For most libraries, it will take a long time to build up a decent-sized collection for their patrons.

When doing readers' advisory, librarians usually ask patrons about the sort of books they like. Children and teens sometimes find this question difficult to answer because they've not found books they enjoy yet. According to librarian Beth Gallaway, trainer/consultant at the Metrowest (MA) Regional Library System, it may make more sense to ask young people about the media they use, such as television, movies, and games, than to ask them about books. Try asking gamers about their favorite games. Game genres correspond quite well to book genres, so knowing the kind of games young people enjoy can help librarians make effective book recommendations. If a patron likes games with fantasy storylines, such as Lineage and World of Warcraft, he or she will probably enjoy fantasy books. For those who like post-apocalyptic, first-person shooter games such as Resident Evil and Half Life, try horror and science fiction books. For gamers who play historical games including Rome: Total War and Civilization, try history and historical fiction. For those who like playing games with mysteries or puzzles, such as Myst and Where in the World Is Carmen Sandiego, try mysteries and thrillers. Most games fit into some genre, and usually librarians will be able to find books that correspond to that genre.[17] Librarians can learn a lot by looking at what young people are doing when not reading books, which makes it important for librarians to keep up with youth culture. If we don't know about popular games, movies, and other media, we are less able to reliably offer readers' advisory services to young adults.

It is clear that libraries are losing Millennial patrons (and, to a lesser extent, Gen X patrons) at an alarming rate. Most libraries have a serious service gap when it comes to patrons in between childhood and adulthood. If teens find that the library has no relevance for them, if they discover that the local chain bookstore is more geared toward their interests and needs, their dismissive attitude will likely persist as they mature. Librarians should try to offer unique services and programs when developing plans for attracting teens to the library, adding value, rather than competing with commercial institutions.

Gaming nights offer teens an activity unlikely to be found elsewhere in the community. These programs are attractive to teens looking for a fun third place where they can hang out with other young people, and they are attractive to parents because the library provides a safe third place for their children to meet. Gaming "reorients teens toward the library, allows librarians insights into youth culture, and brands the library as a technologically advanced, communal third place where people can come for informal social bonding."[18] After gaming programs give you that hook, use your collections, especially those somehow tied to gaming, to transform gamers into readers. Once they become relevant to teens, libraries will find it much easier to remain a part of their lives—and to ensure the future of public libraries.

Endnotes

1. Cathy De Rosa, et al., *Perceptions of Libraries and Information Resources*, OCLC 2005, www.oclc.org/reports/2005perceptions.htm (accessed March 3, 2006).
2. Brian Kenney and Lauren Barack, "Libraries Losing Teens," *School Library Journal*, January 1, 2006, www.schoollibraryjournal.com/article/CA6296513.html (accessed March 3, 2006).
3. "Video Game Makers Missing Opportunities," *Silicon Valley/San Jose Business Journal*, April 1, 2003, www.bizjournals.com/sanjose/stories/2003/03/31/daily22.html (accessed March 4, 2006).

4.   J. C. Herz, *Gaming the System: What Higher Education Can Learn From Multiplayer Online Worlds*, The Internet and the University: Forum 2001, www.educause.edu/ir/library/pdf/ffpiu019.pdf (accessed March 2, 2006).

5.   Paul Bryant, "Gran Turismo Sends Japan's Sports Cars Abroad," *Gaming Age*, December 11, 2002, www.gaming-age.com/cgi-bin/news/news.pl?y=2002&m=12&nid=11-34.db (accessed March 6, 2006).

6.   Catherine Delneo, "Gaming for Tech-Savvy Teens," *YALS* 3.3 (2005): 34.

7.   James Paul Gee, *What Video Games Have to Teach Us About Learning and Literacy*, New York: Palgrave Macmillan, 2003.

8.   Nick DeKanter, "Gaming Redefines Interactivity for Learning," *TechTrends* 49.3 (2005): 27.

9.   Gee, 39.

10. Cliff Edwards, "Class Take Out Your Games," Business Week Online, February 20, 2005, www.businessweek.com/magazine/content/06_08/b3972100.htm (accessed March 5, 2006).

11. Kurt Squire and Constance Steinkuehler, "Meet the Gamers," *Library Journal*, April, 15 2005: 40, www.libraryjournal.com/article/CA516033.html (accessed March 5, 2006).

12. Erin Helmrich and Eli Neiberger, "Video Games as A Service: Hosting Tournaments at your Library," *VOYA*, February 2005, pdfs.voya.com/VO/YA2/VOYA200502VideoGames.pdf (accessed March 6, 2006).

13. Squire and Steinkuehler, 41.

14. John Scalzo, "The Video Game Librarian: GameFest and the Bloomington Public Library," Gaming Target, August 26, 2005, www.gamingtarget.com/article.php?artid=4579 (accessed March 12, 2006).

15. Delneo, 34.

16. John Scalzo, "The Video Game Librarian: It's the End of the Year as We Know It (And I Feel Fine)," Gaming Target, January 25, 2006, www.gamingtarget.com/article.php?artid=4941 (accessed March 12, 2006).

17. Beth Gallaway, "What Libraries Can Do for Gamers (Other than Programming and Collections), Gaming Learning and Libraries Symposium," 2005, gaminginlibraries.org/2005symposium/presentations/bethgallaway.pdf (accessed March 12, 2006).

18. Squire and Steinkuehler, 41.

Chapter 14

What Will Work @ Your Library

Now that you've learned about the different types of social tools, you're probably thinking about how you can use them in your library. Perhaps you find one or two technologies particularly intriguing and are ready to try them out.

But the success of any new technology implementation rests on two key factors. First, any technology must meet your colleagues' or patrons' needs; without the need, only the most technologically savvy are likely to embrace it. Even when social software is implemented in response to patron or staff needs, you will need to provide marketing and training so that people understand and embrace the new tool. Secondly, your library staff must be willing to use and promote the new technology. Telling staff members that they're going to start using a wiki without any dialogue or training is not likely to be met with much enthusiasm. Staff members need to be involved in the planning and implementation process so they can voice their questions and concerns; staff training is also critical to success.

With those factors in mind, here are some guidelines on successfully implementing social software in your library, whether you work for a small law firm or a large university. The following sections revisit some of the uses of social software that were discussed more in-depth earlier; if a specific implementation intrigues you, look for a more detailed explanation in the chapter discussing that tool. This chapter also features interviews with librarians in a variety of settings who share the social software tools they believe to be most valuable for other librarians working with similar populations.

Know Your Population

The mission of any library is to meet the educational, informational, or recreational needs of its service population. How do librarians know what their service population needs? In many libraries, the most vocal patrons get the best service. What about those who are not vocal? What about those who do not even use the library? Librarians should consider the needs of regular library users, as well as the needs of those who use the library infrequently and those who don't use the library at all. Perhaps, if we designed library services with these latter audiences in mind, they would become more frequent users. It is important to get to know your population better and a variety of techniques are available to help you do so, including making informal observations, studying demographic information, and formally surveying your population. In all cases, getting out of the library is crucial to getting to know the people your library should be serving.

Observing your patrons at work and play can give you insight into their interests and needs. If you work in an academic environment, walk around campus and visit the areas where students and faculty congregate. Where do they study? How do they access information and do research? Knowing the answers to these questions allows you to better understand what your population wants from the library. If you work in a public library, walk or drive around your neighborhood. What does your population look like? Where do people hang out? What do young people do after school? Census data can be useful in understanding what your population looks like now and how it has changed over time. If you work as a librarian for an organization, observe your employees at work. How do your patrons access information? How do they use technology? What does their workflow look like and how could the library offer support? Observing your service population outside library walls can offer valuable insights into their needs and what they might like to see inside of the library.

You can also evaluate the needs of your service population through formal surveys. Many libraries create paper surveys for people to voluntarily take while at the library, but this approach fails to collect insights from people who don't use the library. People who volunteer to fill out surveys also tend to have strong opinions (either positive or negative), which will not paint an accurate picture of your service population. If you conduct a simple survey, you need to be proactive in targeting a diverse group of people. Making the survey available on your Web site and handing out copies at other community institutions can help encourage your population to provide feedback.

Sarah Houghton-Jan, Information and Web Services Manager, San Mateo County Library, California

Blogging is an effective tool for getting information out about all types of library services and resources: events, classes, closures, new resources, neat features people might want to know about—just about anything! It's easy for any staff member to submit blog entries using the WYSIWYG interfaces that all blogging software offers today. Blogs are the simplest way to create a constantly updated "what's new at the library" section of your site, and when combined with RSS, they become powerful outreach tools.

People like having information delivered to them. Many adults use RSS, but are sometimes unaware when they're doing so (as through My Yahoo!). RSS saves your users time, a precious commodity to all of us. RSS also guarantees that once someone has subscribed to your feed, your information will be pushed to them ... reaching more people than you would without RSS. Indeed, you'll reach a much different audience than you would with, say, an e-mail newsletter.

People expect us to be available 24/7 online, and that expectation extends beyond our catalogs and databases into our staffing. We need to be where our users are when they want us to be there. That can mean finding resources for a student at 9 PM or helping someone find small business start-up information at 2 AM. It can mean being available 24/7 through a Web-based chat cooperative or being around during business hours on IM. Most adults are, at this time, more comfortable using Web-based chat products, though I would emphasize the importance of offering both services; you'll get two completely different sets of users.

Another excellent way to learn about your patrons—and to make sure you hear from different demographic groups—is to conduct focus groups. Your assessment process can incorporate a number of focus groups, making sure that each is a manageable size of about five to eight people. It makes sense to talk to members of a similar demographic group together. For example, you probably wouldn't conduct a focus group with children and elderly people at the same time, because neither group would feel entirely comfortable speaking freely in front of the other. Choose people of similar ages and backgrounds to interview together. The facilitator should ask each focus group the same questions and make sure everyone voices an opinion. Offering refreshments during each focus group not only encourages people to come, but is a good way to create a relaxed atmosphere where people can share their feelings and ideas.

Even if you are not implementing new technology, it is essential to evaluate the needs of your service population on a regular basis and determine whether your services are meeting those needs. Through a combination of techniques, it is possible to get a deeper understanding of what your service population wants from the library, not just those who visit the library regularly. Once you know your population and have a better sense of their needs, you can see how social software can meet those needs. You will also have a better idea of how your service population would respond to new social software tools and how best to market them to your community.

Different Libraries, Different Needs

There is no "typical library" since libraries exist in so many different settings and serve so many different populations. A corporate librarian serving aerospace engineers will have different needs than a public librarian serving small children. However, both may use the same social software tools to meet those different needs. This section will examine some of the needs common to specific types of libraries or libraries that serve specific types of populations. While there is no way to prescribe specific tools for specific library types, many have similar issues and needs. This section will address a number of these issues and make suggestions about what tools might be best for your situation.

Public Libraries

Public libraries serve diverse populations, struggling to be all things to all people. They must serve every member of their community—essentially

Kelly Czarnecki, Teen Librarian, ImaginOn, Public Library of Charlotte & Mecklenburg County, North Carolina

Some of the best ways libraries can overcome communication gaps with teens and serve them better are to engage them through gaming, podcasting, and synchronous online interaction with chat and IM. Truly involving youth means giving them a variety of tools to create their own stories and interact with others. In my experience at the Bloomington Public Library in Illinois, using these applications to serve teens meant creating a culture, not just a one-time program organized by the Young Adult librarian. This means that you create ongoing programs that build on each other and offer youth the opportunities to create and interact within this space we call "the library."

Furthermore, it means the A/V [audio/visual] librarian at the reference desk IMing teen patrons about the latest movies and music, the network manager creating a gaming guild for teens and texting about what they think of library services while playing the game, or the Web developer going to the local schools to record teens' opinions on the latest games, books, and movies. Not only is it important to interact with teens in these ways, but it is important to use these tools for building relationships.

Teens were given the opportunity to create their own video games through an after school computer club at the library, not just attend video game events or chat online with the network manager. Podcasting allowed teens to share their stories not only with their classmates but their parents, friends, and basically anyone in the world that has access to the Internet. Through interaction and creation of these media they are becoming the creators of their own stories, lives, and worlds rather than just passive consumers of other people's stories, lives, and worlds.

from birth to death—and adapt to a constantly changing population. As a result, public librarians need to keep up with their patrons' changing interests and be flexible in how they serve their community members. Some social software applications are relevant to a range of age groups, helping public librarians find new ways to disseminate information and build community both online and offline.

One of the most important role public libraries can play in young children's lives is that of inspiring a lifelong love of reading. Libraries accomplish this through fun programs, storytime, and readers' advisory. Many of these same efforts can be duplicated online for young people unable to visit the library, or for children and teens to browse between visits. Librarians can create podcasts, screencasts, or videos of stories in the public domain, which allow children to benefit from storytime anytime. When learning to read, children could even listen to a podcast while following along in the book.

Libraries can provide readers' advisory services for all age groups through blogs and wikis. Blogs have been used in libraries for recommending books on different topics, but wikis may be the more appropriate tool since entries can be arranged by subject rather than chronologically. Librarians can create categories such as "books based on games" or "fractured fairy tales," listing the best books on those topics. They can post lists of recommendations based on popular books, such as, "if you liked the *Harry Potter* series, you might also like …". Patrons of all ages could be encouraged to add their own book recommendations or reviews. Libraries can use social software to encourage young readers and offer book recommendations for adults.

Beyond posting content online, public libraries can also use social software to build community and establish the library as a positive and supportive place for young people. Encouraging children and teens to become content creators allows them to express their creativity. They can develop podcasts and vlogs at the library, create book reviews, or even create their own polished broadcasts. Public libraries could set up a podcasting station or video-making area with little more than a computer, a microphone, some free software, and a video camera. Libraries could develop a collaborative blog where teens could post reviews, or offer classes to teach young people how to create their own blogs. Game nights and other social programming encourage teens to see the library as a third place.

Students can become teachers   *old ←→ young*

While people think of social software as something that improves online interactions, it can also encourage social interactions in the physical library.

Children and teens occasionally use the library when they need help with their homework or are writing a research paper. However, patrons aren't always near the library when they need help. Since patrons of all ages can also access library resources from home or work, librarians can make themselves available to patrons at their point of need by offering synchronous reference services, ranging from providing IM reference for a few hours a day to being part of a 24/7 chat reference cooperative. Many adults, children, and teens use IM every day to chat with friends, colleagues, or business clients, so consider it as an alternative for your library as well.

Academic Libraries

Academic libraries have struggled to serve an increasingly tech-savvy, mobile population. Fifteen years ago, the library was the only place to do research. Now, not only can students use commercial search engines to do research, but they usually can access their library's databases from home. If students can research virtually, we need to provide other library services such as reference and instruction virtually as well. In addition, many colleges and universities have seen the growth of distance learning. While the library is sometimes an afterthought in the planning process, library services are integral to quality distance education. Libraries have been scrambling to translate their traditional services into the online medium to provide equivalent services to online learners. Social software tools can connect librarians to their patrons online, provide instructional content, and create a sense of community.

The primary mission of academic libraries is to support research through collections, instruction, and reference assistance. IM and commercial virtual reference software now make it possible to provide live online reference assistance to distance learners on the other side of the world or patrons on the other side of the library. Using SMS, students can even obtain reference assistance without a computer.

Thanks to numerous online databases and e-books, many library collections are now online. However, the growing number of databases makes it difficult to keep up with the online resources that libraries offer. This is where a blog can be useful: Librarians can use a blog to make announcements and offer tips about new online resources. Blogs can also

Stephen Francoeur,
Information Services Librarian,
Baruch College, New York, New York

Among the many social software technologies, the three that are probably the most fundamental for academic libraries are RSS, chat reference, and screencasting. RSS allows data to be repurposed many different ways as you stream it out to your users. There's more to RSS feeds than those for blogs your library may have set up. RSS feeds can also come out of OPACs and databases, allowing users to set up RSS feeds for specific searches or subjects and use the feed as an alerting service. Not only can your users view the feeds in the many different feed-reading devices, RSS feeds can be set up within course management systems (like Blackboard) or on relevant college and library Web pages.

By chat reference, I include not only commercial Web-based chat software but also IM software. Libraries are annually spending enormous sums to maintain virtual libraries on their library Web site; they should be staffing those virtual libraries with reference staff, just as they would staff a physical library.

Screencasting offers librarians a quick and easy way to build mini-demos of how to use various library resources and services. It lowers the barriers for creating online tutorials, much as PowerPoint made it easy for the average person to make presentation slides. They are quite easy to add to a Web site and offer a much richer Web environment.

be used to market resources to distance learners, putting a human face on the very distant library.

To direct students to useful resources, librarians often create subject guides or pathfinders, which can be now done on a wiki instead of a traditional Web site. Wikis have several features that make them superior to Web sites in this case: They are searchable, librarians can assign categories to each resource to improve findability, and wikis require no knowledge of Web design to add content. Another option for creating subject or course guides is social bookmarking. Librarians can assign subject tags to each resource so that these can later be found by subject. Social bookmarking services offer RSS feeds so the bookmarks can be syndicated to other places. You can place your social bookmarks on your library's Web site, rather than asking your patrons to visit another site.

Brian Mathews, Distance Learning Services and Mechanical Engineering Librarian, Georgia Tech Library & Information Center, Atlanta, Georgia

I believe that RSS, or a similar syndication service, will grow in predominance. I envision a blending of the campus portal with the course management system and some other form of social networking, such as Facebook. A lot of librarians have been talking about the need to "be where they are"—which I like; however, simply creating a MySpace account for your library is not proactive enough.

I have not dabbled with VoIP, but as services like Skype increase in popularity, there is potential to reach distance students through this method. However, it's the same as with IM—they have to recognize a need and know who to contact. The real challenge is marketing, and it has been for a long time.

If I had to pick three technologies, I'd have to go with blogs, RSS, and social networking software. Distance students are often disenfranchised, and the goal should be to create a community. As RSS becomes more integrated with Web browsers and/or e-mail clients, it will be important for libraries to push both original and prepackaged content.

Academic librarians can provide instruction online in various ways. They can offer information literacy lectures as podcasts with slides to supplement the presentation. They can also develop screencasts that actually demonstrate and explain the use of various resources. Screencasting appeals to students with diverse learning styles, but files can often be large and difficult for students to download without broadband. Web conferencing software is another option that allows librarians to teach synchronously through a combination of chat, VoIP, and co-browsing. However, Web-conferencing software is currently expensive and often beyond the means of academic institutions. Price will likely become less of a barrier in the future as the software becomes more widely used and less expensive.

School Libraries

Many public school systems have faced budget cuts over the past decade, and school libraries have not been immune. Materials budgets have been slashed and staffing has decreased. In some cases, one school librarian is responsible for serving multiple schools, and, in most cases, librarians have needed to learn to do more with less. Luckily, social software is not only free or low-cost, but it allows librarians to extend their reach beyond the library by offering assistance to students at the point of need.

One important responsibility for school librarians is providing appropriate resources for young people. This can be accomplished by creating Web subject guides, but sometimes librarians do not have the Web design skills or time to develop formal subject guides. School librarians can instead create subject guides on a wiki, which is easier to develop, or create subject guides by tagging resources on a social bookmarking service. Blogs are another option, although their chronological arrangement makes them more suited to highlighting timely resources.

School librarians also provide reference assistance and instruction. If a librarian isn't full time at a single school, or if students with busy schedules don't have time to visit the library, services can be offered remotely. Librarians could offer research assistance after school via IM. Since the number of young people with cell phones is growing at a tremendous rate, it also makes sense to look at how school libraries can provide mobile services. In many schools, libraries are small, crowded, and not conducive to providing instruction. Screencasting lets librarians record lectures and visuals for students to watch at the point of need. While there is no substitute for an in-person class, it's not always possible in every library and for every class. Screencasting or even podcasting could be viable alternatives for librarians to reach a much larger audience.

Christopher Harris, Coordinator, School Library System/Media Services, Genesee Valley BOCES, New York

When school libraries turn to the Internet for electronic resources, they often face the challenge of working through a filter and then still having to preview and review sites to make sure they didn't miss anything. One solution to this problem is the adoption of social bookmarking software within a large district or a library system region. With a local or regional implementation, resources could also be tagged with curriculum standards or performance indicators they address.

There have been quite a few conversations about one-to-one computing, but most of these discussions fail to recognize that quite a few secondary students already have a computer in their pocket—their cell phone. Even if the solution isn't a cell phone, the prevalence of iPods, handheld gaming systems, and other mobile computing devices means there is an existing platform on which we can deploy e-books, digital audiobooks, and digital video.

As teacher-librarians work to support the increased use of digital resources, there will be an accompanying change to how instruction takes place in a school library. When a fourth grade class uses an electronic database, they don't necessarily have to work in the physical library space. The simplicity of new screencasting technology allows the teacher-librarian to deliver instruction on a specific resource with a specific objective in mind.

Corporate and Law Libraries

All corporate and law libraries share one common factor: the importance of institutional knowledge-sharing. Managers want to make the most of their employees' unique knowledge, and they need to find the best way to collect that knowledge to benefit the organization. A wiki is the perfect place to collect individual and institutional knowledge for a number of reasons. First, because it requires no experience with markup languages, everyone can use a wiki. Second, wikis are easy to organize.

Most are already searchable, and librarians can assign categories to different subjects and make them easy to browse as well. Wikis let employees collaboratively catalog best practices, project notes, internal business processes, and any other information the company wishes to collect.

Some corporations and legal offices also may want to capitalize on their employees' social networks. In business and law, who you know is often as valuable as what you know. Social networking software allows each employee to see himself as part of a larger network. Using social networking software, managers can see who their employees are connected to—and who their employees' connections are connected to—and determine how those connections could benefit the company. You never know when a friend of a friend will be your next million-dollar client, or when your college roommate's cousin will be needed as an expert witness. Social networking can be much the same as having a large institutional Rolodex.

In a busy legal or corporate environment, it is important to get relevant information to patrons quickly and remotely, and a few tools can facilitate this. The first is social bookmarking. When patrons read articles online or find Web sites useful to their work, they could use a place to store these links and make them more findable later on. Social bookmarking allows them to assign tags to each link, so that each will be filed away with other similar links. An institutional social bookmarking system enables employees to share bookmarks with their colleagues, allowing them to discover resources they may have missed otherwise.

RSS is another excellent tool for information on-the-go. Busy professionals don't have time to read every journal and visit every Web site with information about their subjects of interest. RSS can push the content from hundreds of Web sites to a single page, which the patron can quickly evaluate and skim for relevant information. Patrons can even subscribe to RSS feeds of database searches to notify them of any new articles in their subject. This significantly decreases the time patrons need to spend searching for current awareness information.

If library patrons travel often or need information when they can't get to the library, library services should be available remotely. Many lawyers and corporate employees own wireless handhelds such as BlackBerrys or Treos, on which they can surf the Web, send e-mail, and read files. Libraries can offer a variety of services for handheld users, including providing IM or

Dave Hook, Manager, Operations Information and Configuration Management, MDA Space Missions, Brampton, Ontario

Generally speaking, I would put wikis as the most important application in corporate libraries. I see wikis playing a huge role in corporations in the near future, similar to how intranets are used in corporations now. Wikis can be used to address two key issues corporations face today: those of knowledge management and of retrieving information fast, efficiently, and economically. Wikis address the first problem by providing a forum for collaboration, knowledge sharing, and knowledge preservation. They can be used to capture business process and best practices, which become "living" documents that quickly evolve to reflect changing business needs. Wikis can be used as a "window" to internal information, thus providing an efficient and economic means of retrieving information.

While wikis can provide a window to information within the organization, RSS feeds create a link to the outside world of information through timely delivery of current awareness information. I see RSS feeds being used in corporations to replace many of the applications for which e-mail has been used. I also believe that we haven't nearly seen the best of what RSS can do—there will be more applications to come that we haven't yet imagined.

Handheld computing has a huge potential in certain corporate environments—particularly where information is needed immediately, and physically interfacing with a library is inconvenient, such as a medical or research environment. Handheld devices such as electronic notebooks can provide not only immediate access to information, but also a means of recording it as it is created.

SMS reference services and making library resources accessible to mobile users. Libraries can purchase reference content that is loaded onto handhelds for instant answers; reference databases including LexisNexis and

Ovid are also now accessible via handhelds. Patrons of corporate and law libraries are often too busy to visit in person, so it's important to bring the library to them.

Medical Libraries

Not all medical libraries have the same mission and goals. The primary mission of a hospital library is to support effective decision making. They provide practical information for doctors, nurses, and patients. The dual missions of an academic medical (or health sciences) library are to support effective decision making with practical information, and to support scholarly research in the medical field.

The most important function of a hospital library is providing evidence-based research as quickly and effectively as possible. When doctors prescribe and diagnose, it helps to have references on hand. Many doctors use handhelds to take notes and record patient histories. Handhelds are also very useful reference tools. Many medical references can be loaded onto handheld devices, so that doctors and nurses have this information at their fingertips. This way, instead of going to their offices and searching the *Physician's Desk Reference* (*PDR*) for a specific drug, they can simply consult the *PDR* in their pocket. All medical libraries should make their Web sites readily accessible via handheld devices, due to their widespread use among medical professionals.

Doctors and nurses in all settings need to keep up with the latest research, and librarians can facilitate current awareness, with RSS as the most useful tool. Librarians can set medical professionals up with subscriptions to various journal tables of contents via RSS, so doctors and nurses can see the tables of contents of new issues in their aggregators. They can then determine if there are articles worth reading. Medical professionals can also subscribe to search feeds in medical databases such as MEDLINE and Ovid. Librarians could use blogs to highlight recent articles of interest in a variety of medical specialties. With medical library blogs, the librarian acts as a filter, finding the best articles in the medical literature. With RSS feeds, content is pushed to the patron without any intervention needed on their part beyond initially subscribing. Both of these tools make it far easier for health professionals to keep up-to-date.

Michelle Kraft, Medical Librarian, South Pointe Hospital, Warrensville Heights, Ohio

Medical professionals (doctors, nurses, etc.) have been using handheld devices in their daily patient care activities for quite a while. There is a lot of medical reference software available for handheld devices, and many of these products are available as an institutional subscription. Traditional medical Web database providers such as MDConsult, StatREF, and Ovid offer handheld products or components to their systems. Medical libraries are purchasing some of these handheld applications and have made the library a sync spot for their handheld devices. Now, with the push for the Electronic Medical Record (EMR), many more hospitals and doctors are looking at handheld devices to be a one-stop shopping tool where they can both look at the patient's medical information and find medical research information.

RSS offers a lot of potential for medical librarians to reach out to their users. Librarians can feature medical news feeds and current library information directly on their Web site, like Cushing/Whitney Medical Library, Yale University (www.med. yale.edu/library). Using RSS feeds, librarians can also display newly available medical books within their catalog directly on their home page. PubMed offers RSS feeds to users as a method to stay current on medical literature. Users can view the latest updates on literature searches in one place, whenever, and faster than waiting for them to be sent via e-mail by PubMed. Medical journals are offering RSS feeds of their tables of contents as well. Unfortunately, most users do not know what an RSS feed is, and this is one area where medical librarians can educate to propel this technology to be indispensable among their users.

Mary Carmen Chimato, Head of Access Services, Health Sciences Library, Stony Brook University, New York

IM reference is huge! We have several distance learning programs, some which are completely online, and being able to reach a librarian via IM is a huge benefit to the students and the librarians. When we started IM reference we actually noticed a decline in the number of phone calls that we were getting from our distance learners; they prefer IM. We have also noticed that we are getting questions, oddly enough, from patrons in the library who don't want to get up and come to the reference desk. They prefer having the entire reference consult at their laptop at an undisclosed location in the library. I think students prefer it because it doesn't break their studying rhythm by having to get up. IM is also a hit with the practitioners and third- and fourth-year med students who can use IM reference from their handheld devices. So this service is really popular and is used by health sciences students as well as the practitioners, faculty, and staff.

RSS is just as important as IM, because, in the health sciences, it is imperative for people to stay current with what is going on in the field and in the literature. We teach classes on RSS and setting up newsreader accounts, and these are a big hit. Many health sciences organizations, like the NIH, WHO, and FDA, as well as many journals, now offer RSS news feeds, and it makes staying current with medical news and research so much easier.

Since health sciences libraries also support academic research, they can benefit from many of the same social software tools as other academic libraries. Screencasts and podcasts can be used to provide instructional content that patrons can watch or listen to online at the point of need. Wikis and social bookmarking software can be used to develop subject guides that point patrons to the best resources in different medical specialties. Blogs can be used to keep patrons informed about new resources and programs. Librarians can provide reference services to busy medical professionals via IM, commercial virtual reference services, and SMS reference. Essentially, health sciences libraries need to provide the services of both a hospital library and an academic library, which is not always an easy task.

Other Special Libraries

Many kinds of special libraries do not fit into the previously mentioned categories. These include government libraries, libraries for nonprofits and cultural organizations, and museum libraries. Many special collections librarians in academic and public libraries also have a somewhat different role from the rest of the librarians in their institutions. These special libraries and librarians all serve different populations, have different missions, and would benefit from adopting different kinds of social software. However, special libraries can learn a lot from the ways that other libraries have implemented social software, since there is a great deal of overlap in populations among libraries.

Special libraries often serve a population with a particular subject interest, making blogs and RSS excellent tools to market the library and provide news and information to patrons. Blogs can be used to provide information about the library and news in the subject area, or to market new library resources. RSS alerts can be set up to push subject-specific information to patrons. This information can be retrieved in an aggregator or can be syndicated onto the library's Web page. In some environments, social bookmarking might also be useful for collecting links to resources useful to patrons; these bookmarks can also be syndicated on the library's Web site. As with company libraries, wikis can be used to collect institutional knowledge and best practices that will benefit the organization. If there is some demand for synchronous virtual reference among the service population, IM or commercial virtual reference are both good options. Online instruction can be provided using podcasting or screencasting. Many of these tools serve common needs across library types.

Some special libraries house special collections such as historical records, manuscripts, photographs, art, and other artifacts. One way to make these materials more accessible is to provide a way for people to view them online. This can be accomplished with photo-sharing software. Librarians can take photos of items in their collection and place them on a photo-sharing service or in gallery software. This allows people who are unable to visit the collection to view it, and, for institutions with rotating displays, it enables people to see what's not currently on display. Librarians can also use this technique to catalog their collection visually, adding descriptive metadata to their online collection with tags that describe each item. For local history collections, patrons with long-time ties to the community can also be asked to scan historical photos and documents (or bring them in for librarians to scan) that can then be made available online without the items being in the library's physical collection.

Elise C. Cole, Local History Librarian & AskUs? Coordinator, Oakville Public Library, Oakville, Ontario

When dealing with special collections and the public that I serve, the top three technologies are as follows:

Blogs: You'll note that I have a blog (canadianlib genie.blogspot.com). I've organized two preconferences to the annual Seminar of the Ontario Genealogical Society titled, "Helping Genealogists Climb Family Trees @ Your Library." In both cases, and particularly when we were in Windsor, where we had participants from the U.S., it became apparent that there was a gap in knowledge about resources dealing with Canadian online family/social history research resources, both fee and free. While the blog is targeted at librarians and library staff providing specialized reference on this large topic, I know it is also read by professional and amateur genealogists.

Synchronous online reference: While I do not yet use this mode of communication with my clients, this is the best method of communication when dealing with researchers at a distance, and also when dealing with more fragile items. Given the fact that many of my researchers are adults, my current delivery of information via e-mail and in response to e-mail inquiries works well for this age group.

Photo-sharing apps: A great deal of information is becoming available due to various heritage photo databases. Since we're a smaller library system and we do not maintain an archive, we aren't able to retain and properly store these photos. In addition, many people and partner heritage organizations do not want to yet donate their photo collections. So I developed our Scanning Bees. We partner with a local group, the Trafalgar Township Historical Society (TTHS), and have a number of days where we have staff, Society volunteers, and scanning equipment set up, and let people stop by with their photos. We scan these photos, the Society Volunteers make notes about the photos and their content, and the member of the public donates the electronic copy to the Society. In turn, we have an agreement with TTHS to use the photos in Oakville Images, which then feeds into Halton Images (images. halinet.on.ca), and then into Images Canada (images canada.ca). People who find one of these photos during a search of any of the above access points and want a copy will be put in touch with TTHS, who can use the photo-reprint service as a fundraiser for their organization.

Selling Social Software to Your Staff

Many librarians have stories about new initiatives, technologies, and services at their library that have failed. In some cases, an initiative seemed to be exactly right for the library, but for some reason didn't work out as well as it should have. Sometimes this failure is due to lack of staff buy-in. An enthusiastic staff is critical to the success of any new program or service, since staff members are generally charged with its implementation. Initiatives that are planned by administrators and simply handed down to staff are more likely to fail than those where staff is involved. If staff members do not feel invested in new technology, they will not support it. If a library director is considering offering an IM reference service, for example, she could simply tell staff members that this is being done—or better yet, she could involve staff in all levels of planning and implementation. An involved staff ensures buy-in.

Encourage staff members to voice their concerns about any new idea. Sometimes staff members may be reluctant to adopt a new technology because they assume it's just the "hot new thing" and won't last. Or perhaps they're afraid of the technology because they fear it will be difficult for them to learn. If you want to engage your staff in the process, you will need to address these concerns—and create an environment where staff members feel comfortable sharing their concerns. Otherwise, they will continue to hold these negative beliefs about the technology and may even just see it as "my supervisor's pet project."

Some libraries have organized committees to evaluate new technologies for use in the library. Michael Casey, Division Director of Technology Services for the Gwinnett County (GA) Public Library, formed an Emerging Technology Committee that examines new technologies and determines which ones might be useful to patrons or staff in the library.[1] It is valuable to involve staff members of different rank, age, and area of responsibility, for three reasons. First, a diverse group is more likely to come up with a wide range of ideas about how to improve the library. Secondly, a diverse group is more likely to think of how the technology could be implemented or why it shouldn't. Finally, any initiative that has a broad base of support in the library is more likely to succeed. If the committee is only made up of young tech-savvy staff or only of supervisors, other staff members may feel their views aren't being represented.

Some librarians may not only have to convince library staff members of a technology's efficacy, but also the information technology (IT) staff that operate the institution's technical infrastructure. Always involve IT staff in the planning process, so that the team can raise important security or technical issues that the library staff may not have considered. IT staff will also be more likely to support an initiative they are invested in and have been involved in from the beginning. Communication between the library and IT is critical, and the more each group understands and respects the needs of the other, the more likely it is that the library will have the freedom to pursue new social technologies.

The final step in assuring staff buy-in is training. Once you have decided to implement a specific technology at your library, you will need to teach your staff how to use it. If staff members are not comfortable using the technology, they will make this clear by not using it at all or by using it less than enthusiastically. When developing staff training, it's important to consider your staff members' levels of technological savvy.

You may have people at both ends of the spectrum. Effective training will neither go over participants' heads nor be at a level that is too elementary. This may entail providing different levels of training to different groups of staff. While training should be mandatory for staff using the technology on a daily basis, it should be open to all library staff. If the reference staff is creating a blog, for example, it will be useful for other staff members to understand what a blog is and to see the tools their library is using to communicate with patrons. In addition to training, documentation about the technology will help staff remember what they've learned later on.

Selling Social Software to Your Patrons

Once you have your staff on board with a new social technology for your patrons, the next step is to get patrons on board. Even when new technology is designed to help patrons, there still may be some resistance, which can be reduced by presenting the benefits of your new technology rather than focusing on the technology itself. Marketing and training often go a long way toward increasing adoption. Ignoring the importance of selling social software to your patrons may negate all of the hard work you did to get your tools up and running.

Patrons' response to a new technology often depends on how you present it. Telling patrons about the library's new "blog" or "wiki" might turn off anyone who's not a technology enthusiast, even if the content on the blog or wiki would be of interest. A blog or a wiki is just a tool; the content is the important element. If you create a wiki subject guide, talk about the new subject guide created by your library where patrons can add their insights. If you create a blog to provide readers' advisory services, talk about your new service to recommend good books. If you implement a social bookmarking tool, talk about how patrons can keep track of Web sites and online articles they might need later. It's much more important to talk about how the tool will benefit patrons than to talk about the tool itself. If an application generates RSS feeds, you don't even actually have to point your patrons to it. A tool like Feed2JS lets your blog look like just another page on your library Web site. No one needs to know that you've started using a social bookmarking service to create a subject guide, if you just syndicate the resources onto your site. RSS allows you to make content from other sites look at home on your Web site. Many of your patrons probably use RSS feeds every day, via My Yahoo! and other popular Web sites, without even knowing it. The more familiar your social software tools look to patrons and the fewer barriers you create to access, the more likely your patrons will be to use your new tools.

Marketing is an important part of launching any new service. How would patrons know about your new IM reference service if you didn't mention it anywhere? How long would it take them to find the screencast tutorials linked on your Web site without hearing about their existence? Marketing can take place in a variety of ways. The front page of the library Web site is always a good place to advertise new services. On a college or university campus, librarians could do radio and print announcements in all of the school publications; tear-off flyers are also a popular option. Librarians working in business, government, and other institutions can advertise their new services through the staff intranet. In smaller offices, word-of-mouth is always an easy and cost-effective way to get the word out. Libraries could distribute bookmarks that advertise the new service, since those will likely get used. Public libraries can place flyers in other popular places in the community—schools, grocery stores, and church bulletin boards—which is also a good way to market to people who may not traditionally use the library. This advertising not only markets the new social software tool, but also markets the library as an institution that is keeping up with technology.

Finally, depending on the tool, it may be worthwhile to offer training to patrons. While many libraries offer basic Internet classes, they often have little available for those beyond that level. Some libraries are starting to offer classes on tools such as social bookmarking, photo sharing, and blogging. These tools can benefit patrons in their everyday lives by helping them share photos and information with friends and keep up with information. When a new technology is introduced at the library, classes should be offered to explain the technology to patrons. When the Orange County Library System in Florida (www.ocls.info/Programs/Computer Classes) began podcasting, they also started offering classes on how to find, listen to, and create podcasts. If your library decides to implement a wiki subject guide, it would make sense to offer classes on how it works and what patrons can do with it. Documentation is also important, but some patrons learn more from taking a class than reading instructions. People who are intimidated by new technologies may be willing to try them in a comfortable learning environment with a knowledgeable instructor.

Social software is more than just a "hot new thing," but when any technology is implemented for cachet alone, it is almost sure to fail. Technology should be implemented in response to a need and should be used in libraries to make librarians' lives easier or to serve patrons better. This requires librarians to have a clear understanding of their patrons' needs, which can be accomplished through a variety of formal and informal assessment methods. Any new technology also must be presented to both staff and patrons in such a way as to assure buy-in. Involving stakeholders in the decision-making process, making sure access to social tools is seamless, marketing new tools, and training staff and patrons are all keys to success for any technology implementation in libraries. While it does require careful planning, the use of social software in libraries can lead to unprecedented online communication, collaboration, and community building.

Endnote

1. Michael Casey, "Your IT Department, Buy-In, and Team Work," Library Crunch, November 22, 2005, www.librarycrunch.com/2005/11/your_it_department_buyin_and_t.html (accessed April 3, 2006).

Chapter 15

Keeping Up: A Primer

In our profession, change is as inevitable as it is constant. People change, communities change, technologies change, and libraries change. Today's service population at most libraries differs dramatically from the communities of the 1990s. Populations may grow more diverse, more affluent, or more tech savvy. As people age, so do their needs, wants, and attitudes toward the library; many likely use the library in different ways than they did 17 years ago. Staffs at libraries have also changed; librarians have different skill sets and different strengths. We also have many more technologies that are growing and changing faster than ever before, making it difficult to keep up with new developments. Librarians, though, must keep abreast of change to provide the best service to their patrons. Effective planning demands that we remain aware of developing technologies, trends in libraries, social and economic forces affecting libraries, the needs and wants of our service population, and the strengths and weaknesses of our organization. Knowing where you are and what you need can help you plan for where you want to be in the future.

By the time you read this book, you will likely have a choice of even more online social tools than described here. While this book is designed to provide an overview of current social technologies and help you determine how to apply them in libraries, you may want to see what's happening now with the ones that interest you the most. You can keep up in a variety of ways: Many classes focus on blogs, wikis, RSS, and social bookmarking. Conferences all over the country discuss social software. You can also keep up with technology in libraries without spending a lot of money. In the following sections, you'll find a number of tips on keeping up with the latest developments in library technology with or without institutional funding. You can design your own professional development plan using materials freely available on the Web, and minimize information overload with RSS and social bookmarking. The Web site companion to this book (www.sociallibraries.com) contains many additional Web resources to help librarians keep up with the newest social software in libraries.

1: Keep Up with the Professional Literature

Print and online journals offer quality articles to help keep you informed of technological developments in libraries. Some of these may be available through your library's online databases or professional collection. If not, your own local public library or a nearby college may offer access to journals in library and information science. You can also read many journals online for free, from trade journals that post full or partial content on their sites to open access journals. Many Web sites also offer the latest technology news and provide current awareness services. While the following list is far from exhaustive, it offers an assortment of quality content to get you started:

- *Ariadne* (www.ariadne.ac.uk) – This British quarterly Web magazine covers technology issues that affect digital libraries.

- *Bulletin of the American Society for Information Science and Technology* (www.asis.org/Bulletin) – This monthly magazine discusses issues that affect librarians and information scientists.

- *Cites & Insights* (citesandinsights.info) – This bimonthly Web journal, authored and edited by Walt Crawford, primarily focuses on technology and policy issues with articles covering discussions in the biblioblogosphere.

- *College and Research Libraries* (www.ala.org/ala/acrl/acrlpubs/crljournal/collegeresearch.htm) – The scholarly journal of the Association of College and Research Libraries covers issues that affect academic libraries. The current year's articles are accessible only to members, but back issues are available free to everyone.

- *Crossroads* (webjunction.org/do/Navigation?category=551) – Each issue of WebJunction's monthly newsletter covers a different subject relevant to technology use in public libraries.

- *Current Cites* (lists.webjunction.org/currentcites) – The editors of this Web site scour the literature in the information technology field to provide a monthly, annotated bibliography of the best recent articles. While some are from print journals, the majority are freely available online.

- *D-Lib Magazine* (www.dlib.org) – This monthly online scholarly journal contains articles related to digital libraries.

- *EDUCAUSE Quarterly* (www.educause.edu/eq) – This peer-reviewed journal with articles about technology issues in education is geared toward educating academic and IT administrators on instructional technologies.

- *EDUCAUSE Review* (www.educause.edu/er) – EDUCAUSE's more mainstream bimonthly magazine covers the use of technologies in education.

- *First Monday* (www.firstmonday.org) – This open access peer-reviewed journal covers Internet development, policies, and trends.

- *inCite* (alia.org.au/publishing/incite) – This journal of the Australian Library and Information Association covers issues affecting libraries, often including articles about technology applications in libraries.

- *Library Journal* (www.libraryjournal.com) – Geared to librarians in all settings, this bimonthly magazine includes articles about emerging technologies and technology applications in libraries.

- *netConnect* (www.libraryjournal.com/index.asp?layout=net Connect) – *Library Journal*'s quarterly supplement focuses specifically on Internet applications in libraries.

- *New York Times: Technology* (www.nytimes.com/pages/ technology) – The technology section of the *New York Times* reports on technology trends, which may affect libraries in the future.

- *SLJ.com* (www.schoollibraryjournal.com) – This online edition of *School Library Journal* offers articles about providing library services to young people. Many of the articles cover emerging technologies in the field.

Librarians can also find quality journal articles about technology in libraries by searching the growing LIS repositories. A repository is a space on the Web where people can deposit documents they have written, on which the author holds copyright or which he has permission from the publisher to archive. Currently, most people who archive their materials in repositories are from outside the U.S., but as knowledge of open access repositories is growing, this may soon change. Notable LIS repositories include DLIST (dlist.sir.arizona.edu), E-LIS (eprints.rclis.org), and SDL (drtc.isibang.ac.in/sdl). These repositories are searchable, and some offer an RSS feed of newly added materials.

Lesson 2: Keep Up with Blogs

Hundreds of bloggers write about library issues, and tens of thousands more write about technology. These bloggers act as filters, keeping up with current technology and often condensing their knowledge about a topic into a single post. This prevents readers from having to do all the research themselves; blog posts also often include additional links to related resources. Many bloggers eagerly try out cutting-edge technologies and review them for their readers. If you have a question about a certain technology mentioned, try contacting the blogger in the comments section of his or her blog or through e-mail; most are happy to engage in discussion.

The sheer variety of blogs makes it difficult to find the best ones for the subjects that interest you. Start by reading a few of the more popular and easy-to-find blogs and see where the links lead. If one blogger you frequently read links to another blog about podcasting, check it out to see if it interests you. Once you start reading several blogs, subscribe to their RSS feeds in an aggregator so you don't have to check each to see if it's been updated. With an RSS, whenever a blog is updated, the updated content will simply show up in your aggregator.

Since blogs come and go quickly, and new blogs may gain prominence after the printing of this book, use the list at the companion Web site (www.sociallibraries.com) to find some of the best blogs for keeping up with social software in libraries. The site also contains an OPML file of those same blogs that you can download and subscribe to in your aggregator. (OPML is an XML format for outlines, and can include a list of RSS feeds that, when placed in an aggregator, will subscribe you to all of the RSS feeds inside that file.)

Lesson 3: Keep Up with Other Librarians in Online Communities

Online communities are a great way to keep up with what's happening in libraries and communicate with other people using social technologies in libraries. Online communities for librarians range from Web sites and online forums to wikis and electronic mailing lists. There are more than a hundred electronic mailing lists dedicated to various types of library services. Try a few different electronic mailing lists for a few weeks to see if the conversation interests you; if not, you can simply unsubscribe. It's important to be judicious when choosing mailing lists, because you can quickly become overwhelmed by the constant flow of e-mails. If you're concerned about receiving too many e-mails, you can often subscribe to a digest, where a number of e-mail messages are condensed into a single post. Here are just a few online communities that may help you learn more about social software in libraries:

- *Blended Librarian* (blendedlibrarian.org) – This online community for academic librarians working to blend technology, instruction, and library services includes discussion forums, live chats, and Webcasts.

- *DIG_REF* (www.vrd.org/Dig_Ref/dig_ref.shtml) – This electronic mailing list is devoted to discussing virtual reference services.

- *LibGaming* (groups.google.com/group/LibGaming) – This Google Group is devoted to gaming in libraries.

- *Library Instruction Wiki* (instructionwiki.org) – This is a space for librarians to share handouts, tutorials, and ideas for providing library instruction.

- *Library Success: A Best Practices Wiki* (www.libsuccess.org) – Librarians can use this space to share their success stories about providing services to patrons.

- *LITA-L* (www.lita.org/ala/lita/litamembership/litaldisclists/litalotherdiscussion.htm) – This electronic mailing list of the Library and Information Technology Association lets community members discuss information technology in libraries.

- *OFFCAMP* (listserv.utk.edu/archives/offcamp.html) – Librarians can tap into this electronic mailing list to provide services to off-campus learners.

- *Web4Lib* (lists.webjunction.org/web4lib) – Use this electronic mailing list to discuss Web applications in libraries.

- *WebJunction* (webjunction.org) – Covering a variety of topics, this online community includes articles, online courses, and discussion forums. While WebJunction was developed to serve small public libraries, librarians from a variety of settings frequent the community.

Lesson 4: Keep Up with Webcasts and Podcasts

Online learning has become quite popular during the past few years, and more online training opportunities are being offered through groups including ACRL (www.ala.org/ala/acrl/acrlproftools/elearning.htm) and EDUCAUSE (www.educause.edu/eli). Some of these e-learning opportunities can be costly and out of reach for many librarians, but a number of organizations offer e-learning for free through self-paced modules, Webcasts, and podcasts. Some of these organizations let users interact in real-time with the speaker; others offer an archive of past Webcasts for free. Some have also started recording podcast interviews with important figures in the field and making them available online for free. While some free e-learning opportunities may not be as structured as for-pay classes, they offer valuable knowledge at a price anyone can afford:

- *Blended Librarian* (blendedlibrarian.org/events.html) – This online community offers free Webcasts on subjects related to Web and instructional design.

- *Engadget* (podcasts.engadget.com) – A companion to the popular blog, this site offers podcasts about the latest gadgets for gaming, music, media viewing, photography, and communication.

- *Infopeople* (infopeople.org/training/webcasts/index.php) – This organization serves California libraries by improving the technology skills of librarians. Infopeople offers live Webcasts for free to California residents but opens up its archives to anyone who wishes to view them.

- *IT Conversations* (www.itconversations.com/index.html) – This listener-supported Web site provides free podcasts with famous tech enthusiasts on a wide variety of technology-related topics, ranging from conference talks to interviews to book readings.

- *OCLC* (www.oclc.org/education/conferences/presentations/ default.htm) – OCLC offers symposia and talks at various conferences on topics related to technology and libraries. Many of these talks are recorded and made available online for those who could not attend.

- *OPAL* (Online Programming for All Libraries) (www.opal online.org) – This membership organization is devoted to offering library-related programming online for free. Programs range from online events for public library patrons to professional development Webcasts for librarians. The Webcasts are free for anyone who wishes to attend and are archived as podcasts after the session.

- *SirsiDynix Institute* (www.sirsidynixinstitute.com) – As an arm of the library automation vendor SirsiDynix, the Institute offers free live biweekly Webcasts featuring important figures in the field. Most of the talks center on information management, information technology, and library trends. Its Webcasts are archived in a variety of formats, including podcasts.

- *Talking with Talis* (talk.talis.com) – This library automation vendor offers free podcast talks with leading thinkers on such subjects as Web 2.0, the Semantic Web, social software, and library trends.

All of the podcasts have a feed you can subscribe to in an aggregator so that you will be informed when a new podcast is available for download. A podcatcher such as Juice (juicereceiver.sourceforge.net) or iTunes (www.apple.com/itunes) automatically downloads the podcasts onto your computer. Some organizations offer subscriptions to an e-mail alert service or a newsletter to alert you to upcoming events. The popularity of online learning is growing, and we will likely see many more free podcasts, Webcasts, and even entire online conferences in the future.

Lesson 5: Keeping Up with Conferences and Continuing Education

Conferences and continuing education courses have always been the gold standard for improving our skills and learning more about our professional areas of interest. Continuing education courses are available online at colleges and universities and through local and state organizations. Some courses are quite affordable, especially for members of the sponsoring organization. Due to the high cost of travel and the growing availability of broadband access, online continuing education courses have become quite prevalent. While synchronous online courses include many of the same elements as face-to-face sessions, they lack some of the social aspects of in-person classes and conferences. Many conference attendees report that the best parts of conferences are the conversations that go on in-between sessions, in lounges and bars, and during meals. During these times, people with common interests can discuss what they are doing at their libraries and share ideas for implementing technology in the future; people can also make valuable connections at conferences with leading figures in the field.

While there are several major national conferences related to library technologies, such as Computers in Libraries, Internet Librarian, LITA Forum, and Access, there are even more regional, state, and local conferences around the world that offer education on many of the same topics. Local conferences often cost less, both in travel and registration, and some continuing education courses offered in your local area may be less expensive than those offered online. Local events also give you the opportunity to meet librarians from other local institutions. This sort of networking is valuable in building future local partnerships.

Many librarians can only afford to attend local conferences, but you can still learn from events you cannot attend in person. Bloggers now often cover every session at the major conferences, describing what the speakers discussed and giving their own impressions of sessions. This is not only useful for those unable to attend the conference but also for attendees who had to choose between two appealing concurrent sessions.

Bloggers often tag relevant posts with the name of the conference so that all of the conference reports can be found together on Technorati. Many conference speakers or conference organizers also archive presentation materials online so you can access PowerPoint slides and/or handouts after the event. Some conferences record their speakers and offer the talks and other materials for sale. Often, conference papers are published in professional journals. If you find a presentation that raises questions or intrigues you, contact the presenter directly; the library profession is full of people who enjoy discussing their work and sharing with colleagues. So while you may not be able to fly across the country to attend a conference, you still may be able to get a great deal from it without ever leaving home.

Lesson 6: Keep Up by Playing with Technology

You can learn a lot from reading about new social technologies and how librarians are implementing them. However, the best way to learn a technology is to use it. Playing with a technology offers valuable insights into its pros and cons. Only when you create your own screencast will you understand whether the benefits outweigh the drawbacks for your institution. Only when you use IM to chat with friends and colleagues will you have a good sense of whether to implement it at your library. Whether you are considering implementing a particular social tool in your library or are just curious about it, you can get a much better understanding of the technology by trying it out.

Most of the technologies mentioned in this book are free or at least have free versions available, and it is usually easy to get an account or download the software. You can set up a hosted blog or wiki and start adding content to it within minutes. You can also start archiving and tagging Web sites or photos after filling out a brief registration form on one of the many photo-sharing or social bookmarking services. Some of the best audio recording software is free or open source. Likewise, some screencasting software is free, and you can often obtain 30-day free trials of the pricier but more sophisticated software products, which gives you enough time to test out the software to determine whether you want to purchase it for your library. Once you have software set up, use it. Bookmark pages, write blog posts, edit a wiki page, create a screencast, vodcast, or podcast, and IM with a friend. You will learn more from actually using the software than you ever could by reading articles about it. Besides, playing with technology can be a lot of fun!

Lesson 7: Keep Up While Keeping Sane

It can be difficult to keep up with new developments in library technology, and you can drive yourself crazy in the process. Key to keeping up with technology in libraries is realizing that you can't keep up with everything. You need to prioritize. What subjects are of greatest interest to you? What subjects are most relevant to your library? Focus on these and worry less about the others. It's good to be aware of other subjects, but you can't be an expert in everything. If your library is unhappy with its catalog, it might be a good idea to keep up with developments from library automation vendors. If you're looking for ways to create tutorials, you may want to look at the social tools that can make that happen for you. If you're interested in the future of handheld computing, focus on that. As your interests or situations change, you can change your focus and start reading different blogs and articles. When designing a plan for keeping up with technology in libraries, it is important to remain flexible and realistic about the amount of time you can devote.

Even after narrowing your focus, you may still have much research to do but no time to do it, adding the risk of missing potentially important information. You may not have the time to read the latest issue of *Ariadne*, for example, and could miss reading a timely article about Web services just when your institution is thinking about implementing a similar project. Your ability to keep up with what's going on in your areas of interest is directly related to your ability to manage information online using RSS and social bookmarking.

Many of the Internet sites mentioned in this chapter offer RSS feeds of some sort. All blogs and podcasts have RSS feeds that notify subscribers when a new post or podcast has been published. Journal RSS feeds usually contain the table of contents of the newest issue, with links to each article. With RSS, rather than visiting each Web site to see if there is new content, you can simply subscribe to the RSS feed and the information will be pushed to you via an aggregator. (You can also convert your RSS feeds into e-mail alerts and have them sent to your inbox if you're more comfortable with an e-mail format.) You can use social bookmarking to help you keep up when you're busy. If you find an interesting journal article but don't have time to read it right away, simply bookmark it and assign tags that will help you find it later. If you're doing research on a particular software product, use social bookmarking to organize your research online. Use your bookmarks as an online filing system, making things findable that you may want to use later.

There is no one "right" way to keep up with technology in libraries. You will need to design your own approach to staying current on subjects of interest, using a combination of tools and strategies. Keeping up requires flexibility and a knowledge of the relevant resources for your interests, funding level, and time you have to devote. While reading journals or blogs may be sufficient for subjects of ongoing interest, when you need in-depth research on a topic, you may want to ask questions on electronic mailing lists, try out software, or take a class. You may also try going outside the field to see how professionals in other areas are using technology. Whatever your strategy, it's important to remember that you can't keep up with everything, and sometimes it's better to file something away for later when you can give it your full attention. While keeping up with technology in libraries can involve a significant investment of time, it will help you better anticipate trends and serve your patrons.

Chapter 16

Future Trends in Social Software

Over the next few years, our information landscape will continue to change. We will see new tools emerge and have new opportunities to provide services to patrons using social software. This book focuses on giving you the tools you need to make practical decisions about technology and how to implement social software successfully in your library. No matter what type of new social software tools appears in the coming years, the fundamental guidelines for successfully implementing technologies in libraries remain constant.

The following sections highlight future trends and new ideas about how technology may impact our library systems. As social software becomes more mainstream, we will see changes in the way people and institutions use these tools and how they are integrated into our daily lives. The proliferation of online content will continue to raise questions about ownership and digital preservation, issues that libraries need to be concerned with. Change is inevitable in both technology and libraries, but the key is to assess your patrons' needs regularly and keep up with their use of technology.

Beyond the Hype: How We Will Integrate Social Software into Our Daily Lives

Currently, much social software is still in the early adopter phase; the general public has, for the most part, not yet caught on to the technologies. Ultimately, some technologies will go mainstream, as blogging and IM have, and some will not. The sheer number of social applications entering the market each year makes it unlikely that all will attract a big enough audience to be profitable over time. Because social sites are only useful with a critical mass of users, 50 different social bookmarking sites or photo-sharing sites can't make it in the marketplace. People may try out many different applications, but ultimately, they will go with those that are most popular or that their friends use. The other issue is that the "coolness factor" will eventually wear off; applications need to offer practical value to consumers. Wikis are a great tool, but people who can't find a practical use for them in their daily lives will eventually stop playing with the software. Other applications on the market right now are fun and clever but don't really provide functionality that people need. Technology will only go mainstream if people see it as a useful addition to their daily lives.

People use many different social software tools—blogs, wikis, RSS aggregators, photo-sharing software, social bookmarking software—and those that endure will likely be those that work well together. For example, photo-sharing software and social bookmarking software should make it easy to send a photo or a link to your blog. You should be able to set up your aggregator to send posts you're interested in to your social bookmarking application in one click. All content should have an RSS feed associated with it so you can take the content and syndicate it elsewhere. In the future, we should be able to view and create content for any of these tools from a central place rather than visiting dozens of different Web sites. Applications that lock content up and applications that don't work well with other social tools ultimately will not survive the competition in the social software marketplace.

The social software applications that do go mainstream will support our activities and interactions in the physical world. For example, people use blogs, wikis, and IM at conferences to enhance their face-to-face interactions. They make plans for the conference and share tips about the venue on wikis. They cover the conference on blogs. Finally, they discuss the conference in real time with other attendees—and nonattendees—using IM or an IRC channel. Essentially, this creates a record of the conference and becomes more than just a collection of talks, people's impressions, and details on what went on behind the scenes. Tagging blogs and photos with the name of the conference lets people easily view all of the collected media from the event. Conference organizers could also add social networking software so people can connect with like-minded conference-goers; spaces for pre- and post-conference discussions of presentations with presenters; streaming audio or video from sessions for those who could not attend; and recorded podcasts of all the talks. Only when social software applications support our personal and professional lives will they become more than a temporary interest. Time will tell which applications will become mainstream and which will never move beyond the realm of hype.

Localization of Social Software

When people started using the World Wide Web in the mid-1990s, one of its most exciting aspects was the ability to connect with like-minded people from all over the world. In the library world, the Web has facilitated an unprecedented sharing of ideas among tens of thousands of librarians internationally. While this connection is very important, we are most concerned with our local environment. We live, eat, sleep, work, and play in our local area. For social software to be truly useful, it must support our day-to-day activities, which are ultimately local. We are starting to see a shift toward local interests in social software; people ultimately want to know about the best restaurants, hair salons, yoga classes, or car mechanics in their local area. They want to be able to find people and get together with those who have similar interests.

While most social software tools, including blogs, wikis, or podcasts, can be globally or locally focused, a number of social software applications are specifically designed for use at the local level. While Facebook is available to qualified users all over the world, each academic institution or organization has its own Facebook, and users are only free to explore the profiles within their institution or organization. You can click to see others at your institution who are interested in similar things and see who is taking the same classes as you. Essentially, Facebook encourages local connections.

craigslist (www.craigslist.org) is designed in much the same way, with craigslists in many areas for buying and selling things, finding jobs, and connecting with people locally. Meetup (www.meetup.com) is also designed to connect people who are interested in certain activities or who have common interests. Judy's Book (www.judysbook.com) is a site for people to rate and post reviews of restaurants, services, or anything else in their local area. People can also post questions about their local area for other knowledgeable users to answer. Local rating systems such as these allow people to discover what their neighbors consider to be the best in their area.

Of course, wikis and recommendation sites are only useful if people use them. In big cities, local sites often have a large number of participants, while in rural areas, recommendations may reflect the views of just a few people. Time will tell which local social software tools are sustainable and how effective they are outside of major cities. Newspapers are also getting into the social software game, allowing readers to review restaurants and other local institutions; newspapers have the added benefit of an existing Web presence that people turn to for local information. In markets overwhelmed by different local social software options, local media that can adapt their business model may be able to create the most sustainable local social software applications.

College and University-Branded Social Software

College students are among the most prolific users of social software, including blogs, wikis, social networking sites, and IM. Colleges and universities have started developing and branding their own social software solutions for a number of reasons. First, campus social software makes it easier for an institution to keep up with what their students are talking about. Second, it's just good PR; schools with their own blog-hosting or social bookmarking software look as though they are keeping up with technology, something that concerns many prospective students. Finally, college-created social software can help students find other like-minded people on campus. Young people blog on many different services, including Xanga (www.xanga.com), MySpace (www.myspace.com), and LiveJournal (www.livejournal.com). Blogs hosted on a university's Web site are easier for classmates to find, which facilitates local social networking.

Many colleges and universities have implemented university-wide blogging initiatives. Many simply offer blog hosting and a directory of all user blogs. The University of Warwick in Coventry, England, however, took a different approach with its Warwick Blogs (blogs.warwick.ac.uk). Warwick Blogs, which was custom-built, resembles a social networking site in design. Each student and every faculty or staff member has his or her own blog, which can be found in the directory by academic area or name. Users can customize the look of their blogs and easily upload images. Using a type of structured blogging, they can also can post reviews of movies, books, music, and television shows, which can be retrieved from a common pot of reviews by type. From the front page of Warwick Blogs, you can get a good sense of the zeitgeist of the university: what people are writing about, what they are photographing, and what they are tagging.

Universities have also started to offer other university-branded social software tools to their students, faculty, and staff. As discussed in Chapter 8, the University of Pennsylvania implemented PennTags as an academic social bookmarking service for members of the university to keep track of research and create bibliographies. A number of colleges and universities have their own special area of iTunes, where students can download lectures and other academic audio content. Universities are also starting to develop official wikis that community members can use as a guide to the institution and area, a project space, a personal space, and more. Case Western Reserve University in Ohio (wiki.case.edu) and the University of Calgary (wiki.ucalgary.ca) both host wikis that members of the academic community can freely add to and edit. This lets student groups, academic departments, classes, and project groups develop their own space in the wiki. With the growing popularity and usefulness of social software, many colleges and universities will jump on the social applications bandwagon in the years to come.

Service-Oriented Architecture and Web Services

Software developers have worked for decades to find a happy medium between simplicity and complexity. In the early days of software development, developers found themselves creating complex applications with functional parts that could not easily be reused. They initially solved this problem by cutting and pasting code from one application into another to achieve the same functionality. But this approach backfired when programmers realized that they would have to fix every instance of the code if a bug was later discovered. Software architects determined that it was not necessarily the specific code but its functionality that they wanted to reuse. So, instead of creating large, complicated individual programs that use pieces of the same code, they can create simple programs that can be joined together in different ways, an approach better known as Service-Oriented Architecture (SOA).[1]

According to Hao He, "SOA is an architectural style whose goal is to achieve loose coupling among interacting software agents."[2] Software agents can be service providers and/or service consumers. All services are self-contained, interoperable pieces of software that provide a specific functionality. Service consumers are pieces of software that need other software to complete a specific function. The service consumer is able to determine which software provides that functionality using a directory service. The consumer then sends a request to the provider in a language the provider understands (typically XML), and the provider offers the requested service. Applications usually contain many of these individual services that can be reused in other applications. Most applications have a specific provider hard-coded in the service; however, functions can be programmed to search the directory for available providers who specialize in the requested functionality. This reduces the dependence of consumers on a specific provider.

Let's use an example outside the computer world to explain the relationship between service consumers and providers. Suppose a woman in ancient Greece seeks an oracle for an answer to a question. (The woman is the service consumer, and the oracle is the service provider.) More than one oracle in Greece might be able to answer her specific question, so she finds the list of oracles (the directory service). The woman will choose an appropriate oracle and pose her question. However, asking an oracle a question involves a specific protocol, in that the question must be asked in a way the oracle understands. When the oracle answers the question, the woman's service has been provided. She does not care how the oracle divined the answer to her question, just as the service consumer does not need to understand the underlying functionality of the service provider. As long as she gets the answer to her question, she has made a successful transaction.

Web services are just one approach to service-oriented architecture, but they are currently the most popular because they are built using commonly used platform independent protocols.[3] Often, an individual application involves many different functions. If a developer codes all of the functionality into one application, it becomes more difficult to separate the different functions if someone wants to combine them differently at a later date. With Web services, rather than building a single application with all of the functions, programmers create a separate, self-contained application for each function. These applications can then be combined in various ways based on the needs of the developer of the larger application. If multiple Web services provide the same functionality, developers can choose which one best meets their needs rather than having to combine applications from the same provider. Because they are developed using the Web services platform, each Web service will work with any other Web service; they are completely interoperable.

Currently, interoperability is one of the biggest concerns in the application development field. Consumers often get locked into a particular software vendor because they need software that works together. For example, a library system might wish to use an Interlibrary Loan (ILL) module from a different vendor, which will not work with their current Integrated Library System (ILS). Hence, they may be forced to purchase an ILL module that is compatible with their ILS vendor, but that does not quite meet their needs. This is common in libraries and other fields. With Web services, all the applications speak the same language, preventing this lock-in and creating a more competitive marketplace, where users are free to choose the best software for their needs. Another benefit of Web services is that no developer is limited to his or her own imagination or talents when designing new software. Since each Web service is self-contained, interoperable, and reusable, developers can build upon the work of others, perhaps using the services in ways the original developers hadn't even imagined.

Web services exist to share and build upon existing functionality, which can be attractive to companies that want to see their applications improved. Many companies write an application programming interface (API) for their products, which they then make available to developers. An API exposes a set of functions that make up the application and can be used in the creation of other applications. This allows developers to access the functions of another application in their own applications, so that they don't need to build the functionality from scratch.

Some companies only make their APIs available to official developers of their software, or make them available for a fee. Others make their APIs freely available so users can extend the functionality of their product far beyond their original intent. This is what happened with Google Maps (maps.google.com). Google let developers embed Google Maps into their own applications using JavaScript. Many developers could see the benefits of adding location information to their applications, and the Google Maps API (www.google.com/apis/maps) offered a way to do this without having to reinvent the wheel. The first application to use the Google Maps API was Housing Maps (www.housingmaps.com), which takes information from craigslist about apartments for rent and lets users see where these apartments are located on a map. When moving to a new city, an individual could see where an apartment was located without knowing any street names. This sort of application ultimately became known as a "mashup," because it involves combining (or mashing up) two separate applications, or an application and data, to create an entirely new one. Google Maps has been used in mashups for reported crimes (www.chicagocrime.org), Census information for a small geographic area (65.39.85.13/google/default. htm), the locations of bike routes in an area (www.andreischeinkman.com/ bikemap), and much more. Any content that would be enhanced by location information—including restaurant reviews, prices at gas stations, job ads, and tourist information—has been integrated with Google Maps.

Suppose your library wanted a Web page to display community information, such as the locations of police and fire stations, library and local parks, and sites for buying parking permits. By incorporating a map, patrons could see how far the locations are, get directions from their current location, and map the routes themselves rather than calling the library for directions. The library could also provide maps with crime information or other demographics such as average housing prices and Census data.

Often, a library does not have a specific book a patron is looking for, and the patron does not have time to wait for the item to arrive via ILL. If the library is part of a consortium, information about member libraries owning that book could be mapped out, so the patron could easily find the closest facility with another copy. Libraries could harness the holdings information from other local libraries—and even bookstores—to show on a map where a particular book can be found.

Currently, though, there are significant walls between different systems and sources of information. While some of our collections are part of our ILS, most online holdings exist as separate islands, which are hidden in many cases. As a result, our collections are not truly integrated: They are difficult to search and locked-in to vendor-specific systems. Library vendors have each tried to invent the wheel themselves, building all-encompassing ILS solutions of proprietary parts with little collaboration or interoperability. Web services encourage sharing this functionality to decrease the programming burden and increase interoperability. Web services are more modular, so self-contained functional pieces can be combined and reused by different vendors. Web services offer methods of separating data from applications, making it easier for software from different vendors to work together. This will require a revolution in vendors' thinking about software development, but it will also produce revolutionary improvements in using library middleware.

Power to the People: Peer-to-Peer and Distributed Computing

When most people hear the term "peer-to-peer," they think of illegal music file sharing. While it's true peer-to-peer can be used for illegal file sharing, there is nothing inherently illegal about the technology. Before peer-to-peer, file sharing required a client to access the file and a server to store the file. With peer-to-peer, though, there is no centralized server; each person's computer acts both as a client and a server. When you begin downloading a movie in a peer-to-peer network, as pieces of that movie are downloaded, they are also made available on your computer to be downloaded by others. So a peer-to-peer network relies on the bandwidth, storage space, and CPU time of all computers taking part. The more people on the network, the faster the downloads, because tasks are distributed across more computers. Peer-to-peer technology is often used to share very large files, particularly video and audio, as well as in VoIP networks such as Skype, where the system runs on the computers of everyone who uses it.

Distributed computing is another way to spread complex computing jobs across many computers. A centralized server or servers use multiple computers to accomplish a specific task, such as complex mathematical problems. The server gives each computer a small piece of a much larger task to accomplish. One notable example of distributed computing is the Screensaver Lifesaver (www.chem.ox.ac.uk/curecancer.html) where participants "could help find a cure for cancer by giving 'screensaver time' from their computers to the world's largest ever computational project, which will screen 3.5 billion molecules for cancer-fighting potential."[4] SETI@home (setiathome.ssl.berkeley.edu) uses the power of many personal computers to help analyze signals from space for signs of intelligent life. Rather than using supercomputers, the program runs in the background of each participant's computer so its presence isn't disruptive to the user.

Peer-to-peer and distributed computing have many legitimate applications that are being used increasingly in academia. The common thread is that all these projects are powered by the computers of many different people who are willing to share their bandwidth and CPU time. They capitalize on the network effect: The more people who use a service, the better it performs. Peer-to-peer file sharers reap some personal benefit, such as faster downloads and access to content. Participants in distributed computing projects usually have an interest in the project, but do not benefit directly from participating. Many peer-to-peer and distributed computing projects are being developed in academic institutions, so we are likely to see many more legitimate applications in the future.

Speeding Up the Net: Broadband Penetration and Internet2

Lack of broadband Internet access is one of the biggest barriers today for creating video content. This is changing rapidly, as broadband becomes more affordable and more readily available, even in rural areas. According to the Pew Internet and American Life Project, between 2005 and 2006, broadband adoption grew 40 percent, double the rate it grew between 2004 and 2005. In March 2006, 84 million Americans had broadband access at home. Broadband adoption grew 30 percent in rural areas, 63 percent among senior citizens, and 121 percent among African-Americans. This indicates that broadband is becoming more mainstream, and its adoption will continue to grow rapidly. While some rural areas still do not have access to Internet via cable or DSL, Internet access by satellite is becoming just as affordable as other broadband options.

Another interesting project that might change the way people use the Web is Internet2 (www.internet2.edu), a nonprofit consortium of more than 200 universities and members from government and the technology industry. The goal of the group is to develop and test the new network technologies that will be part of the future and much faster Internet. They have built an experimental super high-speed (10 gigabits per second as of 2006) Internet backbone, used for research purposes by the participants. Internet2 is developing cutting-edge applications and network infrastructure. Eventually, the research being done by this consortium will lead to new network technologies and faster connection speeds for consumers.

Online Collaboration Goes Mainstream

Sharing online does not always come naturally. Most people have files on their own computer and keep their knowledge locked in their heads. However, sharing is critical to the success of any collaborative work, such as group research projects, Web site redesign, or co-authored papers. Resources, ideas, and writing need to be shared in the most efficient way. While you can e-mail documents and links to your colleagues, it makes more sense to have a centralized space online where this collaboration can take place. Wikis are often used for this purpose, but recently, other wiki-inspired collaborative applications have been developed that offer more user-friendly interfaces and more project-related tools.

A number of companies offer online collaborative project spaces with wiki-like functionality, group calendars and social bookmarking built in. Many collaborative Web-based calendaring programs not only let each person have an individual calendar, but also let each project member view a group calendar with appointment details. People can schedule meetings for members on the group calendar since everyone can see what times everyone is free. More social bookmarking sites are now allowing groups to form where members can bookmark documents in a group pool of links. This is useful for project groups where all members are interested in what the others are bookmarking. Web-based office suites allow users to work on documents and spreadsheets, and then share them with friends. Products such as Zoho Writer (zoho.com) let people collaborate in developing a document in a Web-based word-processing program similar to most commercial products. Unlike wikis, there is no unusual syntax to learn. These products have taken the best features of a wiki and matched them with the ease of use of a word-processing program. The best of these collaborative products offer a comprehensive solution, with collaborative bookmarking, word processing, file sharing, calendaring, and other social features useful to organizing projects.

Issues with Online Content

One side effect of the variety of social software tools is the amount of content people put onto third-party servers. This raises issues around the ownership and preservation of content. Whether you use a hosted blog or wiki or you build a profile on MySpace, you may not have complete control over your content. Terms of service may vary, depending on the company that runs the service. Some companies give many rights to the company and few to the content creator. Many people are posting original music, video, text, and photos on MySpace, for example, without considering the rights they may be granting to MySpace to sublicense or modify their work. Here is an excerpt from MySpace's Terms of Use Agreement as of June 2006 (please note that MySpace has since changed its Terms of Use to make it less restrictive):

> By displaying or publishing ("posting") any Content, messages, text, files, images, photos, video, sounds, profiles, works of authorship, or any other materials (collectively, "Content") on or through the Services, you hereby grant to MySpace.com, a non-exclusive, fully-paid and royalty-free, worldwide license (with the right to sublicense through unlimited levels of sublicensees) to use, copy, modify, adapt, translate, publicly perform, publicly display, store, reproduce, transmit, and distribute such Content on and through the Services.[5]

While many social software services do not claim ownership of or rights to any of their members' content, some do claim complete ownership over anything posted to their service. Future legal challenges regarding services that use people's content without their fully informed consent are quite likely.

RSS feeds are designed for republishing and remixing, but what if the content in an RSS feed is protected by copyright? What if their license limits use to noncommercial purposes, and the feed is published on another company's Web site? With the availability of RSS feeds and the remixing and syndication of those feeds elsewhere, some legal challenges will arise here as well. When content becomes so portable and easy to produce (and reproduce) online, questions about who owns the content and what rights other people have to use it will ensue.

Finally, the question of permanence continues. Many people are putting their words, photos, music, videos, and other content onto services that may or may not exist a year from now. If the company goes out of business, what will happen to your content? How will Web content be preserved, especially if it resides on third-party servers? The content we put online defines our culture, helping to chronicle our history decades from now. While the Internet Archive is a great tool for archiving Web pages and documents, it does not archive pages that are password protected or protected by a robots.txt file (which keeps Web crawlers from indexing a site). How will academic institutions preserve the blog posts of their faculty? How will e-mail messages be preserved? This content is so ephemeral and so easy to delete, but will be so important to painting a full portrait of our history in the future.

Lessons

This book has highlighted many success stories where libraries have improved services to patrons and attracted new populations by using social software. Putting content on the Web doesn't need to be scary or difficult when you have the right tools. While there may be a complicated backend to some of these tools, and people throw around terms such as PHP, JavaScript, and XML, you don't usually need to understand how these things work—you just need to know how to use them, as with most of the technologies in our daily lives, including computers, cars, and microwaves. You don't need to know how to build any of them from scratch or how their internal mechanisms work. The best way to get comfortable with these technologies is to play with them. Since most of the tools mentioned in the book can be used for free—or at least offer a free trial—try them out and see if you can imagine using them in your library. While this book contains plenty of information, you can only learn certain facets of the applications by playing with the tools. So kick the tires and test drive some social software!

In the future of social software, only one thing is certain: Things will change. Some companies may cease to exist, and tools that don't even exist yet will gain sudden popularity. Be wary of hitching your wagon to any one technology or company. While MySpace and Facebook may be the most popular social networking sites for young people at the moment, this may not be the case several years from now. This is not to say that libraries shouldn't use the popular sites of the moment to provide services to their patrons, but any approach to social software should be flexible. If you are using a hosted blog, make sure your posts are being backed up, just in case you need to move your content or the company goes out of business. Read the terms of service for any proprietary service you use and make sure you have full ownership of your own content. Be willing to make changes as your patrons do.

Most importantly, try to keep up with your patrons and be willing to change. Social software offers unprecedented possibilities for communicating, collaborating, and building community with your patrons online, but these technologies are only tools. Your primary focus should always be on your patrons and how to provide them with the best services possible.

Endnotes

1. Sayed Hashimi, "Service-Oriented Architecture Explained," ONDot Net.com, August 18, 2003, ondotnet.com/lpt/a/4108 (accessed 18 November 18, 2005).
2. Hao He, "What is Service-Oriented Architecture?" XML.com, September 30, 2003, webservices.xml.com/lpt/a/ws/2003/09/30/soa.html (accessed November 18, 2005).
3. Hashimi.
4. Screensaver Lifesaver, University of Oxford, May 15, 2006, www.chem.ox.ac.uk/curecancer.html.
5. "MySpace.com Terms of Use Agreement," MySpace.com, May 1, 2006, collect.myspace.com/misc/terms.html?z=1 (accessed June 1, 2006).

Appendix: Referenced Web Sites

Chapter 1

GM FastLane Blog, fastlane.gmblogs.com

Chapter 2

Becker-Posner Blog, www.becker-posner-blog.com

Library Stuff, librarystuff.net

Pitas.com, www.pitas.com

Blogger, www.blogger.com

Movable Type, www.sixapart.com/movabletype

Blog for America, www.blogforamerica.com

The Daily Nightly, dailynightly.msnbc.com

FastLane Blog, fastlane.gmblogs.com

Lessig Blog, www.lessig.org/blog

WordPress, wordpress.org

Annenberg Center for Communication Blog Comparison Chart,
www.ojr.org/ojr/images/blog_software_comparison.cfm

Web Log Software/Platform Reviews from About.com,
weblogs.about.com/od/softwareplatformreviews

librarian.net, librarian.net

Feed2JS, feed2js.org

RSS-to-JavaScript, www.rss-to-javascript.com

Chapter 3

Media Center Blog, mabryonline.org/blogs/media

Marin County Free Library Blog, marincountyfreelibrary.blogspot.com

Ex Libris, www.libraries.wvu.edu/exlibris

West Virginia University Library News, www.libraries.wvu.edu/news

Georgia State University Library News and Subject Blogs,
www.library.gsu.edu/news

Binghamton University Science Library Blog,
library.lib.binghamton.edu/mt/science

First Reading from the Hawaii Legislative Reference Bureau Library,
www.hawaii.gov/lrb/libblog

WisBlawg from the University of Wisconsin Law Library,
www.law.wisc.edu/blogs/wisblawg/

Stark County Law Library Blawg, temp.starklawlibrary.org/blog

Ohio University Libraries Business Blog, www.library.ohiou.edu/
subjects/businessblog

h2oboro lib blog, www.waterborolibrary.org/blog.htm

UN Pulse, unhq-appspub-01.un.org/lib/dhlrefweblog.nsf

Roselle Public Library Blogger Book Club,
www.roselle.lib.il.us/YouthServices/BookClub/Bloggerbookclub.htm

Harris County Public Library eBranch Blog, www.hcpl.net/ebranch/news

Tutt Library of Colorado College Bookends,
library.coloradocollege.edu/bookends

Old Bridge Library Weblog, obpl.blogspot.com

SJCPL Lifeline, www.libraryforlife.org/blogs/lifeline

Ann Arbor District Library, www.aadl.org

Ann Arbor District Library Director's Blog,
www.aadl.org/taxonomy/term/86

AXIS Blog, www.aadl.org/axis

Bethel Park Public Library Children's Department Paperless Notebook,
bpchildrens.blogspot.com

Reference at Newman Library Blog, referencenewman.blogspot.com

Walking Paper, walkingpaper.org

David's Random Stuff, davidrandomstuff.blogspot.com

Catalogablog, catalogablog.blogspot.com

LibWorm, www.libworm.com

Technorati, technorati.com

BlogPulse, www.blogpulse.com

Feedster, www.feedster.com

The Shifted Librarian, www.theshiftedlibrarian.com

PLA Blog, www.plablog.org

LITA Blog, litablog.org

NJLA Blog, blog.njla.org

Information Today, Inc. Blog, www.infotodayblog.com

Chapter 4

CNN, www.cnn.com/services/rss

New York Times online edition,
www.nytimes.com/services/xml/rss/index.html

Washington Post online edition, www.washingtonpost.com/wp-
dyn/rss/index.html

NewzCrawler, www.newzcrawler.com

BlogBridge, www.blogbridge.com

Bloglines, bloglines.com

Rojo, www.rojo.com

Information Wants to Be Free, meredith.wolfwater.com/wordpress

MyYahoo!, my.yahoo.com

Winnetka-Northfield Public Library RSS, www.wpld.alibrary.com/
rsspage.asp

Feed2JS, feed2js.org

RSS-to-JavaScript, www.rss-to-javascript.com

University of Alberta New Books in NEOS Libraries, www.library.
ualberta.ca/newbooks/index.cfm

Seattle Public Library Reader's Corner,
www.spl.org/default.asp?pageID=collection_readinglists

Chronicle of Higher Education's Chronicle Careers, chronicle.com/jobs

Seattle Public Library, www.spl.org

Hennepin County Public Library RSS Feeds,
www.hclib.org/pub/search/RSS.cfm

LibraryElf, www.libraryelf.com

Kansas City Public Library Subject Guides, www.kcpl.lib.mo.us/guides

Georgia State University Library News and Subject Blogs,
www.library.gsu.edu/news

Jay Bhatt's Feeds in Bloglines, www.bloglines.com/public/bhattjj

Englibrary Blog, www.library.drexel.edu/blogs/englibrary

Curriculum Match Factor, www.proquest.com/syndication/rss

University of Wisconsin Ebling Library RSS E-Journal Feeds,
www.hsl.wisc.edu/bjd/journals/rss/index.cfm

OhioLINK Journals, journals.ohiolink.edu

RSS Mix, www.rssmix.com

KickRSS, www.kickrss.com

Netvibes, www.netvibes.com

Pageflakes, www.pageflakes.com

Blogdigger www.blogdigger.com

Chapter 5

Portland Pattern Repository, c2.com/cgi/wiki

Wikipedia, en.wikipedia.org

GNU General Public License, www.gnu.org/copyleft/gpl.html

Creative Commons Licenses, creativecommons.org/licenses

Davis Wiki, daviswiki.org

Ohio University's Biz Wiki, www.library.ohiou.edu/subjects/bizwiki

SJCPL's Subject Guides,
www.libraryforlife.org/subjectguides/index.php/Main_Page

MediaWiki, www.mediawiki.org

University of South Carolina Aiken Gregg-Graniteville Library,
library.usca.edu

University of Minnesota Libraries Staff Home Page, wiki.lib.umn.edu

PmWiki, www.pmwiki.org

ALA Chicago 2005 Wiki, meredith.wolfwater.com/wiki

ALA 2006 New Orleans Wiki, meredith.wolfwater.com/ala2006

Library Success: A Best Practices Wiki, www.libsuccess.org

Library Instruction Wiki, instructionwiki.org

WikiMatrix, www.wikimatrix.org

Chapter 6

ForumMatrix, www.forummatrix.org

Inside Line Forums, www.edmunds.com/insideline/do/ForumsLanding

AADL-GT, www.aadl.org/aadlgt

Slashdot, slashdot.org

LISNews, lisnews.org

March of Dimes Share community, www.shareyourstory.org

PUBLIB, lists.webjunction.org/publib

Fulbright Web, www.fulbrightweb.org

Yahoo! Groups, groups.yahoo.com

MSN Groups, groups.msn.com

Flickr, flickr.com

Zoto, www.zoto.com

SmugMug, www.smugmug.com

Textamerica, www.textamerica.com

Nokia Lifeblog, europe.nokia.com/lifeblog

TypePad, www.typepad.com

Kablog, www.kablog.org

craigslist, www.craigslist.org

Upcoming.org, upcoming.org

Eventful, eventful.com

MoveOn, moveon.org

Amnesty International, www.amnestyusa.org

Bloomington Public Library Flickr page, flickr.com/photos/
    bloomingtonlibrary

LaGrange Park Library Flickr page, flickr.com/photos/60582448@N00

San Francisco Community Services Directory, http://sflib1.sfpl.org:83/

pictureAnnArbor, www.aadl.org/services/products/pictureAnnArbor

It Girl Consulting, www.itgirlconsulting.com

WebJunction, webjunction.org

BlogPulse Conversation Tracker, blogpulse.com/conversation

Technorati, technorati.com

ALA Chicago 2005 Wiki, meredith.wolfwater.com/wiki

Chapter 7

Friendster, www.friendster.com

MySpace, www.myspace.com

Facebook, www.facebook.com

Ryze, www.ryze.com

LinkedIn, www.linkedin.com

Dodgeball, www.dodgeball.com

Socialight, socialight.com

Denver Public Library eVolver on MySpace, www.myspace.com/
denver_evolver

Denver Public Library eVolver, teens.denverlibrary.org

Chapter 8

TripAdvisor, www.tripadvisor.com

Amazon.com, amazon.com

Netflix, netflix.com

Slashdot, slashdot.org

del.icio.us, del.icio.us

Flickr, flickr.com

LibraryThing, www.librarything.com

Walking Paper, walkingpaper.org

Technorati, technorati.com

Furl, www.furl.net

What Should I Read Next, www.whatshouldireadnext.com

Lansing Public Library, www.lansing.lib.il.us

Lansing Public Library on del.icio.us, del.icio.us/lansingpubliclibrary

PennTags, tags.library.upenn.edu

Connotea, www.connotea.org

CiteULike, www.citeulike.org

Chapter 9

Maryland AskUsNow!, www.askusnow.info

ICQ, www.icq.com

AIM, www.aim.com

MSN Messenger, join.msn.com/messenger

Yahoo! Messenger, messenger.yahoo.com

Google Talk, www.google.com/talk

Morrisville State College Talk to a Librarian Live,
library.morrisville.edu/talk.html

Massachusetts Trial Court Law Libraries,
www.lawlib.state.ma.us/chat.html

New Castle-Henry County Public Library, www.nchcpl.org/ask_
librarian.htm

University of North Carolina at Chapel Hill Libraries,
www.lib.unc.edu/house/im_a_librarian.html

Library Success Wiki—Online Reference,
libsuccess.org/index.php?title=Libraries_Using_IM_Reference

Gaim, gaim.sourceforge.net

Trillian, www.ceruleanstudios.com

Fire, fire.sourceforge.net

Meebo, meebo.com

Walking Paper, walkingpaper.org

Skype, www.skype.com

Google Talk, www.google.com/talk

Microsoft NetMeeting, www.microsoft.com/windows/netmeeting

InfoEyes, www.infoeyes.org

iVocalize, www.ivocalize.com

Chapter 10

Nokia Life Blog ,europe.nokia.com/lifeblog

Textamerica, www.textamerica.com

Lane Medical Library at Stanford School of Medicine, lane.stanford.edu

Virginia Commonwealth University Libraries, www.library.vcu.edu/pda

AvantGo, avantgo.com

Feedalot, www.feedalot.com

NewsMob, newsmob.com

Innovative Interfaces—AirPAC, www.iii.com/mill/webopac.shtml#airpac

PubMed for Handhelds, pubmedhh.nlm.nih.gov/nlm

Ovid@Hand, www.ovid.com/site/products/tools/ovidhand/ovidhand.jsp

LexisNexis for handhelds, www.lexisnexis.com/handheld

Factiva for handhelds, www.factiva.com/factivafeedback/wireless.asp

Project Guetenberg, www.gutenberg.org

NetLibrary, www.netlibrary.com

Overdrive's Digital Library Reserve, www.dlrinc.com

Healy Library PDA Loan Program, www.lib.umb.edu/pda/nursing

Harvey Cushing/John Hay Whitney Medical Library PDA Resources & Services, info.med.yale.edu/library/technology/PDA

Ehrman Medical Library PDA Toolkit, library.med.nyu.edu/library/ eresources/toolkits/pda.html

Edward G. Miner Library PDA Complete List, www.urmc.rochester.edu/hslt/miner/selected_topics/pda/pda_ resources.cfm

Altarama, www.altarama.com.au

PDA Resource Page, web.simmons.edu/~fox/pda

Curtin University of Technology SMS a Query, library.curtin.edu.au/contact/sms.html

Southeastern Louisiana University Sims Library's Text a Librarian, www2.selu.edu/Library/ServicesDept/referenc/textalibrarian.html

TeleFlip, www.teleflip.com

Chapter 11

Listen Up!, gpclibraryradio.blogspot.com

Omnibus, www.dowling.edu/library/newsblog/podcasts.asp

Audio to Go, www.wpi.edu/Academics/Library/Borrowing/Podcasts

Click-A-Story, www.fordlibrary.org/clickastory

Grandview Elementary School Library, www.grandviewlibrary.org

Public Domain Podcast, publicdomainpodcast.blogspot.com

LibriVox, librivox.org

Authors On Tour, www.authorsontourlive.com

Lansing Public Library podcasts, www.lansing.lib.il.us/podcast.htm

Alden Library Podcast Tour, www.library.ohiou.edu/vtour/podcast

University of Sheffield iPod Induction Tours, www.lbasg.group.shef.ac.uk/downloads/index.html

South Huntington Public Library, shpl.suffolk.lib.ny.us

Open Stacks, openstacks.net/os

Thomas Ford Memorial Library podcasts, www.fordlibrary.org/yareviews

Bloomington Public Library podcasts, feeds.feedburner.com/bplpodcast

Stanford at iTunes, itunes.stanford.edu

BoilerCast, http://boilercast.itap.purdue.edu:1013/Boilercast/

Room 208 at the Wells Elementary School podcasts, bobsprankle.com/blog

Mabry Middle School podcasts, mabryonline.org/podcasts

Audacity, audacity.sourceforge.net

LAME Encoder, lame.sourceforge.net

OurMedia, ourmedia.org

FeedBurner, www.feedburner.com

podsafe music network, music.podshow.com

Talking with Talis, talk.talis.com

Online Programming for All Libraries (OPAL), www.opal-online.org

Teen Librarian, www.teenlibrarian.com

IT Conversations, www.itconversations.com

Podcast Alley, podcastalley.com

iTunes podcasts, www.apple.com/itunes/podcasts

Yahoo! Podcasts, podcasts.yahoo.com

PodZinger, www.podzinger.com

Podscope, www.podscope.com

Juice, juicereceiver.sourceforge.net

Chapter 12

Camtasia, www.techsmith.com/camtasia.asp

ViewletBuilder, www.qarbon.com/presentation-software/viewletbuilder

Adobe Captivate, www.adobe.com/products/captivate

University of Maine Blake Library Tutorials, www.umfk.maine.edu/
infoserv/library/resources/tutorials

University of Calgary Library Connection,
library.ucalgary.ca/services/libraryconnection/tutorials.php

UCLA College Library's The Road to Research,
www.sscnet.ucla.edu/library/tutorial.php

Calgary Public Library Tutorials, calgarypubliclibrary.com/library/
tutorials.htm

The Distant Librarian, distlib.blogs.com

Steve Garfield's Video Blog, stevegarfield.blogs.com/videoblog

Rocketboom, www.rocketboom.com/vlog

YouTube, www.youtube.com

SCAD On Demand, www.scadondemand.com

Princeton University Channel, uc.princeton.edu

Ulead Video Studio, www.ulead.com/vs

Pinnacle Studio Plus, www.pinnaclesys.com

Muvee autoProducer, www.muvee.com

FeedBurner, www.feedburner.com

Chapter 13

Pogo, www.pogo.com

EA Nation, www.ea.com/nation.jsp

Yahoo! Games, games.yahoo.com

MSN Games, zone.msn.com

Second Life, secondlife.com

Apolyton University, apolyton.net/civgroups/news.php?civgroupid=56

AXIS Blog, www.aadl.org/axis

AADL-GT, www.aadl.org/aadlgt

Santa Monica Public Library, www.smpl.org

Bloomington-Normal Gamefest, www.bngamefest.com

Alliance Library System, www.alliancelibrarysystem.com

Online Programming for All Libraries (OPAL), www.opal-online.org

Chapter 14

Cushing/Whitney Medical Library at Yale University,
    www.med.yale.edu/library

Librarians Helping Canadian Genealogists Climb Family Trees,
    canadianlibgenie.blogspot.com

Halton Images, images.halinet.on.ca

Images Canada, imagescanada.ca

Orange County Library System Computer Classes,
    www.ocls.info/Programs/ComputerClasses

Chapter 15

Social Software in Libraries Web site, www.sociallibraries.com

Ariadne, www.ariadne.ac.uk

Bulletin of the American Society for Information Science and Technology, www.asis.org/Bulletin

Cites & Insights, citesandinsights.info

College and Research Libraries, www.ala.org/ala/acrl/acrlpubs/crljournal/collegeresearch.htm

Crossroads, webjunction.org/do/Navigation?category=551

Current Cites, lists.webjunction.org/currentcites

D-Lib Magazine, www.dlib.org

EDUCAUSE Quarterly, www.educause.edu/eq

EDUCAUSE Review, www.educause.edu/er

First Monday, www.firstmonday.org

InCite, alia.org.au/publishing/incite

Library Journal, www.libraryjournal.com

NetConnect www.libraryjournal.com/index.asp?layout=netConnect

New York Times: Technology, www.nytimes.com/pages/technology

SLJ.com, www.schoollibraryjournal.com

DLIST, dlist.sir.arizona.edu

E-LIS, eprints.rclis.org

SDL, drtc.isibang.ac.in/sdl

Blended Librarian, blendedlibrarian.org

DIG_REF, www.vrd.org/Dig_Ref/dig_ref.shtml

LibGaming, groups.google.com/group/LibGaming

Library Instruction Wiki, instructionwiki.org

Library Success: A Best Practices Wiki, www.libsuccess.org

LITA-L, www.lita.org/ala/lita/litamembership/litaldisclists/litalotherdiscussion.htm

OFFCAMP, listserv.utk.edu/archives/offcamp.html

Web4Lib, lists.webjunction.org/web4lib

WebJunction, webjunction.org

Blended Librarian events, blendedlibrarian.org/events.html

Engadget, podcasts.engadget.com

Infopeople, infopeople.org/training/webcasts/index.php

IT Conversations, www.itconversations.com/index.html

OCLC, www.oclc.org/education/conferences/presentations/default.htm

Online Programming for All Libraries (OPAL), www.opal-online.org

SirsiDynix Institute, www.sirsidynixinstitute.com

Talking with Talis, talk.talis.com

Juice, juicereceiver.sourceforge.net

iTunes, www.apple.com/itunes

Chapter 16

craigslist, www.craigslist.org

Meetup, www.meetup.com

Judy's Book, www.judysbook.com

Xanga, www.xanga.com

MySpace, www.myspace.com

LiveJournal, www.livejournal.com

Warwick Blogs, blogs.warwick.ac.uk

Case Western Reserve University's CaseWiki, wiki.case.edu

University of Calgary Wiki, wiki.ucalgary.ca

Google Maps, maps.google.com

Google Maps API, www.google.com/apis/maps

Housing Maps, www.housingmaps.com

ChicagoCrime.org, www.chicagocrime.org

AnalyGIS, 65.39.85.13/google/default.htm

Bicycle Routes in Chicago, www.andreischeinkman.com/bikemap

Screensaver Lifesaver, www.chem.ox.ac.uk/curecancer.html

SETI@home, setiathome.ssl.berkeley.edu

Internet2, www.internet2.edu

Zoho Writer, zoho.com

About the Author

Meredith G. Farkas is the Distance Learning Librarian at Norwich University in Northfield, Vermont. In this position, she has implemented many of the social technologies discussed in this book, using them with patrons and colleagues. Meredith writes the "Technology in Practice" column for *American Libraries* magazine. She is the author of the Information Wants to Be Free blog (meredith.wolfwater.com/wordpress), writes for the collaborative blog TechEssence (techessence.info), and is the creator of Library Success: A Best Practices Wiki (www.libsuccess.org), as well as several national conference wikis. In March 2006, Meredith was named a Mover and Shaker by *Library Journal* for her innovative use of technology to benefit the profession. Before entering the library field, she worked as a child and family therapist in Florida. Meredith holds a BA from Wesleyan University in Connecticut, and an MSW and MLIS from Florida State University. She lives in Central Vermont with her husband, Adam.

Index

A

H

I